Waterloo General

Waterloo General

The Life, Letters and Mysterious Death of
Major General Sir William Ponsonby
1772–1815

John Morewood

Pen & Sword
MILITARY

First published in Great Britain in 2016 by
PEN AND SWORD MILITARY
an imprint of
Pen and Sword Books Ltd
47 Church Street
Barnsley
South Yorkshire S70 2AS

ISBN 978 1 47386 804 5

Printed and bound in England by
CPI Group (UK) Ltd, Croydon, CR0 4YY

Typeset in Times by CHIC GRAPHICS

Pen & Sword Books Ltd incorporates the imprints of
Archaeology, Atlas, Aviation, Battleground, Discovery,
Family History, History, Maritime, Military, Naval, Politics,
Railways, Select, Social History, Transport, True Crime,
Claymore Press, Frontline Books, Leo Cooper, Praetorian Press,
Remember When, Seaforth Publishing and Wharncliffe.

For a complete list of Pen and Sword titles please contact
Pen and Sword Books Limited
47 Church Street, Barnsley, South Yorkshire, S70 2AS, England
E-mail: enquiries@pen-and-sword.co.uk
Website: www.pen-and-sword.co.uk

Contents

Preface

Major General Sir William Ponsonby achieved immortality by leading the charge of the Union Brigade at the Battle of Waterloo. This was the cavalry charge that wrecked what Napoleon had intended to be the decisive attack to defeat Wellington. In the space of twenty minutes the French 1st Corps of General Comte d'Erlon broke through Wellington's line, tasted victory and then suffered utter defeat at the hands of Sir William's less than 1,000-strong Union Brigade, comprising English, Irish and Scottish heavy cavalry regiments. Sir William chose the timing of the charge and personally led the three regiments to success. However, he was killed in the overwhelming French counter-attack, and the next day the Duke of Wellington added a postscript to his dispatch to the Secretary of State for War:

> Since writing the above, I have received a report that Major General the Hon Sir William Ponsonby is killed; and in announcing this intelligence to your Lordship, I have to add the expression of my grief for the fate of an officer who has already rendered very brilliant and important services and who was an ornament to his profession.

This was a more glowing encomium than Wellington was prepared to give Sir Thomas Picton, a much more famous commander today, who had also been killed at Waterloo. Sir William, like Sir Thomas Picton, had served Wellington well during the Peninsular War. Sir John Fortescue, the historian of the British Army, regarded Sir William as the best cavalry brigade commander after Bock and Arentschildt (and certainly on a par with Le Marchant and Vivian). During the Peninsular War Sir William had led his regiment in the decisive cavalry charge at the Battle of Salamanca and then led a heavy cavalry brigade for the remainder of the war, earning a reputation for bravery and professionalism.

Over time, however, Sir William's contribution was forgotten. Historians, who should have known better, criticised him for allowing the Union Brigade's charge to get out of control and quoted horrendous losses, ignoring the fact that after Sir William's death the Union Brigade had to fight on for another seven hours. His role in the Peninsular War was also ignored. No book has ever been written about him and it is time to set the record straight.

Sir William was not just a very capable cavalry commander. He also belonged to one of the most fascinating and influential families in the land. His uncle was the leader of the Opposition in the House of Commons. His brothers would reach high positions in the Church, the Diplomatic Corps and the Treasury. His sister was married to Earl Grey, who would later become Prime Minister. His second cousin was the infamous Lady Caroline Lamb, whose love affair with the poet Byron was the talk of London. His elder brother had been the preferred lover of the most popular courtesan of the day.

I first came across Sir William many years ago. I grew up in Cumbria where the Ponsonby family originated. My parents, particularly my father, encouraged me in my love of history and this included old Cumbrian families. One day I went into Whitehaven Library and there was a copy of Sir John Ponsonby's work on the Ponsonby family. I'd always been fascinated by the Napoleonic Wars and there in Sir John's book was a chapter headed 'Waterloo General'. That is where I came across Sir William Ponsonby for the first time. I later encountered him again in the wonderful film *Waterloo*, in which he is played by Michael Wilding.

It was not until 1995 that I wrote an article on Sir William, which was published in the *Journal of the Friends of the Waterloo Committee* (now the Waterloo Association), of which I am now the Secretary. And then I did nothing else. Work got busier and life took over. But I had in the back of my mind that I wanted to do something more to tease out the whole story. It was no longer just about a tenuous Cumbrian link to the Battle of Waterloo. I wanted to understand how someone who had such a good professional reputation during the Peninsular War, could have his reputation attacked and shot to pieces by some Waterloo historians. And then there was the tantalising question: how did Sir William actually die at Waterloo? Was he shot, or killed by French lancers? Was he on his own, or with some of his troops? Was he attempting to escape back to the Allied lines, or was he trying to do something else? I was determined to find out.

As you get older you begin to wonder what your legacy will be. I always had the desire to dedicate a book to my father and hand it to him as a thank you. It always seemed there would be plenty of time to do this. And then suddenly, catastrophically, Dad died in November 2009. This book has become a memorial to him, if that makes any sense. I finally started writing it in the dreary winter of 2013–14, on my fortnightly weekend journeys to Cumbria to see my widowed Mum. Now Mum has died and so this book is for both of them, and Sir William of course. Perhaps it may be my legacy too.

I couldn't have written this book without encouragement, help and support from many people. First of all, grateful thanks as always to the wonderful historian and battlefield guide Ian Fletcher, who encouraged me to write the book in the first place, and to another great historian and editor of first-hand accounts of Waterloo, Gareth Glover for providing me with such helpful advice and encouragement. Gareth has painstakingly reviewed the book twice. Also grateful thanks to Mick Crumplin of the Waterloo Association, to Alan Henshaw of the Dragoon Guards Museum at York, Robert Pocock and Alasdair White for helping me find the position of the wood near which Sir William died and most especially to members of the Ponsonby family – Laura Ponsonby, Lord Frederick Ponsonby and Lord Rupert de Mauley – who have been unstinting in their support. I am also very grateful to Pierre de Wit, who brought to my attention firstly Colonel Bro's sketch of how he deployed the lancers to attack the Scots Greys and secondly Colonel Best's account of his finding Sir William's body on the morning after Waterloo. Particularly, as this is my first book, I am very grateful for the support and advice of Rupert Harding and his colleagues at Pen and Sword. Finally a special mention to Elizabeth Phipps of Haile Hall, the original home of the family in Cumbria, and to the staff of the various libraries I have used; in particular the Borthwick Institute at York, the British Library, Durham University Library and the National Army Museum. I should also mention Andrew Field, whose book *Waterloo – French Perspectives* pointed me in the direction of French sources for Waterloo and reminded me that you must use all sources available regardless of whether they have been translated into English or not. That has been a fascinating journey.

Needless to say, any errors are solely my own.

John Morewood
February 2016

Prologue

It is 3pm on the afternoon of Sunday 18 June and an officer in a major general's uniform is riding hard. He has just led his brigade of fewer than 1,000 men in defeating what Napoleon Bonaparte had decided would be the decisive blow that would have won him a crucial battle and reestablished him once again as the military genius of Europe. For this is the battlefield of Waterloo, and the officer is Major General Sir William Ponsonby, the commander of the Union Brigade, a brigade that comprised English, Irish and Scottish regiments. Intoxicated with success, one of those regiments, the Scots Greys, has gone on too far and has attacked Napoleon's Grand Battery of eighty guns. The infuriated emperor has ordered his elite lancers to destroy them. And now Sir William, having ordered his men to return to safety, is riding hard accompanied only by a single trooper. They must both ride hard because at their heels, intent on killing them, are seven lancers armed with 9-foot lances. For a while Sir William and the trooper keep ahead of the pursuers and there is a fleeting hope that they may escape. Then they hit a waterlogged ploughed field and Sir William, realising as his horse slows that there is no longer any hope, hands a locket to the trooper, asking him to give it to his son, and tells him to ride on to safety. He then draws his sabre to defend himself against the seven lancers who cluster around him and then... oblivion.

This is how the wonderful 1970 film *Waterloo* depicts the death of Sir William Ponsonby, a man whom the Duke of Wellington stated had 'rendered very brilliant and important services and was an ornament to his profession'. Wellington said that when the news of Sir William's death reached him he was so shaken that he had to stop writing the Waterloo Dispatch. Sir William, although belonging to one of the most fascinating families of the time, was a career soldier who had led his regiment in the decisive charge at the Battle of Salamanca and served with great distinction as a brigade commander during the Peninsular War. And yet many historians have blamed him for the decisive charge at Waterloo getting out of hand. But did it, and did Sir William die in the way portrayed in the film? This book, which uses family sources, including some of Sir William's own letters, as well as French and

German accounts, seeks to restore Sir William's reputation and, by shedding new light on the battle, help us establish what really happened on the afternoon of 18 June 1815.

Chapter 1

The Ponsonby Family

Sir William Ponsonby's ancestors were minor Cumbrian gentry. For generations they had farmed a small number of acres of poor quality land in West Cumberland, wedged in by the Lakeland fells and the Solway Firth, overlooking Scotland. However, the family that William was born into in 1771 or 1772 bore no resemblance to their Cumbrian forebears. True, Ponsonbys still lived in the 17th-century manor house at Haile near Egremont in Cumbria, but they were very much the poor relations. The main branch of the family had become major Anglo-Irish landowners, with their power base in Ireland.

By the time William was born the family owned tens of thousands of acres of Irish land, with stately homes in the counties of Kilkenny and Kildare and town houses in Dublin and London. They also wielded great political power and influence, being one of the four most powerful families in Ireland. In 1795 Edward Cooke, the Under Secretary of State for Ireland, was able to refer to them as 'the leading aristocratical influence in Ireland', and claimed that they had the viceroy under their control.[1] They also had influence socially, as well as politically. They had family ties to the great English Whig families. The head of the family was the Earl of Bessborough. They went on the Grand Tour, amassed art collections and one of them was rumoured to have been one of the lovers of Princess Amelia, daughter of King George II. The poet Byron would certainly have regarded the Ponsonbys as some of the 'twice two thousand' for whom 'earth was made'![2]

The family's astonishing transformation had begun during the English Civil War. The then head of the family, John Ponsonby, supported Parliament. He was both an experienced soldier and a convinced Constitutionalist.[3] He was given a commission by Parliament as a colonel and instructed to raise a regiment of nine troops of horse, which he commanded on their behalf during the Civil War.[4] In September 1647 he took a regiment of 700 cavalry to Ireland to support the Parliamentarian forces there and helped win the crucial battle of Rathmines, which prevented the Royalists from seizing Dublin. Oliver Cromwell, during his Irish campaigns, regarded John Ponsonby as a very reliable cavalry commander.

Parliament decided to reward John Ponsonby with estates in Ireland, not Cumberland, and he duly departed England and never looked back.[5] Parliament believed that that having more landowners in Ireland who had fought for the Parliamentary cause and were Protestant would help secure Ireland's loyalty to the English government. Taking land from Irish Roman Catholics would also weaken the opposition. In 1641 around 60 per cent of Ireland was owned by Catholic families. In 1662 this had dropped to about 20 per cent.[6] The Restoration of the monarchy in 1662 did not change this. John Ponsonby simply offered his services to Charles II. He was knighted and rewarded with lands near the town of Kilkenny. He subsequently exchanged these for the castle and estate of Kidalton in the Suir valley. He renamed this estate Bessborough in honour of his second wife Elizabeth (Bess). He never returned to Cumberland, dying in Ireland in 1678 and leaving his Irish lands to his eldest son by his second marriage, William.

William (1657–1724) further extended Ponsonby power by following three major strategies, which were also adopted by his descendants. Firstly, he actively supported the English Crown. Secondly, he married into a well-connected family. Thirdly, he increased his landholdings and ensured his new acquisitions allowed him to influence the election of MPs. During the troubles in Ireland following the Glorious Revolution in 1688, William raised a regiment to protect the Protestants in Kilkenny and Waterford and marched it across Ireland to defend Londonderry. He helped repel some of the assaults on the town and was celebrated in rhyme as 'Ponsonby [the] Brave who saved the threatened walls of Derry'. He became an MP and a Privy Councillor and in 1721, as a reward for his loyalty, was created Baron Bessborough. In 1722 he became Viscount Duncannon. The Ponsonbys were now members of the Irish aristocracy.[7]

William's eldest son Brabazon (1679–1758) joined the army, became an MP and Sheriff of Kilkenny and Kildare, and was appointed to the very lucrative position of Commissioner of Revenues. In 1739 Brabazon became Earl of Bessborough. Now only those with the title of Marquis or Duke were higher than the Ponsonbys in the aristocratic hierarchy.

Brabazon, like many of the male Ponsonbys, was a larger-than-life character. He breathed life, challenged convention and women loved him. As a young officer in the Inniskillings, Brabazon spent more money than he had, so he decided to marry a wealthy heiress. He pursued a wealthy widow, Mrs Sarah Colvill, the granddaughter of Archbishop Margetson of Armagh, the Primate of Ireland, but could not persuade her to marry him. So he decided on a stratagem. There was a custom in Ireland at that time that newly married couples would be wakened the morning after their wedding by a band playing outside their house. Imagine Mrs Colvill's surprise when one morning she was awoken by a band playing below her bedroom window in a building in which she had rented rooms. She went to the window, opened it, and saw a large crowd, who cheered her. The cheers increased when a couple of minutes later Brabazon, wearing a nightgown, opened the window of the bedroom next to hers (but in the adjoining suite of rooms, which he had deliberately hired) and thanked the crowd and band (which he had paid for)! To outsiders, who did not know that the windows belonged to two different suites, it appeared that Brabazon and Mrs Colvill had spent the night together. Mrs Colvill protested, but no one believed her, and to save her reputation she agreed to marry Brabazon. Besides money, she also brought to the marriage 2,000 acres of lands in Kildare, centred on Bishopscourt, and English lands in Leicester, which allowed Brabazon to become Baron Ponsonby of Sysonby and a member of the English House of Lords.[8]

Brabazon devised another strategy for advancing the Ponsonby family's cause. Normally, the family title would have to pass to the eldest son, but Brabazon made provisions that ensured that if his eldest son lacked political acumen, then the political leadership passed to the next in line and this is what happened with his two sons William and John.

Brabazon's son William (1704–1793) became Private Secretary to the Duke of Devonshire, Lord Lieutenant of Ireland in 1739, Member of the Irish Privy Council, and MP in the Irish and then English House of Commons. He also held the lucrative position of Postmaster General. He was a great connoisseur of art and a leader of London society and had houses in Pall Mall and at Roehampton. But his greatest coup was marrying the Duke of Devonshire's eldest daughter Caroline in July 1739. The Ponsonbys were now tied to the leading Whig family of the 18th century.[9]

Although William held the title of 2nd Earl of Bessborough, he did not have the political capability to look after the Ponsonby interests in Ireland. These passed to his younger brother John Ponsonby (1713– 1787), grandfather of the William Ponsonby this book considers. John

Ponsonby was for a time the most powerful man in Ireland. He spent the first part of his life at Bishopscourt, which had come into the family's hands following his father's marriage to Sarah Colvill. He cemented the links with the Duke of Devonshire by marrying Lady Elizabeth Cavendish, another daughter of William, the third duke, in 1743, four years after his elder brother had married the duke's eldest daughter. In Hardy's life of Lord Charlemont Ponsonby is portrayed as a dignified, affable gentleman, who had great influence not only by reason of his connection with the main Whig families in both countries, but also because of his persuasive personality. Hardy described him as 'open, affable, and familiar with a peculiar dignity of person at once imposing and engaging.'[10] He entered the Irish House of Commons in 1739 and became Secretary to the Revenue Board and its First Commissioner in 1744 (another lucrative appointment). In 1745 he raised four companies of horse to counter any Jacobite stirrings in Ireland. He was thanked for his loyalty and more important positions followed. In 1748 he became both a Privy Councillor and Speaker of the Irish House of Commons. This was a position of great influence, which he continued to hold until 1770. The role of Speaker, combined with his position as head of the Revenue Board, gave him great control, influence and patronage in Ireland, as well as money. The Speaker's salary in the 1770s was £4,000, around £240,000 in today's money.

By 1750 control of Ireland by the English Government was exercised by the Lord Lieutenant, or Viceroy, who was usually an English aristocrat appointed by the government in London. The Lord Lieutenant would reside in Dublin for two or three months a year, mainly to see that parliament did what the Crown wanted. During this period the position of Speaker was critical as the Lord Lieutenant relied on the Speaker to ensure the Irish House of Commons voted through government measures. John Ponsonby held the position of Speaker for twenty-two years. For the remaining nine months of the year the government of Ireland was in the hands of a few families: the Boyles, Beresfords, Connollys and Ponsonbys. These families became known as 'the Undertakers', not only because they ensured English rule was maintained in Ireland, but also because they were allowed to control appointments to all the key positions in the Irish administration.

This arrangement continued throughout the period of the Seven Years War (1756–1763) and for the first years of George III's rule. However, the English Government then decided to reassert control over its territories in America and Ireland. A new Lord Lieutenant, Lord

Townsend, was appointed to Dublin. To break the power of the Undertakers he dismissed Ponsonby, but following riots in Dublin had to reinstate him. A second attempt was more subtle and Ponsonby was outmanoeuvred. He resigned and passed control of his party to his two sons, William and George, who would become our William's father and uncle respectively. They started to transform the political following they had inherited from their father into a Whig party with an ideology. It was this that allowed the Ponsonbys a second opportunity to take the lead in Irish affairs. They established close links with the Whig party in England and in particular with the inspirational leader Charles James Fox. No doubt the Ponsonbys' connections with the leading Whig families helped. But there is also evidence that the English Whigs regarded George and William Ponsonby and their followers as important allies and the representatives of Whig ideology in Ireland.

Our William's father (1744–1806) was educated at Pembroke College, Oxford and in 1764 entered the Irish House of Commons. He sat in Parliament for twenty-two years until his death in 1806. He was appointed a Privy Councillor in 1784 and between 1784 and 1789 he held the lucrative position of Joint Paymaster General. Burke, the great Whig political theorist, wrote of him 'Ponsonby if I am not mistaken in the opinion I have formed of him, is of a manly decided character with a clear understanding.'[11] Existing letters show that William's father took his parliamentary duties very seriously. In 1803, on at least one occasion, he did not leave the House of Commons until 5am.[12] As was expected of him, he married well. His wife (our William's mother) was Louisa Molesworth, fourth daughter of the Rt Hon Richard Molesworth, 3rd Viscount Molesworth of Swords, an old established Irish family. She brought a dowry of £20,000 (£1.2 million in today's money).[13] Louisa was strong-minded and it is clear that theirs was a loving marriage. He referred to her in his letters as 'Dear Lou'. They shared the same interest in politics and when William was away he would write to her about political events.

As was also expected of him, William lived life to the full. He lived at Bishopscourt in 'the most princely style' and he kept 'the best hunting establishment in Ireland'.[14] Such high living had two consequences: poor health and financial difficulties. These problems, particularly the financial difficulties, would have an impact on William's son in the future.

George, our William's uncle (1755–1817), was educated at Trinity College, Cambridge. He decided to specialise in law. This in itself was very unusual for a member of such an elite family as the Ponsonbys. He was called to the Irish Bar in 1780 and enjoyed various positions including First Counsel to the Commissioners of the Revenue. Later he made a name for himself defending Irish radicals in high-profile legal cases. He would become Lord Chancellor of Ireland in 1806–07 and leader of the Whig Party in the English House of Commons. He was MP for Wicklow in 1778, Innistiogue 1783–1790 and Galway 1797–1801. He would later be MP for Tavistock and Peterborough. He married Mary, daughter of the 2nd Earl of Lanesborough, in 1781. Although he also enjoyed hunting he seems to have been more self-controlled than his brother. He would prove to be a key influence on our William throughout his life.[15]

It is important to remember that William's father and grandfather, although very influential, represented a junior branch of the family. They did not carry the title 'Earl of Bessborough' or control the vast landed estates that belonged to the senior branch of the family.[16] Nonetheless, as William grew up his grandfather, father and uncle demonstrated to him that the family could exert considerable influence in the Irish Parliament.

Chapter 2

William's Early Years
1772–1798

We do not know exactly when our William was born or where. His eldest brother John was born in about 1770, and his younger brother Richard was born in October 1772. However, we do know that William was aged nineteen in February 1791. It is likely that he was born between March 1771 and January 1772.[1] His brothers followed in quick succession: Richard in 1772, George in 1773, Frederick in 1774 and finally a sister, Mary, in 1776. All, with the exception of Frederick, would lead exceptional lives (See Appendix 1). William could have been born in the townhouse in Henrietta Street, Dublin, or at Bishopscourt, or even at Bessborough.

Information about William's early years is also sparse. Despite a family belief that he attended Eton, the college's records show that he was never a student there. It is likely that he was educated, as many of his family had been, at Kilkenny College. He must have displayed some intellectual ability or he would not have been sent to Cambridge University. Attending university was not a prerequisite for the family. William's elder brother John did not attend university, nor did his brothers George or Frederick. His younger brother Richard studied at Trinity College, Dublin.

William's father had attended Oxford and, in an age when son usually followed father, the change must have reflected a concern for William's education and his father's belief that the Oxford experience was not what he wanted for his son. It might also indicate the influence of his uncle, George Ponsonby, who had studied at Trinity College, Cambridge. On 22 February 1791, aged nineteen, William entered Trinity College as a Fellow Commoner, following in his uncle's footsteps.

William went through the ceremony of matriculation at Easter 1791 and graduated with a BA in 1795. His tutor was William Collier, aged 39. Collier had studied at Lincoln's Inn, been ordained a deacon in the

Church of England and was Regius Professor of Hebrew at Cambridge. He was an expert in the Classics and particularly well versed in modern languages, which was unusual in Cambridge at that time. He was also a poet and a 'notorious gourmand'.[2]

A Cambridge education did not mean that William was destined for an academic career or the Church. It was the natural progression for a young man of good standing who had some intellectual ability and was not destined to enter the Royal Navy.[3] Contemporaries who attended Oxford or Cambridge included William Pitt, William Wilberforce and William Wordsworth. The only time a university education was felt to be inappropriate for the sons of the landed classes was if the young man did not have sufficient intellectual ability or the family could not afford it (both of these applied to Arthur Wellesley, later 1st Duke of Wellington!). Indeed, William's future career seems to have been chosen before he entered Cambridge: he was going to be in the army.

Past members of the Ponsonby family had served in the army, including Colonel John Ponsonby in Cromwell's time, and other members of the family had raised troops of horse. However, only one ancestor had actively pursued a military career. This was Major General the Honourable Henry Ponsonby, who had fought at Dettingen in 1743 and was killed at Fontenoy in 1745. So it seems that pursuing a military career was William's own idea and his family encouraged him in his interest.

Although William would make his reputation as a cavalry commander, his first experience would be in the infantry and this was normal practice. Lord Portarlington, a fellow member of the Protestant Irish Ascendancy, obtained a commission for his son in an infantry regiment in order for him to gain basic military training, fully expecting him to join the cavalry later if he wished.

William seems to have gained short-term experience in a number of regiments while he was at Cambridge. Perhaps it was what we would call today 'work experience' or an 'internship'. On 30 September 1790 he became an ensign in the 6th (1st Warwickshire) Foot and in 1793 an ensign in the independent company of Captain Bulwer. A lieutenancy in Captain Davis' independent company followed. Then, on 3 December 1793, he became a lieutenant in the 109th Foot. In September 1794, before William graduated from Cambridge, he became a captain in the newly formed 83rd Foot. The 83rd had been raised in Dublin and was based at the royal barracks there as part of the city's garrison. It then moved to Bath and in May sailed to the West Indies. By then William had left the regiment, becoming a major in the Loyal Irish Fencibles on

15 December 1794. It was here that his military career really began. His first experience of battle would not be in Europe, but sadly in his home country of Ireland.

The Protestant Irish Ascendancy, to which the Ponsonbys belonged, liked to think of Ireland as being like England, with Dublin the second city of the British Empire. But Ireland was not England. It had its own problems, which were rapidly reaching crisis point. Like England, power was concentrated in Ireland in the hands of the few, but in England there was a national identity and the bulk of the population had the same Protestant religion as those who exercised power.

In Ireland there were two separate forces. The Protestant Ascendancy was a small ruling Protestant elite that had negotiated a new deal for Ireland during the War of American Independence (1776–1783). This New Deal had amounted to quasi-independence, with a repeal of the onerous taxes that had previously put Irish trade at a disadvantage. An Irish volunteer army, composed of the ruling Protestant gentry, had been formed, ostensibly to protect the country against the French, but also to ensure these concessions were maintained. Ireland had prospered. The Protestant ruling class had never had it so good and was able to demand a measure of self-government as the price for loyalty, to which the Government in England, as it was at war, felt it had no option but to agree. The agreement made the Irish parliament theoretically independent and equal to that in Westminster. And that was what the Protestant ruling class wanted. They provided the Viceroy with his cabinet and these men ensured that reform for the disadvantaged Catholics, which they believed would weaken their position, did not occur.

The second group were all those outside the Protestant Ascendancy. For the Catholics, who made up the mass of the Irish people, benefits were few. Ireland was fundamentally an agricultural country with many of the population at subsistence level. They suffered from harsh taxes and a land system of uneconomical small holdings. Their religion was outlawed and they could not hold any positions of responsibility in civilian or military life. There was, however, an emerging Catholic middle class, which wanted equal rights, as did those aristocratic families who followed the Roman Catholic faith. The more the Protestant upper class were seen to grow in power, the more aggrieved the Roman Catholics became. Their frustration was also felt by those Protestants who were not members of the established Church of Ireland and were precluded from office. These Nonconformists were very strong in Ulster.

Having effectively gained independence, economically and politically, there were very few in the Protestant Ascendancy who wanted to adopt a more liberal and fair approach to help their Catholic countrymen. The exception was the Irish Whigs, led by Henry Grattan, to whom the Ponsonbys belonged, but they could not force through reform. The situation became much more difficult after 1789 when the political landscape totally changed. The French Revolution established a more liberal regime in France. But in 1793 the French declared war against Britain and encouraged other countries to overthrow their governments. Those in Ireland wanting reform looked to the French model, which was delivering results, and away from the Foxite Whigs who were themselves in a difficult position. They could not give up their principles, but nor could they afford to be seen to support France.

William's father and uncle had transformed their political following from one based on family loyalties to an ideological framework based, as always, on loyalty to the Crown, but also embracing the Whig principles of liberty and toleration, including Catholic emancipation. Now, with the outbreak of war, it seemed that they were in a no-win situation. The politicians supporting the Crown were reactionary, Tory and enemies of reform. The politicians in favour of reform supported a foreign government with which Britain was at war.

Despite the best endeavours of William's father and uncle, it was the extremists on both sides, not those occupying the small middle ground, who would determine what happened next.

Indeed, the Ponsonbys had inadvertently raised Irish hopes and seen them dashed. In 1795 the Prime Minister William Pitt, as the price of obtaining support from some of the English Whigs, appointed a powerful Whig magnate, Lord Fitzwilliam, to be Viceroy of Ireland. The Ponsonbys in particular had close links with Fitzwilliam – indeed William's widowed mother would marry him in 1823. Unfortunately, Lord Fitzwilliam blew his chance to resolve the crisis in Ireland. He knew what had to be done. As always the problem lay in the approach taken. He charged at the problem head on, when a more circumspect strategy was needed. He removed at a stroke many of the leading members of the government in Dublin who were opposed to reform. He stated his support for the immediate admission of Catholics to Parliament and pressed for Catholic emancipation, which raised Catholic hopes. All this he did without consulting his cabinet colleagues in England and within a two-month period. He was seen as too much of a loose cannon. Political strings were pulled and Fitzwilliam was recalled by Pitt. He had only been in office from January to March 1795, but the damage he had caused was disproportionate to the time he had been Viceroy. He had encouraged expectations and then had not delivered. People who had supported the Irish Whigs now felt that their trust had been misplaced and started to consider a more radical approach. Support started to trickle away from George and William Ponsonby to the more extreme elements on either side. Ireland was gripped by extremist forces. By mid-1795 the country had become a powder keg in danger of exploding.

On one side there were the radicals, who now believed that reform would only come through armed insurrection supported by France. They were disillusioned with the Ponsonbys' and Whigs' approach to politics following Pitt's recall of Lord Fitzwilliam. Younger more radical leaders grew in popularity. Wolfe Tone (1763–1798), one of the main leaders in the 1798 rebellion in Ireland, had been a member of the Ponsonbys' loyal opposition to the Irish Government in the Dublin Whig Club. In 1791 he had helped to form the Society of United Irishmen, which encouraged Catholics to make common cause with those Nonconformist Protestants who were also excluded from office. The society had been founded originally to press for Parliamentary reform and full Catholic emancipation by constitutional means. Now Wolfe Tone started to transform it into a secret army, swelled by alliance with the Catholic Defenders movement and looking for French aid to establish a republic in the French style.[4]

To accomplish its aims the society needed the support of the Roman Catholic majority. In Ireland economic conditions had worsened and discontent grew. The war with France caused a slump that crippled the Irish economy, increasing resentment of the war. To the poorer Irish the landlords who charged high rents and paid low wages were seen as the main problem. The Catholic Defenders movement started to arm its members in Leitrim. In some counties radicals began disseminating French revolutionary ideas and intimidating landowners and their supporters, and indeed anyone who opposed them. Lawlessness in the countryside increased. Houses were set on fire. Militia men, magistrates, witnesses to law breaking and servants of unpopular landowners were killed.

The catalyst for what was about to happen was that for all those disillusioned with the Irish government there was now the prospect of outside help. The revolutionary leaders in France believed the Revolution's principles of liberty, equality and fraternity should be applied to all nations. After successfully repelling the attempts to invade

France in 1792, the revolutionary armies went on the offensive and took their principles with them. When France declared war on England in 1793 the option of French military intervention in Ireland, or at the very least French support for an Irish insurrection, which in its turn would hinder the English government in prosecuting a war against France, became possible. Wolfe Tone went to France in 1796 and asked the French to send a large force of 15,000 to 20,000 men under a well-known general – so that there would be a revolution rather than an insurrection and civil war. The French government approved the plan.

The situation was exacerbated by the extremists on the other side. None of the Protestant Ascendancy members of the Irish government would consider reform. The government increased its informers and spy network. The advocates of reform were spied upon and harassed by the Irish Government, which saw the spectre of republicanism everywhere. Even William's father and uncle were watched and their movements reported on. With local magistrates unwilling to do their duty, and reports of a rebellion about to happen, the Government reacted with a policy of total repression. The Irish government forced through legislation in an attempt to stop the lawlessness. In 1796 alone this included an Indemnity Bill, an Assassination Bill and an Insurrection Bill. The Habeas Corpus Act was then suspended to allow the government to hold indefinitely any suspects that had been arrested. William's uncle George spoke against the motion. 'The Irish Ministers', he said 'were men of vindictive spirit, and he would not sacrifice the liberty of the subject to the lovers of vengeance'.[5] In previous years he would have received great support, but times had changed and he was defeated by 137 votes to seven.

The Irish parliament then legalised the creation a of a home defence force, the Irish Yeomanry. This was raised and officered by the Protestant landed gentry in the countryside and municipal bodies in towns and cities. The Dublin government then instructed the military to take action. Discontent reached fever pitch.

William obviously had knowledge of Irish politics and conditions. He would have heard his father and uncle discussing the issues and also seems to have developed an interest in politics, which he maintained throughout his life. He was chosen to represent seats in which the Ponsonby family, or other connected families, had an interest. Family connections ensured he sat in the Irish House of Commons from the age of 24. In 1796 the Devonshire interest had ensured that he was returned as MP for Bandon Bridge (1796–97) and in 1797 another relative, Lord

Lismore, made sure he was returned as MP for Fethard Borough, Co. Tipperary, a seat he held until 1800. He would have listened to the debates in the Irish House of Commons and shared the despair his father and uncle felt.

When he was not in Parliament, William carried out his duties in the Loyal Irish Fencibles. At this time the Fencibles were one of four elements that made up the military establishment in Ireland. The Irish military totalled approximately 83,000 men. However, their experience, skills and roles differed widely, which would cause problems in the future.

Firstly, there were the regular troops of infantry and cavalry, supposed to number 15,000 men. They included the 5th Dragoon Guards, whom William would soon join. Many of the troops were under strength, as regiments were frequently sent to Ireland after arduous campaigning or serving overseas (in the West Indies, for example, vast numbers of men died of disease) to recruit and retrain.

Secondly, there was the militia: about 22,000 in number. They tended to be officered by Protestant landed gentry with the rank and file drawn mainly from conscripted Catholics, who served for four years. The original plan was for the militia to number 15,000 men. As they had to be scattered around the countryside in small detachments on policing duties, very few had any training.

Then there was the newly formed yeomanry of about 35,000 men. As volunteers they lived at home and again had very little military training. Some units only received their weapons on the very eve of the uprising.

The fourth group, in which William was now an officer, were the Fencibles. The name derived from 'defencible' and their purpose was to defend the country against threat of invasion and to provide garrison and patrol duties, thereby allowing regular army units to perform offensive operations. Their great strength was that although the rank and file were local volunteers, they had regular army officers in charge. It was very much the eighteenth-century equivalent of the Territorial Army. After the regular troops they were the best-trained military forces in Ireland. Outwardly they were virtually indistinguishable from regular troops, being organised, clothed, equipped and trained in the same way. Although most regiments of Fencibles serving in Ireland during the rebellion were Scottish, two regiments of cavalry and four of infantry were established as Fencibles in Ireland. William's commanding officer in the Loyal Irish Fencibles was Colonel William Handcock. The lieutenant colonel was William Reynell and William was major. In addition there were seven captains, eleven lieutenants, seven ensigns, a chaplain, adjutant, quartermaster and a surgeon, as well as all other ranks. The Loyal Irish Fencibles had been established in November 1794 and had two battalions.

In Ireland at this time the role of the British military was threefold. Firstly, there was the need to ensure any unrest was suppressed before it reached armed revolt. This meant searching and seizing arms and apprehending ringleaders. Information would be received from a very extensive intelligence network run by the government, and then it was up to the local military authorities to decide how to act. Only in Dublin did the Government have a small counter-insurgency force. Everywhere else it was totally dependent on the militia and the regular forces.

Secondly, there was the need to provide a field army of regular (trained professional) troops to counter any French invasion if it occurred or to crush any revolts which broke out.

Thirdly, there was the need to provide the normal 'police service' for Ireland. In the absence of a police force, the military had to combat crime and lawlessness, including smuggling, just as the army had to do in England.

The Loyal Irish Fencibles would undertake the first and third of these roles. We have no details of their operations, but as they were an infantry regiment they would provide garrisons for the major towns and attempt to quell any unrest in surrounding areas. It was during this period that William would develop his leadership skills, because as a major he was one of the three most senior officers in the regiment. However, being a major in the Fencibles was not the same as being a major in the regular army. By 1798 William had decided on a change which would dramatically impact his future career. He decided to move from the infantry to the cavalry, and in particular the heavy cavalry. The regiment he chose was Ireland's premier cavalry regiment, the 5th Dragoon Guards, which had a long history of distinguished service.

> Commissions signed by His Majesty for the Army in Ireland
> Major William Ponsonby from the Loyal Irish Fencibles Infantry
> to be Major in the 5th Dragoon Guards vice Major Charles Craven
> who exchanges their commissions at the regulated Difference.
> Dated March 1 1798.[6]

The transfer would prove to be a mixed blessing, as Ireland was about to erupt.

Chapter 3

Into Action for the First Time: the 1798 Rebellion in Ireland

The 5th Dragoon Guards had been founded as a regiment of horse in 1685 and had always been heavy cavalry. This meant that they were shock troops, used in battle to charge opposing cavalry or infantry and cut them to pieces. The 5th Dragoon Guards had a legendary reputation. They had served in Belgium, Ireland and Bavaria and had won glory at Marlborough's great victories at Blenheim, Ramillies, Oudenarde and Malplaquet, taking part in the great cavalry charges. As part of a government financial review in 1788 they were reclassified as Dragoon Guards, which meant that they fulfilled the same role but the government paid them less.

From 1714 to 1793 the regiment never left Ireland. Indeed, by 1767 the regiment, with the exception of one foreigner, was composed exclusively of Irishmen. The principal duties of the troops were to assist the civil power by putting down gangs of highway robbers on the roads and making expeditions to round up bodies known as 'Rapparees' and 'Whiteboys', who terrorised and plundered those who were not strong enough to protect themselves. Another duty was to assist the excise officers in capturing smugglers, as there was a great contraband trade with France and Spain with goods distributed along the rivers. The regiment also took part in various concentrations of troops that were ordered to repel threatened invasions, although none occurred before 1793.

In 1793 all this changed with the beginning of the war with revolutionary France. Just as twenty-two years later, the plan was to invade France across her frontiers. In Belgium a British army commanded by George III's favourite son Frederick 'The Grand Old Duke of York' collaborated with Austrian troops. The 5th Dragoon Guards arrived in September 1793 and in April 1794 won fresh glory at the battle of Le Cateau. In this battle, fought in fog, two French columns totalling 32,000 men and seventy-nine guns were defeated by a combined Anglo-Austrian cavalry force of seven regiments including the 5th Dragoon Guards. More than 3,000 Frenchmen were killed and twenty-two guns captured, and the enemy was routed. The 5th Dragoon Guards sustained losses of nine men and twenty-three horses killed, ten officers and men and nine horses wounded and four men and twenty-three horses missing. The Duke of York stated 'the conduct of the British cavalry was beyond praise'. Unfortunately the rest of the campaign was not as successful, and in November 1795 the regiment returned to England. There it stayed until October 1796 when it was ordered to return to Ireland because the Lord Lieutenant claimed that the forces at his disposal were entirely inadequate to meet the projected French invasion of Ireland.

In 1796 the 5th Dragoon Guards, comprising nine troops totalling approximately 330 men, marched to Bantry Bay to oppose the French landing that Wolfe Tone had been working towards for so long. However, stormy weather forced the invasion fleet to return to France and the regiment went into camp on the Curragh, just outside Dublin, with other cavalry regiments. There it was inspected and General Wilford, one of the inspecting generals, said it was the best mounted regiment in the camp. In the autumn of 1797 the regiment was moved to Dublin and it was there that William Ponsonby joined it in March 1798.

The post of colonel of the regiment was not as much an honorary one then as it is now. Andrew Bamford, in his excellent book *Gallantry and Discipline – the 12th Light Dragoons at War with Wellington* has shown that at least one colonel, Sir James Steuart of the 12th Light Dragoons, concerned himself with the operations of his regiment, including matters of discipline and promotion, as well as providing the regiment with its horses. The colonel of the 5th Dragoon Guards was Lieutenant General Thomas Bland, who was 62 years old in 1798. He was a distinguished soldier and, although undoubtedly interested in the regiment and its activities, left active operational control in the hands of the two lieutenant colonels. These were the Honourable Robert Taylor and John Ormsby Vandeleur. Robert Taylor, as senior lieutenant colonel, actively commanded the regiment from 1792 to 1801. He had joined the regiment as a cornet in 1783 and had worked his way up, becoming lieutenant colonel in 1792. He had commanded the regiment in Flanders in 1793–95, leading it in all the major actions there. He had a reputation for maintaining the regiment at the highest levels of operating efficiency. However, from February 1798 to July 1799 he served as brigadier general in Ireland and would be second in command to General Lake, the Army Commander in Chief, when the French invaded, so we do not know how active a role he had with the regiment at this time.

The other lieutenant colonel was John Vandeleur, who had also served in Flanders with the regiment. He had been second lieutenant colonel of the 5th Dragoon Guards from 1794. He was the eldest son of John Ormsby Vandeleur of Maddenstown, County Kildare, so his and William's families would be well known to each other. It is possible that he encouraged William to join the regiment.

The senior major, William Sherlock, was also very capable. He had been a major in the 5th Dragoon Guards since 1794 and had also served in Flanders. It is likely that he was quite old, as he retired from army command in 1801. As the fourth most senior active officer in the regiment William must have felt he had a lot to live up to, knowing at the same time that the regiment was in very capable hands. Given what was about to happen this was just as well.[1]

By 1798 the Irish government could have been forgiven for thinking that it was winning the struggle to prevent a rebellion. In 1797 troops had succeeded in seizing enormous quantities of weapons stored by the rebels – 48,000 guns and 70,000 pikes according to one source.[2] A Dutch attempt at invading Ireland had been foiled by the Royal Navy at the Battle of Camperdown. In May 1798 the Dublin authorities succeeded in arresting the United Irishman's chief leader Lord Edward Fitzgerald, as well as members of his central coordinating committee. Lord Edward was a son of Ireland's most important aristocrat, the Duke of Leinster, and his arrest was seen as a major coup.

However, on 23 May the rebellion broke out as planned, although it lacked the coordination that Lord Edward would have given it. Lord Edward had claimed he could mobilise 280,000 United Irishmen against government forces who numbered 83,000 and had drawn up detailed plans to secure the capital. Dublin was the second most important city in the British Empire, but although it had a castle this was really just a collection of government buildings. There were no proper fortifications and the rebels believed they had only to assassinate the Government ministers in order to seize control. The arrest of Lord Edward and the Leinster region's leaders prevented this from happening. Set against the rebels was a very efficient government security system based on paid informers, a city police force and soldiers, mainly infantry. Outside the city were camps for cavalry to prevent attacks on the city. And it was here that the 5th Dragoon Guards were situated.

Outside Dublin the situation was very different. There is no doubt that the government underestimated the size and ferocity of the rebellion that would occur, which resulted in the deaths of 70,000 people. The government's lucky arrest of the national ringleaders was not as catastrophic as it could have been, as they had already sent out the timetable and instructions for the rebellion. Some counties did not rise as planned, but others did. Kildare and the south east rose up in rebellion, as did Antrim and County Down. In these areas the fighting was savage. Death among civilians was high and destruction of property widespread. Both sides committed appalling atrocities and for many the regular army was the only force to show any discipline and protect the innocent. The 5th Dragoon Guards were used to protect Dublin, but had their strength weakened as squadrons and troops were sent to help defeat the rebels in the affected areas.

On 9 June one squadron of the 5th Dragoon Guards, comprising two troops of sixty men under Major Sherlock, was detached from Dublin into the counties of Wicklow and Wexford. It saw action against the rebels at Arklow, Ballycarnen, Gorey, Vinegar Hill and White Hills between 9 and 21 June.[3] The 5th Dragoon Guards Museum in York holds a regimental silver medal belonging to Captain Moore, for service at Arklow on 10 June 1798.[4] With Sherlock actively involved in southeastern Ireland, responsibility for providing protection for Dublin and taking action against the rebels closer to home, including in his own county of Kildare, fell on William's shoulders. The Adjutant General's Office in Dublin ordered all house-dwellers to post the names of those who were living in the houses. Lights had to be placed in the windows of the middle floors of houses in Dublin and a curfew was enforced from 9pm to 5am. Another detachment of the regiment was employed in the county of Kildare, clashing with different groups of insurgents. William's lifelong friend Denis Pack, then a captain in the 5th Dragoon Guards, charged a group of rebels at Rathangan on 21 May and on 19 June charged 100 rebels near Prosperous, killing twenty to thirty on the spot.

Although it failed to prevent atrocities, and for a time lost control of key towns, the beleaguered government in Dublin gradually reasserted control. More troops arrived from England and the Royal Navy frustrated the French in their invasion plans.

By August the rebellion was nearly suppressed, but on 22 August a small French army of 1,000 men under General Humbert managed to evade the Royal Navy and land at Killala in the west of Ireland. They gained support from the Irish rebels and, having defeated General Lake's army of militia and regular troops at Castlebar, they headed towards Dublin. All nine troops of the 5th Dragoon Guards were mobilised and formed part of the army that Marquis Cornwallis, the new Viceroy of Ireland, led out of Dublin to confront the rebels. The troops were transported along the Grand Canal to Tullamore. Between them Cornwallis and Lake had 25,000 troops. Their plan was to trap Humbert at Castlebar. Humbert, however, gave Cornwallis the slip on 4 September and headed into central Ireland. Cornwallis ordered Lake to pursue him with 5,000 men while he moved his larger force, including the 5th Dragoon Guards, across country to cut Humbert off before he could join a rebel force in the midlands and threaten Dublin.

On 8 September the rebels were caught between the two armies of Marquis Cornwallis and General Lake and defeated at Ballinamuck. After a short battle Humbert and his French force (ninety-six officers and 746 men) surrendered and became prisoners of war. The 1,500 Irish were hunted down without mercy. After the battle Cornwallis selected the squadron of the 5th Dragoon Guards commanded by William to escort him back to Dublin.[5]

It is estimated that the death toll in the rebellion was around 70,000. About a dozen towns had been partially or totally destroyed by the military, the rebels or both. 'In the capital', according to one traveller 'the streets were crowded with the widows and orphans of those who had fallen in battle. In the country I beheld villages everywhere burned and razed to the ground.'[6] Although the suffering was lessened by one of the best harvests of the century, scattered groups of insurgents still committed violent attacks on the civilian population from remote hideaways. On the Wexford-Wicklow border there were shootings and chapel burnings. There were disturbances in Galway and a rising in Clare. The insurgents needed to be hunted down. And so William Ponsonby and the regiment remained in Ireland. But by mid-1799, with political prisoners being sent to Australia or forced to join the army or navy, and others choosing to emigrate of their own free will, the government felt comfortable enough to be able to send the 5th Dragoon Guards to Europe as part of the larger war effort.

Chapter 4

In Command

There were very good reasons for the British government taking a more positive view of the Irish situation. In 1797 the naval mutinies had collapsed and there had been major naval victories over France's allies, first over the Spanish at Cape St Vincent and then the Dutch at Camperdown. The rebellion in Ireland had been crushed, and the defeat of Humbert and the mopping up of the remaining insurgents had coincided with news reaching England of Nelson's great victory at Aboukir Bay in August 1798, in what was being called the Battle of the Nile. Bonaparte's fleet had been annihilated without the loss of a single British ship. At a stroke a range of dazzling possibilities opened up. The French government, which a few months before had sent Bonaparte to carve out a French empire in the Middle East and perhaps progress on to India, was now on the back foot. There was the possibility of a new coalition against France comprising Austria, Russia, Naples and the Ottoman Empire, and further good news soon followed. On 12 October Sir John Warren intercepted a French fleet of nine ships bound for Ireland carrying 3,000 French troops, a huge amount of stores and a considerable amount of artillery, as well as the rebel leader Wolfe Tone. Warren captured all but two of the French ships and with them Wolfe Tone and 2,500 French troops. The remaining ships managed to get back to France. When Wolfe Tone died, having attempted suicide, the Irish rebels lost their last leader. The British government reasoned correctly that the French government would have to abandon all military ventures against Britain and Ireland.

In May 1799 the combined forces of the East India Company and the Nizam of Hyderabad defeated the troops of France's potential ally in India, Tipoo Sultan, who died defending his capital Seringapatam. Closer to home Austrian and Russian forces reversed the French conquests in Italy so that by the end of June 1799 only Genoa and adjoining territory remained in French hands. The British government decided to finance a joint expedition with Russia to force the French out of the Netherlands. The first British forces landed in August 1799. As in 1794 they were commanded by the Duke of York and, as before, they had initial success. The 5th Dragoon Guards were chosen to serve in the campaign, but the situation quickly deteriorated and the army had to be evacuated in October. Events unfolded so quickly that the 5th Dragoon Guards were stopped in transit and disembarked at Liverpool.

Instead of going on overseas service, however, they were ordered to keep the peace in Gloucestershire and Herefordshire. This was not as unusual as it might appear, although it was definitely an anti-climax after the events in Ireland and the prospect of serving abroad. At that time in England, just as in Ireland, there was no police force and cavalry and infantry regiments had the role of undertaking operations against smugglers and quelling civilian unrest. Outbreaks of popular rioting did not reach the levels they would in the nineteenth century during the Chartist, Corn Law and Reform Bill agitation, but they could still occur and would have to be dealt with by whatever forces were in the area. The fact that Britain was at war exacerbated the situation. Income Tax had just been introduced, although those with incomes below £60 were exempt. Of greater impact was the threat of food shortages. The value of wages fell and the cost of wheat and oats rose. The winter had been very bitter; in some areas the coldest in living memory. Snow drifts prevented goods being transported and in some areas deliveries of coal to provide warmth could not be made. There was no hay for the horses, livestock suffered and the price of meat rose. The harvest was bad. The price of flour had increased five times since the war began, so that many people could not afford to buy it to make bread. Even when the harvests were good the price stayed high, suggesting farmers were restricting supplies to ensure higher prices. Workmen sold furniture and pawned clothes to feed their families. Employers started laying off their workers, who formed unions to object to this and the impact of new machinery that reduced both the number of workers needed and the skills required. The government reacted by passing Combination Acts stipulating that anyone trying to strike, or meeting to discuss wages and conditions, could be prosecuted. The militia were needed to make the arrests, backed up by the yeomanry and the regular army. Sometimes unrest occurred unexpectedly. In February 1800 there was a riot in Sunderland when a dealer charged high prices for corn. He was pelted with mud, the inn where he took refuge was attacked and his carts were pushed into the river. The magistrate fled after reading the Riot Act and the militia had to load their muskets and go through the motions of preparing to open fire in order to dispel the crowds that had appeared out of nowhere. Hunger encouraged republican feeling and in 1800 posters started to appear calling for liberty, more food and an end to the war.[1]

The 5th Dragoon Guards were based in Gloucester between 1799 and 1801, with detachments placed in Hereford, Cheltenham and Tewkesbury to ensure riots did not occur.

In October 1801 a peace treaty was signed with France, which lasted until 1803, but this did not mean that the regiment stayed put. Indeed it seems to have been standard practice to move regiments on a regular basis. The 5th Dragoon Guards moved to Worcester and stayed there until 1802. Eighteen months were spent in Northumberland with the headquarters at Newcastle; six months were then spent in York and four months in Manchester, ending in April 1804.

Although war had ended, discontent about conditions had not. The new government of Addington put new taxes on beer and other commodities to help pay interest on the National Debt. The army and navy reduced their manpower greatly and many returning sailors and soldiers found it hard to find work. In the West Country, where the 5th Dragoon Guards were situated, ex-soldiers and sailors were a source of cheap labour for mill owners, and unemployed weavers attacked carts carrying the finished materials and burnt a number of the mills. The militia were regularly called out and it is likely the 5th Dragoon Guards were called out on occasions too.

Nevertheless, despite the unrest, the years 1799–1805 were relatively peaceful ones for the regiment and William. On 1 January 1800 he was made a brevet lieutenant colonel and in 1803 was formally appointed one of the two lieutenant colonels in the 5th Dragoon Guards. The *London Gazette* on 1 March 1803 announced from the War Office that on 24 February:

> 5th Regiment of Dragoon Guards, Brevet Lieutenant Colonel William Ponsonby to be Lieutenant Colonel by purchase vice Vandeleur who retires.

Peace, however, was short lived. Napoleon and Addington distrusted each other's intentions. The agreed terms of the Treaty of Amiens were not adhered to and in May 1803 Britain declared war. Napoleon made plans to invade and established a network of camps along the Channel coast. But to invade England he needed control of the Channel, and this the Royal Navy denied him.

In Britain the problems of a country at war resurfaced. Business slumped everywhere. The 5th Dragoon Guards were moved to Scotland and based at Piershill Barracks in Edinburgh. As before, separate squadrons were based at different centres and they were rotated between them every two months. Besides having a number of squadrons at Edinburgh, the 5th Dragoon Guards also had squadrons at Perth, Haddington and Hamilton.

Although there were radical elements in Edinburgh called the United Scotsmen, life for the regiment was the same: undertaking operations against smugglers and quelling civilian unrest. Ralph Heathcote, an officer in the regiment (1st Royal Dragoons) who took over the Edinburgh posting after the 5th Dragoon Guards, gave an account of the barracks and life there. It was probably the same for the 5th Dragoon Guards. The barracks were a mile from Edinburgh, very near the sea 'and in a most delightful situation'.[2] A typical day was as follows:

At about nine o'clock the trumpets sound for foot parade when the different troops being formed before the stable doors march towards the centre of the barrack-yard and after being formed in line are examined by the Major (viz their dress and arms are inspected); then the serjeant's guard mounts and the officers leave the regiment; their business being done; then the serjeant major exercises the regiment, with which we have nothing to do. At 10 o'clock I breakfast with some others in the mess room, many officers preferring to breakfast in their own rooms. At eleven all the subaltern officers (those below the rank of captain) are to go to the riding school and at twelve the same subaltern officers have to attend the foot drill, and then your business is done for the day. If a field day is ordered (we have about four a week) there is neither riding school nor foot drill. By field day is meant exercising the whole regiment on horseback. As we exercise on the sands of the seashore, we must regulate our time according to the tides of the ocean, and then I leave it to you to judge how fine it must be riding on the hard sand, having a most beautiful sea view before you, adorned by the shores of Fife. ... At five the trumpet sounds for dinner (for the officers I mean; the privates dine at twelve). We generally sit down twelve of us, married officers not belonging to the mess. Our dinner is excellent; our knives and forks and spoons are silver with the cipher of the regiment upon them; this is upon all the plates, glasses, decanters etc and forms a most elegant effect.[3]

For recreation the officers read, sketched, formed musical societies and attended balls, theatres and receptions in Edinburgh. In the summer there were horse races at Leith, which the officers entered, followed by balls, plays, concerts and assemblies, the balls lasting until seven the next morning. The officers would also visit families they knew in the area. Thus on 21 October 1804 we find Lady Louisa Stuart writing to Lady Portarlington from Bothwell Castle, the home of Lord and Lady Douglas:

> there is a Colonel Ponsonby here for two days, Mr Ponsonby's second son, a very well looking man and agreeable in his manners. He commands a regiment at Leith barracks, of which there is one troop at Hamilton.[4]

If the senior officer of the regiment was married he tended to rent a house close to the barracks. However, Heathcote says that if the senior officer was not married he would mess with the rest of the officers, and this is probably what William did.

Although not engaged in any military action, it is clear that William was determined to ensure the regiment maintained the highest standards. The visiting general who undertook the 1804 annual inspection of the regiment stated:

> The men are uncommonly fine and well set up. The regiment rides well and manoeuvres with rapidity and precision. The saddlery and appointments are kept in excellent order and the system of stable duty and interior economy appears to be very good. I think this is a most excellent regiment of cavalry. The officers and non commissioned officers and men are remarkably zealous and more than commonly intelligent in the execution of every duty in which I have had the opportunity of trying them. I may venture to add that Your Lordship cannot have a regiment of cavalry under your command upon which I should be disposed to place more confidence in a day of difficult service.[5]

In 1804 the 5th Dragoon Guards received a great sign of royal favour. The Prince Regent had an only child, a daughter Charlotte who, if she survived him, would be heir to the throne. In 1804 the regiment was renamed the '5th (Princess Charlotte of Wales) Regiment of Dragoon Guards'.

Between 1805 and 1808 the regiment again served in Ireland, being based at Portpatrick, Belturbet, Dublin, Cork and Donaghedee. During this time William concentrated on up-skilling the regiment. Before this date there had been no training manuals for cavalry. But in 1804 Sir David Dundas published his *General Regulations for Cavalry and Infantry*. In 160 pages he covered such diverse cavalry issues as the duties of officers commanding at out quarters, troops, subalterns and adjutants, quartermasters, sergeant majors, non-commissioned officers, trumpet majors and privates. The *General Regulations* also covered parades, internal economy of troops, inspections, stable duties and care of horses in stables and on the march. The duties of riding masters, the medical and veterinary departments, orderlies, guards, sentries and dragoon servants, as well as regimental tailors, were also listed.

In the library of the 5th Dragoon Guards Army Museum at York there is a copy of the *General Regulations* 'printed by George Grierson of Dublin Printer to the King's Most Excellent Majesty'. The book is headed up 'Standing Orders of the 5th Princess Charlotte of Wales Dragoon Guards'. The inscription reads:

It is General Bland's command that the following articles shall be considered as the standing orders of the 5th or Princess Charlotte of Wales' Dragoon Guards and be obeyed accordingly.
W. Ponsonby, Lieutenant Colonel
Princess Charlotte of Wales Dragoon Guards
Dundalk Barracks. 3rd October 1805

When William was not busy with the regiment he could pursue the life of an eligible bachelor belonging to one of the leading Whig families. In those days upper-class England was polarised: you were either a Whig or a Tory, and that depended on family. Whigs attended Harrow and Cambridge, Tories Eton and Oxford. There would be actors, poets, portrait painters and publishers who were only patronised by Whigs, with others patronised only by the Tories. In London the Whig social scene revolved around Holland House, Spencer House and the Prince Regent's residence at Carlton House. For Tories it was Northumberland House and St James. For clubs the Whigs had Brooks' and the Tories Whites'. Outside London the Whigs had Chatsworth,

Woburn and the Brighton Pavilion; the Tories Stowe. Whigs married Whigs. Tories married Tories and the divides were never crossed. As Leslie Mitchell commented in his book *The Whig World*:

> It is perfectly reasonable to talk of a Whig state of mind and of a Whig lifestyle. Such a person probably lived in London rather than the country, had more sympathetic views about French and Frenchmen, had doubts about revealed religion and what passed for conventional morality, and behaved in a way that his fellow Englishmen would regard as too clever by half. To be a Whig was a matter of whom you dined with, whom you borrowed money from and whom you slept with. It was about preferences in reading and architecture, and therefore about whom you patronised. Whigs were likely to have had the same educational experiences, even the same tutors. They of course married each other. Long before a young Whig entered Parliament, he already had had innumerable points of contact with those men who were now to be his political allies.[6]

At the centre of this Whig world were the Cavendish and Spencer families, and two sisters, Georgiana and Henrietta Frances Spencer. They were the 'it girls' of their day, beloved by the media and setters of social fashion. However they were also political activists in their own right. In fact it could be said that they were more actively 'Whig' than their husbands. Georgiana (1757–1806) was the wife of the 5th Duke of Devonshire. Henrietta (1761–1821) was the wife of Frederick Ponsonby, 3rd Earl of Bessborough (1758–1844), a cousin of William's father. William was aquainted with both and featured in their social circle. Georgiana Duchess of Devonshire had given birth, in 1792, to the daughter of Charles Grey (1764–1845), William's friend and a leading light in the Opposition to the government led by William's uncle. Charles Grey subsequently married William's sister Mary. Another prominent member of the Opposition was Samuel Whitbread, who had married Charles Grey's sister. The playwright Sheridan was also a Whig MP and had been one of Henrietta Bessborough's lovers. Everybody in the Whig world was interconnected.

The palatial Devonshire House in Piccadilly was the social hub of this Whig world. Within five minutes' walk was Spencer House in St James, built to the orders of Henrietta's father. The Earl of Bessborough had a grand London house at No.2 Cavendish Square, not so far away.

Further afield were Chiswick House, owned by the Devonshires, Wimbledon Park, owned by the Spencers, and Bessborough House at Roehampton, owned by the Bessboroughs. London was so much the centre of the Whig world that the Countess of Bessborough's first visit to the Irish estates from which she took her title took place in 1808 – twenty-eight years after her marriage![7]

William had access to all these grand places and received invitations to attend parties and other functions. But his immediate family also had residences in London. Admittedly these were not as grand as those of the Bessboroughs or Cavendishes, but they were still situated within the fashionable part of Whig London. Boyle's *Fashionable Court and Country Guide* shows that his father had a town house at 3 Tilney Street and later one at Seymour Street. His elder brother John and his wife Fanny had a house at 31 Curzon Street in Mayfair. His uncle George Ponsonby and his wife Lady Mary lived at 10 Holles Street, as well as having a house at Newlands in Dublin. As George's political importance grew, he was able to upgrade his property, so he moved to 19 Curzon Street. William's younger brother George lived at 14 Arlington Street. 3 Tilney Street, the Arlington Street and Holles Street properties have all had modern makeovers and their façades are now unrecognisable, but the two Curzon Street properties still look as they did in the days of George and John. It is striking how close the properties are to one another. This allowed William to stay with family when he was attending Brooks', the great Whig club, where he was elected a member in December 1800. His membership was proposed by Lord George Cavendish, again demonstrating the closeness of the Ponsonbys to the greatest Whig family of all.

William could not play a very active role in politics during these years as he no longer had a parliamentary seat. The Act of Union had abolished the Irish House of Commons, and although there were 100 MPs in the English House of Commons representing Irish constituencies they were not as many as when Ireland had had its own parliament. William had supported his father and uncle in their opposition to the Union, being one of the few MPs to vote against the Act. Many other MPs, however, took bribes to vote in favour of the Union and the Act came into force in 1801. From then on William was without a seat.

In 1806 William stood as MP for the county of Londonderry. This was an attempt to expand the Ponsonby family's political influence beyond its usual area, into Ulster. To do this William needed the support of other families. Securing a county seat was a very different proposition from a borough seat. At the very least you needed to hold property in the county and so William leased a proportion of Goldsmiths Hall in County Londonderry. Despite the influence of the Grenvilles, a noted Whig family, William was unsuccessful, but in a surviving document we do hear his voice, his principles and the regard in which he was held. The *Morning Chronicle* of Tuesday 2 December 1806 printed the 'address of the Linen Merchants of the City and County of Londonderry to the Honourable Lieutenant Colonel William Ponsonby', and his reply.

We the undersigned Linen Merchants of the City and County of Londonderry, in quality of independent members of the Community take this opportunity of congratulating you Sir together with every friend of Liberty and the genuine constitution on the favourable prospect now afforded through your exertions (seconded not less by the most respectable proprietors than by the affections of the people) of rescuing this county from its hitherto abject state in respect of its elective franchise.

The liberal principles of your Family afford us a gratifying conviction that in cultivating a connection with you we shall strengthen the cause of Freedom in general and ensure to our County the purest and most honourable exercise of its Delegation.

In the character of Landlords the distinguished Personages now at the head of your Family are equalled in few counties and surpassed in none. With regard to commercial interests, we are still more particularly bound to acknowledge the extent of their information and of their protection.

Nor should we omit to recognise to those of your connection a distinction equally peculiar and appropriate in as much as they have advanced to the regard and confidence of their King through the footsteps of our most Patriotic Statesman and in the paths of our Antient [sic] Constitution.

Such are the grounds on which we earnestly hope and shall zealously struggle in our common cause.

Permit us to add that we are justly sensible of the amiable character which you bear in private life and that in the progress of a more permanent connection we promise ourselves the sincerest satisfaction in regarding you as the protector of our local interests and the guardian of our public rights.

William replied:

Gentlemen, it is with the most heartfelt satisfaction and an honest pride that I beg leave to return thanks for this highly flattering testimony of your approbation and esteem. The approbation and esteem of the independent and reflecting part of the community being in my mind the most honourable distinction that can be bestowed on any Family or individual.

The linen manufacturers have been ever universally considered as the source of those preeminent advantages enjoyed by the Northern Counties of Ireland arising not more from the habits of industry and consequent increase of wealth than from the improvement of the mind and genuine spirit of independence by which its progress is every where distinguished.

Backed by the free and zealous exertions of the Linen Merchants a body of such important and well merited consideration and supported by a great portion of the landed interest of the county I look forward with the most sanguine expectation of the attainment of the object of my ambition, and so far as my humble efforts can go, they shall ever be directed to the maintenance of our constitutional rights and to the prosperity of the City and County of Londonderry.[8]

On 5 November 1806 William's father died in his London home at Seymour Street. He was 62 years old and in his final year had been raised to the peerage as 1st Baron Ponsonby of Imokilly, County Cork. It seems he had been unwell for at least two years, the whole situation being exacerbated by his lifestyle. As Uncle George wrote to John, William's elder brother: 'I have never from his first attack considered him really recoverable. I was always sure he would never submit to that regularity of life and exercise which can alone sustain a broken down constitution.'[9]

William's father had drawn up a will in 1803, providing for his wife and their children. The land holdings described were substantial and situated in three counties: Cork, Kildare and Londonderry. The bulk of the lands in Cork and Kildare went to John, as the elder brother, but William specifically received the land in Londonderry: 'to my second son William Ponsonby now Lieutenant Colonel in His Majesty's 5th Dragoon Guards my estate in the county of Londonderry and I will and direct that my said son the said William Ponsonby shall release my heirs, executors and administrators of a legacy of £1,000 bequeathed to him by his great uncle the Reverend William Usher and which sum of £1,000 has been heretofore paid to me by the executors of the said William Usher.'[10] Possession of the Londonderry estate would give William the qualifying right to fight the Londonderry election again at a future date.

However, in the next few years it would become apparent that William's father had used his lands as security for his borrowings, which were considerable. The scale of the indebtedness was not yet known but, when it was, it would plunge the family into a crisis.

In 1806 the Whig leader Charles James Fox died. The Whigs looked around for another leader, but none of the mercurial talents in the party commanded sufficient support across all the factions. George Ponsonby succeeded to the leadership in the unenviable position of a compromise candidate. He did not want the role and wrote to William's elder brother John:

> I am likely to be obliged to undertake the lead of our Friends in the House of Commons. When I say 'obliged' I mean that contrary to my wish and inclination. I feel it to be a duty indispensable to comply with their desires in order to prevent a disunion which I understand is likely otherwise to take place and the reproach of which would be on me.... I really feel myself unfit for the situation.... I am too old and entirely ignorant of men in England. Also I am an Irishman.'[11]

Many people today are unaware that George Ponsonby actually led the Opposition to the Government in the House of Commons from 1806 until his death in 1817. This in itself potentially posed huge problems for William's future advancement. As a serving lieutenant colonel, his career depended on his military commander, who was appointed by the British government. His uncle was now the leader of the Opposition to that government and his brother-in-law and great friend Charles Grey was one of its strongest critics. Would he lose any chance for promotion due to his family's political allegiances, or would the establishment allow him to progress on merit?

Against this troubled political backdrop, on 20 January 1807 a much happier event occurred. William got married, at the age of 35. The marriage registry entry at St Pancras is very simple: 'Ponsonby Wm batchelor (St George's Hanover Square) = Fitzroy Georgiana spinster'.

The Fitzroy family were another great political family, but were also of royal blood, being descended from Charles II's liaison with Barbara Villiers, Countess of Castlemaine. Their son Henry had been created 1st Duke of Grafton. The second Duke had been Lord Lieutenant of Ireland and the third Duke had been Prime Minister between 1768 and 1770. The third Duke's younger brother had been a lieutenant general and had been created 1st Baron Southampton. He had employed the celebrated architect Robert Adam to create Fitzroy Square in London and Georgiana was his sixth and youngest daughter. Georgiana was ten years younger than William. She was born on 13 October 1782 and died on 6 February 1835. Three of her brothers pursued military careers and one of them, Lieutenant General the Honourable Charles Fitzroy, (1762–1831), would be one of William's executors.

It is difficult to form a view of Georgiana. There is a family story that she was a stern woman who beat her children if they were wayward. The marriage, however, seems to have been a relatively happy one. William's letters show he genuinely cared for his wife and worried about her being lonely when he was abroad on military service. We know she was distraught with grief when William died in 1815.

Georgiana and William had four daughters. Anne Louisa was born on 4 April or May 1808; Charlotte Georgiana was born on 18 June 1809. Mary Elizabeth was born on 21 February 1811, and Isabella Frances was born on 24 February 1812. A son, William, was born on 6 February 1816, after his father William's death.

In 1808 William's regiment returned to England to undertake more peacetime duties. They disembarked at Liverpool in July 1808. During the next three years William and the regiment spent time at Dorchester, Guildford, Colchester and Norwich. As always their role was to counter any rebellious behaviour by the local population and to this task they added crushing the smuggling operations prevalent on the Norfolk and Suffolk coasts. Georgiana accompanied William as he moved from barracks to barracks. Their daughter Charlotte was born at Fingringhoe, Colchester, in 1809 when the regiment was based there.

On 25 July 1810 William was appointed a brevet colonel. This was another indication of his increasing seniority, but without a larger command the appointment did not mean much. However, in 1811 fate intervened.

On 2 June 1811 the regiment was ordered to move to Kingston on Thames. On 8 July the regiment was reviewed on Wimbledon Common by their Royal Highnesses the Prince of Wales and Frederick, Duke of

York who expressed their approval of its appearance and the rapidity and brilliant execution of its movements. A few days later orders were received to prepare the regiment for foreign service. Its destination was Portugal and the Peninsular War.

It was in the Peninsula that William would make his reputation, which would eventually lead Fortescue, the historian of the British army, to state that he was one of the best British commanders of a cavalry brigade.

Chapter 5

Fighting in the Peninsula
Part 1: 1811–12

In 1805 there had been a number of events that defined the next ten years of the struggle between Britain and France. The success of the Royal Navy in first blockading the navies of France and its Allies and then its decisive defeat of the Franco-Spanish fleet at Trafalgar persuaded Napoleon that he would not be able to invade Britain. Within six weeks of Trafalgar he had systematically defeated both Austria and Russia at Ulm and Austerlitz. In 1806 it was the turn of Prussia to be defeated at the battles of Jena and Auerstadt. In 1807, after the battles of Eylau and Friedland, Russia sued for peace and her Tsar Alexander and Napoleon divided Europe up between them.

It has been said that France dominated the land and Britain the sea and the result was stalemate. Certainly the British government would have been happy with this. For twenty months after Trafalgar it had been able to land troops wherever it wanted, but when it had chosen to send expeditions to Buenos Aires, the Dardanelles and Egypt they had been defeated. There had been one minor success when a small British army commanded by Sir John Stuart defeated a French army at Maida in southern Italy. However, with French troops converging upon them in overwhelming numbers, the British army had hastily re-embarked and sailed back to Sicily, so there were no tangible gains from the victory. Much better, politicians argued, to concentrate on winning the colonial war and not to throw away resources on expeditions to the European mainland that had a track record of failure.

But for Napoleon there could only be one victor. Britain had financed the other European powers in raising armies to attack France and could do so again. As Napoleon could not defeat Britain by military methods, he decided to do so by economic means, striking against Britain's trade. As Britain's productive capacity soared due to the developments known collectively as the Industrial Revolution, she needed markets to sell her goods. Napoleon, in a series of measures, banned all trade with Britain and forced this ban on any country he defeated. Britain responded by banning all trade with France except through Britain. The effects were serious in both France and Britain, as there were now only three European countries classed as neutral that could accept British goods: Denmark, Portugal and Sweden. Bonaparte planned to neutralise the two Baltic countries. Although Britain seized the Danish fleet, Denmark signed an alliance with France in 1807 and Sweden, with a mad king, would not cooperate with Britain and was in awe of Russia. This left only Portugal, Britain's oldest ally.

The two Portuguese cities of Lisbon and Oporto acted as huge centres for British goods entering the Continent. Napoleon determined to seize Portugal and dispatched an army, which marched through Spain. The Royal Navy evacuated the Portuguese court and escorted them to the safety of Brazil, which was then part of the Portuguese empire. A French army occupied Portugal and Napoleon decided he might as well annex Spain, even though the Spanish were nominally his allies. The French poured troops into Spain. The Spanish royal family abdicated in favour of Napoleon, but the Spanish people rose in revolt and sent a delegation to Britain requesting help.

A British army was sent to the Iberian Peninsula in 1808 under newly promoted Lieutenant General Sir Arthur Wellesley. It had originally consisted of only 9,000 men, but had won victories at Rolica, Vimeiro, Corunna, Oporto, Talavera and Bussaco. The most recent French invasion attempt by Marshal Massena in 1810–11 had been thwarted and a bloody defeat inflicted on the French troops at Fuentes de Onoro. The fortresses of Almeida and Elvas, guarding the major invasion routes into Portugal, were in allied hands. The Portuguese army was being thoroughly reformed by Wellesley's second in command Marshal Beresford and seconded officers from the British Army, and was becoming an effective fighting force. The Royal Navy controlled the seas around the Iberian Peninsula and could land and supply troops, attack French coastal defences and assist the bands of guerrillas which terrorised the French soldiers. With Portugal secure everything was now ready for Wellington to go on the offensive and take the war to the French in Spain. Not only would this safeguard Portugal, but also, by driving the French from Spain, he would encourage other European states to attack the French, something that had not occurred since Austria's defeat in 1809.

To do this Wellington needed more troops. The Spanish armies were the obvious source, but past experience was not reassuring. In the Talavera campaign Wellington had collaborated with the Spanish, relying on their ability to provide troops, but they had not supported him and when they acted independently they were, with a few exceptions, thrashed by the same French marshals Wellington had already proved he could beat.

If Wellington was going to go on the offensive he needed more British troops, both infantry and cavalry. At the battle of Fuentes de Onoro in May 1811 Wellington's army had numbered approximately 37,600, of which only 1,860 were cavalry. At Albuera the army totalled 20,300, of whom 2,000 were cavalry. Wellington particularly needed more heavy cavalry, led by a good cavalry general who could use them decisively but keep them under control.

In overall command of Wellington's cavalry from June 1810 was Major General Stapleton Cotton (1773–1865). Cotton had a track record of serving in both the light and heavy cavalry. He had served in Flanders, the Cape of Good Hope and India (where he met Wellington) before the Peninsula. Despite a penchant for wearing flashy uniforms and being quick to take offence at perceived slights, he was a steady cavalry commander whom Wellington could trust not to jeopardise the small numbers of cavalry at his disposal. The same could not be said for some of his subordinates, including 'Mad Jack Slade' and Sir William Erskine. It was therefore important that not only were more cavalry sent out, but also that they were led by capable commanders.

In 1811 the Government authorised a new heavy cavalry brigade to be formed. It would comprise the 3rd Dragoons and the 4th and 5th Dragoon Guards. It was commanded by Major General John Gaspard Le Marchant (1766–1812) from Guernsey, who had greatly increased the effectiveness of the cavalry by designing the 1796 light cavalry sabre, producing sword exercises and insisting on cavalry training. He was the founder and first principal of the Royal Military College, the officer school that would one day become Sandhurst. His combat experience was, however, limited to the Flanders campaign of 1794 in which he had served in a junior capacity, so he had no experience of brigade command.

The 3rd (King's Own) Dragoons were under the command of Lieutenant Colonel Mundy. The 4th (Royal Irish) Dragoon Guards were under the command of Lieutenant Colonel Francis Sherlock. Although the 4th Dragoon Guards had not had much combat experience, this was not the case for their commanding officer. Sherlock had started his career with the 8th Light Dragoons in the Flanders campaign of 1794, having on one occasion had his horse killed under him and being mentioned in dispatches for his attack on the village of Bourbeque. He had served in the colony of the Cape of Good Hope with great distinction, reaching the rank of major, but the climate had weakened his constitution and he had returned to England in 1803. He became a major of the 4th Dragoon Guards in 1803 and one of its two lieutenant colonels in 1809. Of Le Marchant's three lieutenant colonels Sherlock had most experience. Indeed, he had more active combat experience than Le Marchant himself.

As for the 5th Dragoon Guards, there was no doubt that it would be William who would lead them into action abroad. Commanding the regiment in the field was the responsibility of the regiment's lieutenant colonel. The 5th Dragoon Guards had two, William Ponsonby and Robert Taylor. Robert Taylor was the senior, with experience of active service in the Low Countries and in Ireland in 1798. However, since 1801, when he was appointed major general, his involvement in the regiment had decreased. Now he was a lieutenant general and outranked Le Marchant, the brigade commander. William had been most recently involved with the regiment and so he was appointed to command the 5th Dragoon Guards in the Peninsula.

Although the regiment had ten troops, it was decided that four would form the depot based at Canterbury. Six troops would serve abroad, comprising in total 544 officers and men.

William had a very reliable group of staff officers to assist. The regimental adjutant from 1808 to 1823 was Joseph Jackson. He had joined the regiment from being a troop quartermaster in the 4th Dragoons and would be present at all the regimental actions in the Peninsula. Thomas Coates had been surgeon of the regiment from 1795. The paymaster was James Bruncker, who had been promoted from the ranks and had served as cornet, lieutenant, captain and adjutant before becoming paymaster in 1806. John Brown Stanley was the regiment's first veterinary surgeon, having been appointed in June 1798. Richard Haslam was the quartermaster. He had served in Flanders and was present at the battle of Le Cateau. He had become troop quartermaster in 1795, regimental sergeant major in 1809 and then in the same year was promoted to quartermaster for the regiment. The current regimental sergeant major was John Hunt Cochrane. He had joined the regiment as a private and served in the Flanders campaign.[1]

The Regimental Army List for 1 January 1811 shows there were two majors, ten captains, twelve lieutenants and six cornets. With the regiment being put on an overseas service footing, numbers were increased at the junior levels and we know that at least one major, six captains, ten lieutenants and eight cornets served in the Peninsula, with the others staying to run the depot and four troops at Canterbury.

The two majors, in order of seniority, were William Jones and William Brooke. William Jones had joined the regiment as a captain in 1798 after being a captain in the 5th Royal Irish Dragoons. He had become major in 1802 and brevet lieutenant colonel in 1809. He would retire in December 1811, but served in the Peninsula with William from September to November 1811. The second major, William Brooke, was born in 1770 and came from County Kildare. He had been a major in the 96th Foot, commanding the garrison on St Domingo in the West Indies between 1795 and 1796. He had transferred into the 5th Dragoon Guards as a major in 1805. He would not travel out with the regiment in 1811, as being second major in seniority he would be in command of the depot at Canterbury. When he did arrive in the Peninsula it was to be as officer in charge of court-martials at Lisbon, a post he held from September 1812 to April 1814.[2]

The six captains who served in the Peninsula from 1811 were, in order of seniority: Prescott, Aicken, Irwin, Ormsby, Osbourne and Walker. Excluding any operational experience in Ireland, only one had had active military experience abroad, so William and Major Jones had officers who could command, but who were mainly inexperienced in battle conditions.

Sergeantson Prescott, the senior captain, was the son of Major General Prescott who had inspected the regiment in 1791. He was born in 1784 and had been a lieutenant in the 91st Foot, transferring into the 5th Dragoon Guards as a lieutenant in 1807. He became a captain in 1810 and replaced William Jones as major in December 1811. He would command the regiment and be wounded at Llerena. He was very capable and William would appoint him to command the regiment after Salamanca. Francis Aicken had joined the 5th Dragoon Guards as a captain from the 21st Dragoons in 1803 and would be wounded at Salamanca. William Irwin, although an Irishman, had been in the Dumfries Fencible Cavalry and had joined the 5th Dragoon Guards as a cornet in 1798, progressing to the rank of captain in 1801. Adam Ormsby, another Irishman, did have military experience. He had served in the Flanders campaign in 1794, having joined the regiment as a cornet in 1791. He had become a lieutenant in 1795 and a captain in 1803.

Keane Osbourne's captaincy dated from 1810. Previously he had been a lieutenant in the 4th Dragoons. He would participate in the charge at Llerena and at Salamanca, where he would be killed. The last captain, William Walker, had joined the regiment as a cornet in 1810 and was the most junior captain, having been appointed in August 1811.[3]

The ten lieutenants who served in the Peninsula were Bradshaw, Brunkshill, Houghton, Kellett, Walker, Gordon, Bradshaw, Hamilton, Jackson and Richards. It is not known whether Francis Bradshaw and George Bradshaw were related. Both would serve with the regiment throughout the Peninsular War. John Brunkshill had been adjutant in the 1st Fencible Cavalry in 1799 and had joined the regiment as a cornet in 1800. He had been a lieutenant since 1804. Edward Houghton, like William Irwin, had served in the Dumfries Fencible Cavalry. He had become a cornet in the 5th Dragoon Guards in 1801 and a lieutenant in 1805. He had served as regimental adjutant until 1808 and would serve with the regiment throughout the Peninsular War, as would the other lieutenants, Edward Kellett, Stephen Gordon, George Hamilton, Charles Walker (severely wounded at Llerena), Joseph Jackson (the adjutant) and William Nunn Richards. The same was true of the cornets: Braithwaite Christie (who would be William's ADC after Salamanca and at Waterloo), Giles Miles, Joseph Pattison, Edward Barrington, Thomas Matthews, Henry Brooke, George Spence and John Clarke.[4]

What is remarkable about the officers of the regiment is how very few of them chose to leave it by transferring to other regiments. Other cavalry diaries record officers transferring or resigning, but of these twenty-five officers only one, Captain Francis Aicken, chose to leave the regiment while it was in the Peninsula: he transferred to the 1st Royal Dragoons in 1813. This paints a very revealing picture of morale in the regiment and reflects positively on the *esprit de corps* William was able to create.[5]

An anonymous trooper of the 5th Dragoon Guards wrote an account of his experiences in the Peninsula. He had previously enlisted in the King's Royal Artillery in Dublin, but had joined the 5th Dragoon Guards in August 1810. He would later serve in India, where he wrote up his account of his time in the Peninsula, which he had kept on scraps of paper. He wrote:

> The Regiment was inspected by the inspecting general of cavalry and all those men who were considered unfit for active service were selected out, of whom some were discharged and the rest

kept to form a depot and furnish recruitment parties. A great many horses were likewise cast and sold off by public auction.[6]

In addition to selecting the best men and horses, all the necessary supplies had to be organised. William also had to find a house for Georgiana and their young family to live in while he was abroad, and of course he did not know how long he would be away. Ireland was out of the question, although Bishopscourt was no doubt offered. The house had to be close to Georgiana's family, who were developing the area of London now called Fitzrovia, in which they had a house, as well as William's own family. Given the precarious state of the Ponsonby family finances, and the fact that William was dependent on his regimental pay, they could not afford to buy a house, but instead chose to rent one at Hampstead, which was of the requisite size but further from central London than they might have wished.

On Monday 22 July 1811, the *Hampshire Telegraph and Sussex Chronicle* was able to tell its readers that on Saturday 20 July:

> The 5th Dragoon Guards marched into Horsham on the 18th and 19th instant on its route for Chichester. Four troops after moved to Arundel barracks. It is supposed the whole will very shortly proceed to Portsmouth to embark for Portugal.[7]

The aim was to reach Lisbon in about seventeen days, but this all depended on fair winds and fitting in with the schedules of other convoys. Le Marchant had some of his brigade embark from Plymouth. The 3rd Dragoons were still waiting to sail on 3 August. On 6 August the *Hampshire Telegraph* reported that Le Marchant and the 3rd Dragoons had sailed. The 5th Dragoon Guards were delayed until at least 17 August:

> The *Wolverine* Captain Kerr takes a convoy to Portugal and sails when the wind is fair. Sir Thomas Hardy will go out in her to resume command of the *Barfleur*. The 5th Dragoon Guards consisting of six troops have embarked this week for Portugal. They will sail with the *Wolverine*.[8]

The *Wolverine* was a brig sloop well used to the work that protecting convoys demanded, and had an enterprising commander. The fact that Sir Thomas Hardy, of Nelson and Trafalgar fame, was travelling on board as a passenger back to his ship the *Barfleur* gave William a chance to meet one of the naval legends of the age. The convoy was also transporting two regiments of infantry and pieces of artillery and comprised twenty-seven transports.

Such a sea crossing was trying for the men, but much more so for the horses, which were kept in specially constructed stalls in the holds of the transports. Everyone prayed for a quick, uneventful crossing. Unfortunately, these prayers were not answered. The convoy was hit by a hurricane. Some ships were driven on to the coast of Holland and lost. The convoy had to reassemble at Falmouth, but the weather played foul again. On 3 September the convoy was again dispersed and had to be reassembled a second time, at Torbay. From there it was able to progress to Lisbon. Disembarkation began on 12 September. Thirteen horses had been lost due to the rolling of the vessels in the storms.

Horses and men landed at Black Horse Square, named after the equestrian statue of King José I erected in 1775. The statue is still there, but is now green as a result of exposure to the elements. From there the troops were marched to their barracks in the vacated palace of Belem. Here there were plentiful supplies of water and vegetables. The horses were housed in stables previously occupied by the cavalry of the Portuguese Royal Guard: 'The stables for horses were well paved and commodious, containing racks, mangers and cisterns to hold water.'[9]

Unfortunately for the troopers, their living conditions were not as good:

> We were obliged to shift in the best way we could our only bed being a kind of platform full of holes whence issued whole squadrons of rats which often left the marks of their teeth upon the faces of those who lay down top heavy over night. This together with swarms of bugs and fleas and mosquitoes could not fail to render our quarters very uncomfortable.[10]

For William and his officers, living conditions were better. They stayed in the royal palace, or in nearby townhouses vacated by the nobility. There were theatres and receptions to attend.

Most accounts from arriving troops pay tribute to the views of the city from the River Tagus, the number of churches, the viaduct and so on. The reality, however, was not as picturesque as the first impressions. The soldiers commented on the filthy streets, into which the inhabitants threw rubbish and waste out of upper windows without warning. They also noted the religious practices of the inhabitants, and explained that the troops couldn't wait to leave the city.

After becoming acclimatised to Portugal, six weeks later the brigade was moved up country. The aim was to prevent General Reynier marching on Lisbon in a surprise attack while the rest of the British army was in winter quarters in northern Portugal. Part of the brigade was posted on the right bank of the Tagus, while William and the 5th Dragoon Guards were moved to Tomar on the left bank. Progress was slow. There were heavy rains and the lack of a pontoon bridge delayed the regiment crossing a river. From Tomar the regiment moved to Abrantes.

All round the town are handsome gardens, olive groves and olive plantations… At this place our camp equipment was completed and ammunition and flints issued to each man.[11]

There was also the prospect of action.

We were immediately ordered in pursuit of a small body of the enemy with whom we had a smart skirmish but with little loss on either side. Great sickness prevailed among our men at this time.[12]

The issue of sickness of men and horses and finding sufficient forage for the horses was a greater problem for William than fighting the enemy, particularly as Reynier decided to make no move against Lisbon.

On 25 October 1811 George Murray, Wellington's quartermaster general, wrote to Sir Stapleton Cotton:

My dear Sir Stapleton, Lord W thinks of sending General Le M's brigade into the valley of the Zezere. I am therefore to request that you will suspend the intended march of General Alten's brigade in that direction. Lord W's idea is that it is of importance to put the newly arrived regiments into the most quiet and comfortable cantonments we can give them. Perhaps you would upon this ground recommend the villages towards Lamego but the objection to them is their distance to the left in case anything should occur to make it necessary to reinforce suddenly the corps in the Alemtego. I hope to have reports from you soon about the supply of forage in the valley of the Zezere.[13]

This preparation period was crucial for both the men and the horses. An officer of the 1st Royal Dragoons who served during the Peninsular

War, in his monograph *The British Cavalry on the Peninsula,* talked about the need to bring the horses to performance by degrees due to the change in climate and forage. A horse eats ten times as much as any human and providing them with suitable food was always a problem. In Portugal there were no oats for the horses to eat. The Indian corn that took its place was edible, but the horses had to get used to it. In addition, many cavalry horses in the Peninsula suffered from a disease called sore back, which was only prevented once the troopers learned how to correctly stuff a saddle and fold the blanket.[14]

The men, too, needed to acclimatise:

But perhaps time was most necessary to initiate the dragoon in the proper division of his time in performing his many duties of cleaning his horse and appointments, furnishing long forage for the horse and food for himself. In England he had been in the habit of having those duties performed for him, or at the least the arrangements for their accomplishments are so good as to occupy very little of the soldier's time.[15]

The troopers also needed to get used to what they could eat and drink. In an age when water was not fit to drink, beer and wine were the fluids consumed, but drinking wine that had not been sufficiently aged could cause great sickness. This was a problem facing many regiments in the Peninsula. Wellington himself wrote of one cavalry regiment:

Of 470 men they could only produce 230 and these looked more like men come up out of the hospitals than troops just arrived from England. All the newly arrived regiments of cavalry are in nearly the same state.[16]

Given the shortage of British cavalry in the Peninsula, the 5th Dragoon Guards were expected to undertake duties traditionally associated with light cavalry alongside their own. This mainly meant outpost duties: operating in small groups ahead of the main part of the army, to get early warning of the presence of the enemy and prevent it from attacking the main body. Given previous operations in Ireland, and operating in scattered groups to enforce law and order, the 5th Dragoon Guards were well suited to this work. They were helped in their task by lighter horses, which although of sufficient weight for a powerful charge, were also light enough to carry out the role of light cavalry.

While ensuring that preparations were effective, William had additional duties. During this period we come across references to William presiding at two courts-martial. In October he heard the case of two privates of the Royal Marines who had left their guard post, broken into a Portuguese house and stolen goods from it. William and the court sentenced the offenders to 800 and 1,000 lashes respectively. In November, William officiated at the court-martial of a deputy assistant commissary general of the fort at Peniche, who had abused his position towards the local inhabitants: 'he beat the people employed under him and insulted the inhabitants of the fort by conduct and language which a gentleman ought not to have used.' William and the court sentenced him to be suspended from rank and pay for three months and to be severely reprimanded.[17]

We don't know how William spent Christmas 1811, but in early January the brigade was ordered to move into northern Portugal. Wellington had decided to attack Ciudad Rodrigo, the French-held fortress that commanded the northern approach into Spain and mirrored Almeida, which Wellington already held. If he took Ciudad Rodrigo he would not only safeguard northern Portugal, but also be able to invade Spain along the major road whenever he chose.

However, Wellington did not want to be attacked by a French relieving force while he was besieging Ciudad Rodrigo. He needed cavalry to give advance notice of French troops marching to relieve the fortress and prevent any attack.

Wellington ordered Le Marchant to move his cavalry brigade to Ciudad Rodrigo. The journey took only three days, but it was very cold with snow on the ground and the roads had been neglected for so long that they were virtually impassable. The villages en route were deserted and in a state of ruin, so the cavalry had to carry sufficient food for themselves and their horses.

> On 8th January the weather being unfavourable we were ordered with a detachment of light infantry to Castella Branca. We then passed Vilha Velha to Niza leading our horses the whole of the way and moving in single file in consequence of the rugged and steep nature of that part of the country. Our orders were to intercept a body of the enemy that were hovering about that quarter with the intention of succouring Rodrigo but we compelled them to relinquish this attempt.[18]

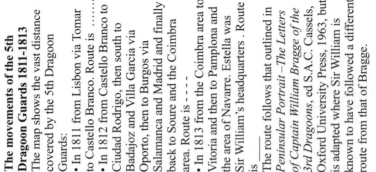

The movements of the 5th Dragon Guards 1811-1813

The map shows the vast distance covered by the 5th Dragoon Guards:

• In 1811 from Lisbon via Tomar to Castello Branco. Route is ······

• In 1812 from Castello Branco to Ciudad Rodrigo, then south to Badajoz and Villa Garcia via Oporto, then to Burgos via Salamanca and Madrid and finally back to Soure and the Coimbra area. Route is - - - -

• In 1813 from the Coimbra area to Vitoria and then to Pamplona and the area of Navarre. Estella was Sir William's headquarters . Route is ───

The route follows that outlined in *Peninsular Portrait –The Letters of Captain William Bragge of the 3rd Dragoons*, ed S.A.C. Cassels, Oxford University Press, 1963, but is adapted where Sir William is known to have followed a different route from that of Bragge.

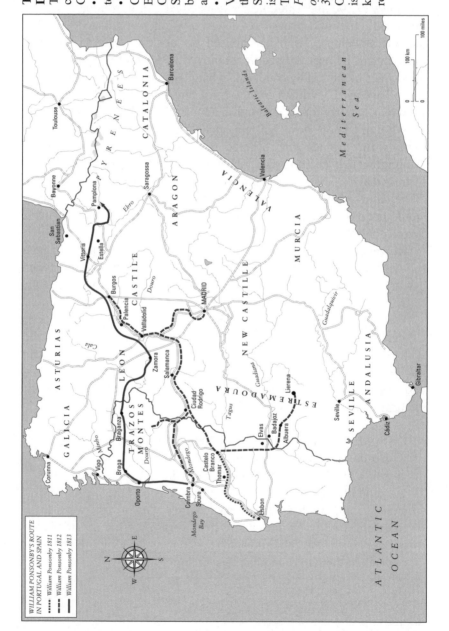

WILLIAM PONSONBY'S ROUTE
IN PORTUGAL AND SPAIN

······ *William Ponsonby 1811*

- - - - *William Ponsonby 1812*

─── *William Ponsonby 1813*

The fortified city of Ciudad Rodrigo was stormed on 19 January 1812. Wellington then turned his attention to Badajoz, the French-held fortress that commanded the southern approach into Spain. By holding Badajoz, as well as its Portuguese neighbour Elvas, he could decide to invade Spain from the south as well as the north. But Badajoz was more formidably fortified than Ciudad Rodrigo. The French would not be caught unawares and, having lost control of the northern approach to Spain, they would do everything they could to prevent Badajoz from falling.

Le Marchant's brigade moved south, probably with relief, as the forage for the horses had been consumed and the animals had been forced to eat oak leaves, which made many sick. A French attempt to relieve the pressure on Badajoz by making a move towards Oporto caused William and the 5th Dragoon Guards to march to Oporto, but the French had withdrawn before they arrived.

In February 1812 the brigade was reorganised. The 4th Dragoon Guards had suffered greatly from sickness and were transferred to General Slade's brigade. They were replaced by the 4th, or Queen's Own, Dragoons. The 4th Dragoons had served in the Peninsula since 1809 and had seen action at Talavera, Albuera and Usagre. They were commanded by Lord Edward Somerset, the elder brother of Wellington's military secretary, who belonged to a family on very good terms with the Duke. Lord Edward Somerset had joined the 10th Dragoons as a cornet in 1793 and had become lieutenant colonel of the 4th Dragoons in 1801. He was therefore senior to William in length of service. He was popular but prone to attacks of gout.

On 17 February there was some light relief when Stapleton Cotton gave a ball at Cavilhan. Then the marching began again. On 21 February the brigade moved from Castello Branco to Villa Vicosia, which they reached on 5 March. The landscape dramatically changed. The soldiers were now on the vast plains of the Alantejo, punctuated by holm oaks and ideal cavalry country. The brigade was dispersed among the neighbouring villages, which were well populated and flourishing due to their vineyards and the absence of any French attacks. On 15 March the brigade crossed the Guadiana into Spain to keep in check any French attempts to relieve Badajoz. The cavalry headed towards Villa Franca, Zafra and Bienavida, which they reached on 25 March. On 1 April an attempt to bring the French to action near Albuera was unsuccessful when the French were warned by a deserter from the Brunswick Oels regiment of hussars.

From March to the end of May 1812 the cavalry of both sides played a game of cat and mouse in the area around Badajoz. Firstly the British army forced the French to relinquish the Spanish town of Alivenza. Then the British planned to surprise Usagre, sending forward a detachment of light infantry, guns and a squadron each of the 3rd Dragoons and the 5th Dragoon Guards. Unfortunately the French were tipped off by a private of the 3rd Dragoons who deserted to them. The French then attacked at daybreak with a combined force of cavalry and infantry. The 5th Dragoon Guards trooper wrote: 'we retreated in the best manner that we could and not until we had 28 men killed and taken prisoner belonging to our two squadrons besides 13 wounded.'[19]

Stapleton Cotton arrived, with the rest of Le Marchant's brigade and light cavalry, and it was the turn of the French to withdraw. William probably brought up the two remaining squadrons of the 5th Dragoon Guards in this relieving force.

Besides helping prevent the French from relieving Badajoz the regiment also protected the besiegers from attacks from the city: 'On 6th April the cavalry were ordered to take up a position which opposed us to galling fire from the enemy's batteries and the citadel.' On a previous occasion they 'covered the guns from dusk to daylight'.[20]

Badajoz finally fell on 6 April. The 5th Dragoon Guards were not involved in the assault, but they achieved their first major combat success at Llerena on 11 April 1812.

On April 10 Stapleton Cotton had discovered that the French cavalry ordered to observe the British forces were encamped between Usagre and Villa Garcia, with the closest infantry support at Llerena. He determined to cut them off by threatening their front with light cavalry commanded by William's second cousin Frederick Ponsonby, forcing them to retreat towards Llerena, where they would find Le Marchant's brigade waiting for them. The French cavalry discovered the British advance and, as they outnumbered Frederick Ponsonby's brigade, prepared to charge. They had not, however, seen Le Marchant's brigade emerging from a defile in the heights on their flank. Le Marchant led the 5th Dragoon Guards into the attack and five French cavalry regiments were rolled up and pursued for four miles. The French losses were one lieutenant colonel, two captains, one lieutenant and 134 other ranks captured, along with 113 horses and fifty-three men killed or wounded. The 5th Dragoon Guards' losses were fifteen men killed, twenty-seven wounded and twenty horses killed or wounded. This was about two-thirds of the losses in the action.

A detachment of the 5th Dragoon Guards escorted the captured prisoners back to the main Portuguese fortress of Elvas before rejoining the regiment at its base at Crato. Since 16 March when they left Villa Velha they had not had a day's halt. Even after Llerena there had been no respite. The bulk of the regiment had left Zafra on 13 April and was at Zebra, 150 miles away, on the 23rd. Only at Crato was there a chance to draw breath. From Crato, on 7 May, Adjutant Jackson sent to the regimental depot in England the cavalry and brigade orders praising the 5th Dragoon Guards' conduct. William was not present at the action at Villa Garcia. His second in command Major Prescott led the regiment. We don't know why William was not present. Perhaps he was sick, but it did not stop him from praising his command:

SIR – I have great pleasure in communicating to you by direction of Colonel Ponsonby the cavalry and brigade orders issued on a late occasion when the FIFTH DRAGOON GUARDS attacked a very superior enemy and forced him to retire with the loss of about one hundred killed and wounded, besides one lieutenant colonel, two captains, one lieutenant and 140 men taken prisoners with near 100 horses. This affair presents a pledge of the future good conduct of the regiment whenever an opportunity again appears of meeting the enemy and must be peculiarly gratifying to you and the remainder of the corps at the depot in England to hear from such undoubted authority, that the regiment still continues to support that high character which it gained on many former glorious occasions, and in our estimation this last is not the least: the regiment, having previous to the attack on three times its numbers of the enemy's best cavalry, made a forced march of upwards of 60 miles without halting – four of the last of which was at a very brisk pace, through a difficult country, over rocks, ravines, and stone walls; then forming with unexampled celerity and charging with equal and regular rapidity through a grove of olive trees until it came in contact with the enemy, who retired in great disorder under the cover of his infantry and guns. Our loss in this brilliant affair was comparatively trifling as will be seen by the subjoined statement of the names of the brave men who fell.

W. JACKSON
Adjutant[21]

Chapter 6

Fighting in the Peninsula
Part 2: The Battle of Salamanca

The victories at Badajoz and Llerena had occurred in April, right at the beginning of the 1812 campaigning season. Wellington still had a good six months at his disposal and he was determined to make the most of it, particularly as his victories at Ciudad Rodrigo and Badajoz had given him the opportunity to take the initiative and defeat the French forces in Spain. His situation had changed greatly from his previous crossing into Spain and the Talavera campaign of 1809. He was no longer so dependent on Spanish army support that he had to comply with Spanish views, even though he disagreed with them. The question was, who to attack?

Nominal control of the French armies in Spain rested in the hands of Napoleon's brother Joseph, whom the Emperor had made king of Spain. The reality, however, was rather different. Each of the regions of Spain was controlled by a marshal, the highest rank in the French military hierarchy. Each of the marshals believed, quite justifiably, that they were better military commanders and knew more about soldiering than Joseph. They would collaborate with each other if the Emperor was present and commanded them to do so, but in 1812 Napoleon was preoccupied with preparing to invade Russia – the invasion began in June. The marshals remaining in Spain regarded their territories as personal fiefdoms and would not automatically come to each other's assistance if one was attacked. They did not respect Joseph and would try to ignore his orders if they could. Wellington knew all this thanks to his excellent spy network.

One option was for Wellington to attack Marshal Suchet, who was operating in Catalonia and Valencia, but to get to Suchet Wellington would have to fight his way across the centre of Spain, so this option was speedily discounted. Another option was to attack the French forces in the north of Spain in Navarre or the Asturias, but this would have allowed the French forces in central Spain to invade Portugal while Wellington's back was turned, or even worse attack him in the rear. There were two more sensible options. The first was to use Badajoz as a bridgehead and from there attack marshals Soult and Victor in the south of Spain, where they were controlling Andalucia and besieging the Spanish government in Cadiz. Such a move would have pleased the Spanish, but it did not have any other benefits.

The preferred option was to attack what the French called the Army of Portugal, based in Central Spain under its new commander Marshal Marmont. Marmont had already made moves against Ciudad Rodrigo when Wellington moved on to Badajoz. He was the marshal most willing to collaborate, and if Wellington had moved against Soult and Victor he might have come to their aid. Wellington reasoned, quite correctly, that if he attacked Marmont, Soult and Victor would not march to his aid. They concentrated on Cadiz and Andalucia. Soult had been unable to raise the siege of Badajoz, so it was unlikely he would now try and recapture it if Wellington moved to attack Marmont. But just to be on the safe side, Wellington firstly persuaded the Spanish General Ballasteros to deploy some of his troops to further preoccupy Soult. Secondly, he instructed his trusted subordinate, Lieutenant General Sir Rowland Hill, to destroy the crucial bridge over the River Tagus at Almaraz. This bridge would be used by French troops from Soult's army if they wanted to reach Marmont quickly. Once it was destroyed they had to follow a much longer route. At the same time Wellington had his engineers restore the damaged bridge at Alcantara, enabling Hill and his 18,000 men to reinforce Wellington before Soult could reinforce Marmont, even if he wanted to.

To complete Marmont's isolation Wellington encouraged plans for British troops from the garrison in Sicily to mount an expedition to the east coast of Spain, where Marshal Suchet operated. Wellington also ensured that the guerrilla leaders in northern Spain stepped up their attacks on the French. In this he was assisted by Spanish army units and a British naval squadron with a large contingent of marines, who carried out raids along the coast.

As a result of these measures, Wellington could be reasonably certain that Marmont would only be able to look for support from the 15,000 men under Joseph and his chief of staff Marshal Jourdan. If he could defeat Marmont before they arrived, their support would have no impact.

Wellington moved his army north and began to concentrate it. On 1

June William and the 5th Dragoon Guards, as part of Le Marchant's brigade, began to move northwards. At the same time Marmont fell back from besieging Ciudad Rodrigo and left a garrison of 800 men in three forts in the old university town of Salamanca, which was the next city in Spain on the road from Ciudad Rodrigo. In order to feed his army Marmont spread the remaining 25,000 men among cantonments twenty miles north of the town and waited to see whether Wellington would become bogged down in taking the forts and give him an opportunity to counter-attack.

Wellington now had a marked superiority in numbers. The 5th Dragoon Guards had marched via Castel Branco, Alcaniz, Caria, Castelheira and Gallegos to join his forces, which now numbered 48,000 men. On 13 June they crossed the River Agueda into Spain and on 17 June reached Salamanca. On 19 June Wellington left the 6th Division, commanded by General Clinton, to capture the forts and positioned the rest of his army on the heights above the village of San Cristobal, from where he could forestall any attempts by Marmont to relieve the forts. Le Marchant's brigade and the other cavalry units were used to give ample notice of any moves that Marmont might make and block any attempts.

Marmont advanced on 20 June, but despite some skirmishing he had only 28,000 infantry and 2,000 cavalry against Wellington's 37,000 Anglo-Portuguese infantry and 5,000 cavalry. This was because he only had five of his eight divisions available. Nevertheless, he used his artillery effectively and Le Marchant had thirteen horses killed in two of his regiments, although there were no trooper casualties.

On 21 June Marmont was joined by two more of his divisions, numbering just over 9,500 men and giving him parity in infantry but not in cavalry. Some manoeuvring occurred and on 24 June Le Marchant's brigade was sent to support the two heavy cavalry regiments of General Bock when the French crossed the Tormes at Huerta. Marmont withdrew, but not before subjecting the heavy cavalry to a heavy artillery cannonade, which inflicted a number of casualties on both men and horses. This proved to be his final opportunity to relieve the forts, which fell on 27 June. The fall of the forts freed up for Wellington the 6,000 men of Clinton's division and moved the balance of resources back in his favour.

With the fall of the forts and the news that he could not expect any reinforcements from the French forces in northern Spain, Marmont withdrew northwards from Salamanca on 28 June and Wellington followed. Marmont took up a strong defensive position behind the River Douro near Valladolid, about seventy-five miles north-east of Salamanca. Wellington deployed his forces south of the Douro and waited.

Wellington's force outnumbered Marmont's and, on 3 July, William and the 5th Dragoon Guards, together with the 3rd Dragoons, were detached to support the 5th division at Polos in an attempt to cross the Douro by a ford and break Marmont's line. The attempt failed as the French were well provided with artillery and the 5th Division did not have any. Thus the watching game resumed. On 7 July Marmont was joined by his final division of 6,500 men, commanded by Bonnet, which restored overall parity in numbers. The French had slightly more infantry than Wellington, slightly fewer cavalry and more artillery.

The key to understanding what happened next is that Marmont believed he would not get any more reinforcements and had reached his maximum strength, whereas he believed Wellington could increase his numbers further if he ordered Hill to join him with his 18,000 men, which would obviously turn the balance decisively in Wellington's favour. Marmont therefore felt he had to bring Wellington to battle as soon as possible. He was actually wrong on both counts. Firstly, Wellington had ordered Hill to remain in the south watching Soult. Secondly, very unfortunately for Marmont, King Joseph and Jourdan had assembled a force of 14,000 men to march to his assistance. They had sent messages, but guerillas intercepted all of them and Marmont never knew. If he had he might have delayed and waited for the Royal Army to arrive, bringing a decisive advantage. As it was, the crucial battle was fought and won before the royal troops arrived.

Marmont's defeat at the Battle of Salamanca has encouraged historians to ignore the brilliant tactical approach he adopted in the days before the battle. First, on 16 July he hoodwinked Wellington into thinking that he was going to cross the Douro and head towards Salamanca by the shortest route. Wellington moved the bulk of his forces to counter this. During the night the French army marched to the other end of the line and crossed over the Douro there, putting at risk two of Wellington's divisions, which now lacked support. On 18 July Wellinton sent in the heavy cavalry brigades of Bock and Le Marchant to cover the withdrawal of the two isolated divisions. This was achieved and over the next few days Wellington used his cavalry to support his infantry as Marmont made various feints to see if he could open up a gap in Wellington's lines and make a decisive strike. He was unable to find one, but in the course of a few days Marmont had succeeded in bringing his army back into a position from which he could threaten Salamanca. The evening of 20 July saw Wellington call a halt and position his army in front of San Cristobal, covering all the approaches to Salamanca from the north and north-east. Marmont was in front of him, but then made another gruelling march to secure the fords over the river and threaten Wellington's southern flank.On the 21st Marmont moved his army across the river, much to Wellington's annoyance, as they were now too far away for the infantry to intervene. However, the cavalry could still have an influence and the trooper of the 5th Dragoon Guards wrote:

> Our brigade was furnished with three days provisions with strict orders to get them cooked without loss of time. We had been then two days and part of the third without rations. Fires were therefore lighted and camp kettles got ready with alacrity but before they had been allowed time to boil the orders were countermanded, the provisions were thrown away or left on the ground and also obliged to leave our horses' corn behind us on the field, and ordered to mount with precipitation, the enemy having crossed the River Tormas and were advancing with their whole force upon Salamanca. We succeeded in turning their left flank and took three field pieces together with a number of prisoners.[1]

Le Marchant halted his brigade near the ford and village of Santa Martha, situated on the River Tormes close to Salamanca. The 5th Dragoon Guards trooper stated:

> Our brigade with a body of infantry and three guns halted at a small village apart from the main body of our army, both men and horses much fatigued and in want of food. The evening closed in with a threatening look and the clouds gathered thick and heavy all around. The clouds continued to collect together over the face of the sky and the atmosphere foretold an approaching storm.
>
> We rolled ourselves up in our cloaks to snatch a little rest of which we were much in need, when we were roused from our slumber by the bursting of the storm; the rain poured down in torrents, accompanied by thunder and lightening more terrible than ever I remember to have witnessed. To add to our misfortunes many of our horses broke loose and galloped about in all directions. Some found their way to the enemy's camp and

several of our own men had their legs and arms broken by them. In the meantime the French were secure and under cover in a large forest near the Arapiles.[2]

Many additional accounts refer to the storm. Although a number of cavalry regiments lost horses, all agree the storm's effects were particularly felt by the 5th Dragoon Guards because a lightning bolt struck their position. Some of the horses that ran away returned during the night and the following morning, but by daybreak thirty-one mounts were still unaccounted for. The effect of this was twofold. Firstly, the regiment was below strength in horses for the battle. Secondly, eighteen soldiers had been seriously injured when the frightened horses trampled them, and thus could not take part in the ensuing battle. Although William had received reinforcements from England on 17 July, he could have done without losing men and horses before the battle even started. Needless to say he could not have got much sleep that night.

The next day, Wednesday 22 July, was hot and sunny. Even after the downpours of the previous night, moving troops made clouds of dust as they moved into position. Neither army was concentrated: 6,000 of Wellington's best infantry were north of the River Tormes, for example, but the total numbers at each commander's disposal only gave a slight superiority to Wellington. Numbers are always difficult to establish, but the best estimate[3] is as follows:

	French Army numbers	% of the army	Wellington's army numbers	% of the army
Infantry	41,500	84%	45,400	87%
Cavalry	3,400	7%	5,000	10%
Artillery	3,400 manning 78 guns	7%	1,300 manning 62 guns	2.5%
Miscellaneous	1,300	3%	250	0.5%
Total	49,600		51,950	

There was very little difference between the two armies in terms of infantry. One-third of Wellington's infantry was Portuguese, but under Beresford's training they proved themselves the equal of the British troops. The French troops were of good quality and still believed that they would win any battle they fought. The French generals who commanded them were also men of great experience who had commanded troops in the French Revolutionary wars. The one exception to this was Marmont himself. He was the youngest of Napoleon's marshals, being 38 at the time of Salamanca. He had distinguished himself at the battles of Lodi and Marengo and so far in the game of cat and mouse with Wellington had done well, but he had never commanded an army in action. Wellington, on the other hand, was an immensely experienced battlefield commander, although on 22 July he did not have many of his experienced subordinates with him. Lord Hill was still in the south, Sir Thomas Graham had had to return to England because of problems with his eyes and Sir Thomas Picton was recovering from the wounds he had sustained at Badajoz. Apart from General Leith Wellington's divisional commanders were relatively inexperienced.

What was to prove very telling was the weakness in French cavalry. The French usually ensured they had superiority in cavalry to turn a defeat of their enemies into a rout. Marmont had realised this and had commandeered infantry officers' horses and intercepted reinforcements heading for Soult, but he had not had time to ensure the horses were trained and for men and horses to get used to each other. Those cavalrymen that had their own horses were light cavalry, who did not have the experience of the heavy cavalry in being shock troops. Wellington of course had five regiments of heavy cavalry (the three regiments of Le Marchant's brigade (900–1,000 men) and the two Dragoon regiments of Bock's King's German Legion (comprising 700 men) and they were in superb condition. So the discrepancy in cavalry strength was even more in Wellington's favour than the numbers suggested.

All this might not have mattered if 22 July had turned out to be just another day of marching, with Marmont teasing Wellington in the hope he would make a mistake and Wellington avoiding doing so. From Marmont's point of view he still had some positioning to do before he would be in the position he required. He had to finish moving the rest of his army across the river and then move slowly south, aiming to then turn south-west to cut the road to Ciudad Rodrigo, which was Wellington's line of retreat to Portugal. Having completed this manoeuvre he would be between Wellington and Portugal and in a position to attack.

Le Marchant's brigade was ordered to move south from Santa Martha to join the main army, a distance of about four miles. They moved out of the village at 7am. Wellington held a position on a rough north–south axis from the River Tormes at Santa Martha, along a range of heights running south to a hill called the Lesser Arapile, one of two hills close to the village of Los Arapiles, which was held by the light companies of the Guards. From the Lesser Arapile the heights become a ridge facing west for about a mile; in effect the Lesser Arapile is the hinge point of an L-shaped ridge. Behind this ridgeline Wellington was able to hide some of his units from the French. D'Urban's Portuguese cavalry and Packenham's Third Division of 6,000 men were north of the Tormes, guarding a ford to prevent Wellington being taken in the rear.

Marmont occupied the ridge facing Wellington and began concentrating his army so it stretched from the River Tormes to the village at Calvarrasa de Arriba. Beyond was a wood of holm oaks that covered most of the rough countryside to Alba de Tormes eight miles away. Between the two armies was a valley just over a mile in width, separating the two armies with a stream called the Pelegracia.[4] Today the battlefield is relatively unspoiled, but the wood has disappeared.

The morning was spent in a fairly desultory exchange of shots between both sides' pickets, but two key manoeuvres took place. Between 8am and 9am Marmont seized the dominant hill, called the Greater Arapile. This gave him the hinge point for his own L-shaped ridge, pointing west for about three miles as far as the village of Miranda de Azan. As the Greater Arapile is only about half a mile from the Lesser Arapile, this ridgeline was very close to Wellington's L-shaped ridge, but it would allow Marmont to turn Wellington's position and cut him off from Portugal more quickly than taking a more circuitous route. Wellington did prepare to attack the Greater Arapile between 11am and 12 noon, and this may have confirmed in Marmont's mind that Wellington was preparing to retreat, causing him to hurry to move his army to the south-west. Of more significance was Wellington's conclusion that whatever happened would be on the south bank of the Tormes, and that he could therefore order Pakenham's 3rd Division and D'Urban's Portuguese Horse to cross the Tormes and take position four miles north-west of Los Arapiles near Aldea Trajeda. Here they would be ideally placed to support a retreat or check any moves by Marmont to cut the line of the retreat. They would arrive at their position, unseen by the French, at about 2pm. At the same time Wellington realigned his army, keeping the 1st, 5th, 7th and light divisions, an independent Portuguese brigade, Bock's heavy cavalry and some light cavalry, totalling 26,200 men, facing east, and the 4th, 5th, 6th and 7th divisions, with a Portuguese and Spanish brigade and heavy and light cavalry, comprising in all 19,000 men, facing south.

During the rest of the morning each side reconnoitred the other. The unknown trooper in the 5th Dragoon Guards recalls being sent as part of a squadron to reconnoitre the French positions. They came under artillery fire and were forced to withdraw.[5] On another occasion troops from Le Marchant's brigade escorted Wellington on a reconnaissance and again had to withdraw from French artillery fire. At one point Le Marchant's brigade had to support some light cavalry who came under attack from Boyer's dragoons in an attempt to persuade Wellington to move his forces back north.[6]

Between 1pm and 2pm Marmont gave the order for the French to begin to move south-west to turn Wellington's left flank and cut off his line of retreat to Portugal. Although this was his intention all along, he was probably confirmed in his decision by seeing two dust clouds. One was the Allied army's heavy baggage moving from Salamanca towards the Portuguese frontier. The other was probably from Pakenham's and D'Urban's troops, which Marmont misinterpreted as troops leaving the area. Actually, they were heading towards it.

The French troops began to advance along the L-shaped ridge on to the Monte de Azan. They were divided up into divisions arranged as follows:[7]

Division	Number of infantry	Commanded by	Supported by
5th Division	5,200	Maucune	Curto's light cavalry of 1,900 men and several batteries of artillery
7th Division	4,500	Thomières	
2nd Division	6,600	Clausel	
6th Division	4,600	Taupin	
Total	22,800		

In addition Marmont positioned a regiment from the 8th Division to cover the area between the Greater Arapile and the Monte de Azan. The French divisions were to keep close enough to provide supporting cover to each other.

Then things started to go wrong. The exact instructions given to Maucune and Thomières are unknown, but there were enough reputations at stake after the battle to cast doubts on the veracity of any statements made afterwards. Suffice it to say that Maucune stopped opposite the village of Los Arapiles and deployed his artillery and infantry to attack that part of Wellington's line at about 3pm. Thomières' division simply passed him by and kept on going along the ridge. Clausel's division stopped further back, where it could not support Maucune. Taupin's division stopped behind Clausel. This meant that Maucune's and Thomières' divisions could be picked off one by one if Wellington hit them with a superior force and defeated them in detail. Marmont spotted the danger and sent urgent orders to his divisional commanders on the right wing to march to support the centre and for Taupin to move further left. He then left his command position on the Greater Arapile to sort out what was happening on the left. Unfortunately for the French, at that moment he was badly wounded by a shell fired by Wellington's artillery and took no further part in the battle. In a separate incident his second in command Clausel was also wounded by a British shell and so was having his wound treated. The third in command, Bonnet, was then wounded by British artillery. For a crucial hour before Clausel returned, the French army was without an overall leader and the fate of the French advance passed totally into Wellington's hands. Obviously Wellington did not know that Marmont and the French command were *hors de combat*, but he had all his troops positioned so that he could take the offensive. At a stroke he proved to the French what his opponents in India had known: he could win an attacking battle as well as a defensive one.

Wellington, on seeing the French advance, had moved the 5th and 7th divisions from facing east so they could now deploy southwards. He now had 31,000 men facing south to oppose 23,000 French, and this did not take into account Pakenham's division. Wellington now rode three miles to Pakenham's 3rd Division of 5,800 men and instructed it to attack Thomière's division of 4,500. Then he instructed General Leith, commanding the 5th Division of 6,700 men, to attack Maucune's division of 5,200 men once Pakenham was engaged with Thomières.

But this was only part of Wellington's plan. He intended to administer a devastating *coup de grâce* by hitting the French infantry with cavalry while the French were locked in a firefight with the British infantry. To accomplish this he ordered the 1,080 cavalry of D'Urban and Arentschildt to support Pakenham and defeat Curto's French cavalry of 1,900 men. Le Marchant's brigade was ordered to support Leith in attacking Maucune's division, which did not have cavalry support. If all

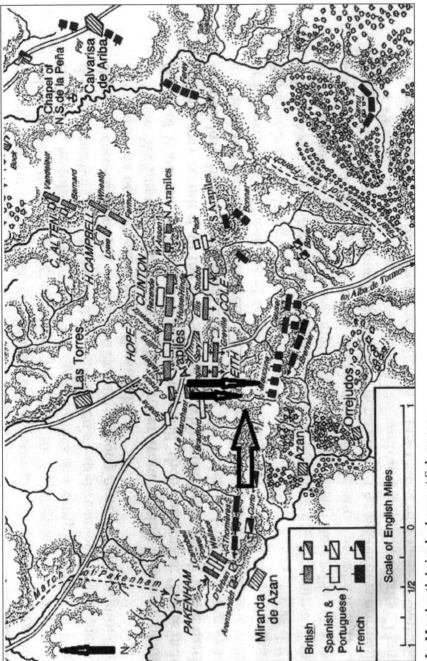

Le Marchant's brigade charge at Salamanca

On this map from Sir Charles Oman's *A History of the Peninsular War* Pakenham's division attacks Thomières' division, while Leith's troops attack Maucune's division. Le Marchant's brigade manoeuvres so that he attacks the retreating Thomière's division and then Taupin's, while William Ponsonby and the 5th Dragoon Guards attack Maucune.

went well the French left would be destroyed before the French centre or right could support it.

It seems that on his ride to Leith to give him his orders, Wellington stopped and gave orders to Le Marchant, ignoring Stapleton Cotton, the overall cavalry commander. He instructed Le Marchant to use his brigade to attack the French at the first opportune moment, telling him 'You must then charge at all hazards'.[8]

At about 3.30pm Pakenham began his attack. His advance was hidden from Thomières by a low range of wooded hills to their front. Curto's cavalry seems to have been riding in parallel to the infantry and not in front to protect it. The attack from both Pakenham's infantry and D'Urban's cavalry caused Thomières' division to collapse. Thomières was killed and his men ran back to Maucune's division for protection.

Leith had been ordered by Wellington not to commence his attack until he could see that Pakenham had been successful. At about 4.15pm Leith's division began its attack on Maucune. Maucune pulled his men back onto the reverse slope and waited for Leith. Although the French fired a volley, in which Leith was wounded, the British returned their fire, cheered and then followed up with the bayonet, at which Maucune's men began to give way. At that very moment Le Marchant led his men into the charge.

Le Marchant's heavy cavalry of between 900 and 1,000 men, 750 being rank and file, was halted on low ground in front of Las Torres, out of sight of the enemy. Le Marchant had ordered the troopers to dismount and lie down so they could not be seen. He sent two officers to reconnoitre the ground they would have to cross and post vedettes to give warnings of difficult points. Like Leith he had been told by Wellington only to advance when the time was right. When the time to advance arrived, the troopers moved forward in two lines at a walk. On the left were two squadrons of the 5th Dragoon Guards under William Ponsonby, with one squadron kept in reserve just behind. In the centre were two squadrons of the 4th Dragoons under Lord Edward Somerset and on the right were two squadrons of the 3rd Dragoons with one squadron kept in reserve just behind. The brigade frontage was about 600 yards. It was about 4.45pm.

Le Marchant led his brigade into the gap between Thomières' and Maucune's divisions. This was beginning to be filled by Thomières' defeated battalions. At this stage Cotton joined Le Marchant and they exchanged heated words as to the actual direction the attack should take. The 3rd and 4th Dragoons hit the French 62nd and 101st regiments, which had already suffered from Pakenham's attack. From then on the brigade was split as Le Marchant turned the 3rd and 4th Dragoons slightly right to deal with the 22nd Ligne from Taupin's division.

William Ponsonby led his regiment on the route that had been planned and into Maucune's division. He did not leave an account of how he felt leading his regiment into the charge, but it must have been an unforgettable experience to lead 300 men into battle to do what cavalry were meant to do and come through it unscathed. Perhaps it was a mixture of dread and intoxication. Richard Webb, the trumpet major to the 2nd troop of the 5th Dragoon Guards, who sounded the charge, stated much later to one of his descendants:

> I trembled all over as I lifted the trumpet to my mouth for I could see what the boys had before them but as soon as my lips touched the mouthpiece fear left me and I blew such a charge as I never had before or could afterwards.[9]

William first attacked the 66th Regiment de Ligne in the flank while it was being attacked from the front by Leith's division. His regiment's speed had now increased from a trot to a canter. The speed would increase to a gallop only if needed, as there was then the danger that the charge would run out of control, with the horses' and the troopers' blood being up. Instructions were communicated above the din by trumpet calls, and the trumpeters in each of the troops took their instructions from the brigade trumpet major, riding next to William and to whom William would shout his orders. The men were in great spirits. Corporal John Douglas of the First Foot (Royal Scots) in Leith's division, which was attacking the French 66th, remembered some of the 5th Dragoon Guards crying out to his regiment 'Now boys lather them and we'll shave them.'[10]

The 66th Ligne of two battalions was the first to feel the hacking cuts of the 1796 heavy cavalry sword. Then it was the turn of the three battalions of the 15th Ligne and then the 82nd Ligne. For any infantry the worst nightmare was to be caught unawares by cavalry, and this is what had happened. The French had not been able to see the heavy cavalry's approach as it was masked by a combination of the advancing infantry, the smoke from the discharge of the muskets and the sun shining into the eyes of the French. When William's cavalry appeared some infantry tried to resist, some feigned death and the rest ran away – some even begged the attacking British infantry to protect them!

A number of accounts give an impression of what the charge must have felt like for William and the 5th Dragoon Guards. Firstly there is Napier's wonderful, atmospheric account. Napier was at Salamanca, but it is important to note that he did not take part in the charge.

A front had been spread on the southern heights but it was loose and unfit to resist; for the [French] troops were some in double lines, some in columns, some in squares; a powerful sun shone full in their eyes, the light soil, stirred up by the trampling of men and horses, and driven forward by a breeze, which arose in the West at the moment of attack came full upon them mingled with smoke in such stifling clouds that scarcely able to breathe and quite unable to see, their fire was given at random.

In this situation while Pakenham bearing onward with a conquering violence was closing on their flank and the fifth division advancing with a storm of fire on their front, the interval between the two attacks was suddenly filled with a whirling cloud of dust which moved swiftly forward carried within its womb the trampling sound of a charging multitude. As it passed the left of the third division Le Marchant's heavy horsemen flanked by Anson's light cavalry broke forth from it at full speed and the next instant 1,200 French infantry though formed in several lines were trampled down with a terrible clamour and disturbance. Bewildered and blinded they cast away their arms and ran through the openings of the British squadrons stooping and demanding quarter while the dragoons big men on big horses rode onwards smiting with their glittering swords in uncontrollable power and the third division followed at speed shouting as the French masses fell in succession before this dreadful charge.[11]

The trooper in the 5th Dragoon Guards who actually took part in the charge tells a similar story:

The smoke clearing away, our artillery men were enabled to distinguish the enemy and ploughed through their ranks without giving them time to close them up. We then rushed to the charge and heedless of the mass of bristling bayonets in the front cut down and trampled everything beneath us. In this charge the gallant Le Marchant lost his life. ...I also received a musket ball in my right leg but did not quit the field.

Sir William Ponsonby then assumed the command of our brigade. The enemy at length then gave way in all quarters. Great confusion took place throughout their columns thus giving our troops every opportunity of following up and taking every advantage of the disorganised enemy. At length it became a complete carnage.[12]

Lt Norcliffe of the 4th Dragoons, also a participant in the charge, wrote a letter to his father three weeks after the battle:

My beloved father
Thanks to the Almighty, and the very great care of my surgeon, I am quite out of danger from the severe wound I received but it was perhaps the most hairbreadth escape that was ever heard of, the skull was just injured and the tenth part of an inch more must have consigned me to an eternal rest. We were pursuing the French infantry which were broken and running in all directions. I was cutting them down as well as I could when in the hurry and confusion I lost my regiment and got with some soldiers of the 5th Dragoon Guards; on looking behind me I could only see a few of the 5th and we were in the centre of the enemy's infantry amongst whom were a few Chasseurs and Dragoons. Nothing now remained but to go on as we were in as much danger as by going any other way.
I rode up to a French Officer who was like the rest taking to his heels and cut him just behind the neck: I saw the blood flow and he lost his balance and fell from his horse. I perceived my sword was giving way in the handle so I said to the officer who lay on the ground 'Donnez moi votre epee'. I really believed he was more frightened than hurt; I sheathed my sword and went on with his. I had not gone 10 yards further before my horse was wounded in the ear by a gunshot, he turned sharp round and at the same instant I was shot in the head. I turned giddy and fell off. I can recollect a French Dragoon taking away my horse. I was senseless a few seconds and when I recovered I saw the French Dragoons stripping me of everything.[13]

Norcliffe later managed to escape and wrote:

it was a glorious day for our brigade. They behaved nobly. 4 men killed of the troop I commanded and several men and horses wounded. It was a fine sight to see the fellows running and as we held our swords over their heads fall down on their knees, drop their muskets and cry Prisonnier Monsieur.[14]

The charge had covered two miles and lasted about an hour. The French left was broken and survivors streamed for the safety of the woods. It was 5.45pm.

There is a great lack of accurate information about the actual charge, in particular as to the order in which French regiments were attacked. However, there is no doubt about the combined impact of Leith's attack and Ponsonby's charge. Maucune's division was broken and took no further part in the battle. The 66th Ligne sustained 588 casualties from 1,169 all ranks (50 per cent casualties), while the 15th Ligne sustained 607 casualties from 1,667 (36 per cent). The 82nd Ligne sustained 272 casualties (27 per cent). Leith's division alone took 1,500 prisoners.The French regiments attacked by Le Marchant and Somerset, along with Pakenham, sustained even higher casualty figures.[15]

The charge was perfectly timed and executed. The French infantry had been caught already shaken, disordered and broken. It converted their defeat into a rout and spread fear and panic throughout the whole French left wing. Three divisions of infantry, half the enemy's cavalry and a good part of its artillery were on the French left. After Le Marchant's charge none of it could be brought to face the allies again except the two remaining regiments of Taupin's infantry.

The casualty figures for the cavalry were very low considering what they had achieved: 105 were killed, wounded or were posted missing. The 5th Dragoon Guards suffered the highest casualties with sixteen killed, forty-four wounded and three missing. Captain Osborne was killed leading his troop, as were two sergeants, one corporal and twelve privates. Among the wounded was Lieutenant Braithwaite Christie, 3rd son of Admiral Alexander Christie of Baberton, near Edinburgh in Scotland. On recovering from his wounds he would become William's ADC for the rest of the war and at Waterloo. However, Le Marchant had been killed leading a late attack against some formed infantry close to the woods, and with his death Wellington lost a very capable cavalry commander.

The casualty figures sustained by the brigade would have been higher if the French cavalry had intervened when the heavy cavalry started to split into smaller groups and become fragmented at the end of their charge, as happened at Waterloo. But one of the remaining unknowns of the Battle of Salamanca is why Curto's cavalry were so ineffective and did not attack Le Marchant's dispersed troopers.

Although the French left had been destroyed, this did not mean that the battle was won. An attack on the French centre was repulsed. Clausel, now back in charge, led an all-out attack with his 2nd and Bonnet's 8th Division, but they were stopped by Clinton's 6th Division and a Portuguese brigade and forced to retreat. A fighting rearguard action by the French divisions of Sarrut and Ferey, which involved an hour-long firefight with Clinton's 6th Division, was finally defeated when Leith's troops attacked them in the flank. The French broke and fled for safety through the woods as night fell and the Battle of Salamanca was over. Wellington's army had suffered 5,200 casualties, but the French had about 14,000, as well as losing twenty guns, six colours and two eagles. Just as importantly, French morale had been dealt a devastating blow.

William Ponsonby was presented with a gold medal for his conduct. The 5th Dragoon Guards were rewarded with the honour of bearing the word 'Salamanca' on their standards. The staff of the drum major of the 66th French regiment of infantry was captured and William, at his own expense, had it mounted and presented to the regiment, which still parades it.[16]

After Le Marchant's death a new commander was needed for the brigade and Wellington appointed William Ponsonby, announcing this in his order of thanks to his victorious army, written the next day.

Col the Honourable Wm Ponsonby is appointed Colonel on the Staff till the pleasure of HRH the Prince Regent is known and is to command the Brigade of cavalry commanded by the late M Gen le Marchant.[17]

William's appointment was a testament to Wellington's view of his abilities, as it could be argued that Lord Edward Somerset was a more obvious choice. Somerset belonged to a family that was close friends with Wellington. They shared the same politics. He was the elder brother of Wellington's secretary. He had been a lieutenant colonel longer than William, and had served in the Peninsula for longer. Despite the problems of having a brigade commander who had an uncle and a best friend leading the opposition to the war effort in the House of Commons, and who would, on promotion to the army staff, have access to confidential papers which could be dynamite if they fell into the wrong hands, Wellington was obviously certain that William was the right man for the job.

Wellington's official dispatch on the battle appeared in the main newspapers, although there was a much longer delay than would be the case nowadays. Cobbett's *Weekly Political Register* carried the news nearly a month later, in its eighth issue dated Saturday 22 August 1812.

OFFICIAL PAPERS Battle of Salamanca
War Department – Downing Street August 16 1812
Lord Clinton Aide de Camp to the Earl of Wellington arrived this morning at the war department with Dispatches addressed by his Lordship to Earl Bathurst dated the 21st, 24th and 28th ultimo of which the following are extracts.

Flores de Avila July 24th 1812
The cavalry under Lieutenant General Sir Stapleton Cotton made a most gallant and successful charge against a body of the enemy's infantry which they overthrew and cut to pieces. In this charge Major General Le Marchant was killed at the Head of his brigade and I have to regret the loss of a most able officer....

It was dark before this point was carried by the 6th division and the enemy fled through the woods towards the Tormes. I pursued them with the 1st and light divisions and Major General William Anson's brigade of the 4th division and some squadrons of cavalry under Lieutenant General Sir Stapleton Cotton as long as we could find any of them together directing our march upon Huerta and the ford of the Tormes by which the enemy had passed on their advance but the darkness of the night was highly advantageous to the enemy many of whom escaped under cover who must otherwise have been in our hands. – We renewed the pursuit at break of day in the morning with the same troops and Major General Bock's and Major General Anson's brigade of cavalry which joined during the night and having crossed the Tormes we came up with the enemy's rear guard of cavalry and infantry near La Serna...

I am much indebted to ...Colonel the Honourable William Ponsonby commanding Major General Le Marchant's brigade after the fall of that officer...[18]

Contrary to what is recorded, the 5th Dragoon Guards' exertions did not end after their charge on the French left. Cannon's *Historical Record*

of the 5th Dragoon Guards, published in 1831, says that the left
squadron of the 5th Dragoon Guards was sent to support Major General
Bock's brigade of KGL Heavy Cavalry.[19] The 5th Dragoon Guards'
trooper recalls pursuing the French until darkness fell, when the French
entered the woods and further pursuit became impossible.

Much to Wellington's annoyance, the Spanish troops had left their
position blocking the bridge across the River Tormes at Alba de Tormes.
If they had held it, the French would have been prevented from crossing
the river and Wellington's army would have taken even more prisoners.
So on the next day, 23 July, the pursuit was resumed and the brigade
plus von Bock's KGL dragoons attacked the French rearguard:

> We took a number of prisoners together with a variety of stores
> of all descriptions. Shortly after Lord Wellington arrived and
> ordered our brigade to halt until the rest of the army arrived and
> the wounded and prisoners to be sent back to Salamanca. Many
> of our men when they dismounted were scarcely able to stand so
> stiff and chafed were they from being such a length of time on
> horseback, the poor horses were also terribly galled and
> completely knocked up. The Germans (at Garcia Hernandez) had
> taken a great many sheep and pigs from the enemy; also a content
> of biscuit and flour. Their General ordered us to be furnished with
> a sufficient quantity for our present consumption and we set about
> cooking in the best way that we could. As the greater part of us
> had eaten nothing for four days previous our method was naturally
> very expeditious, the point of a sword served as a toasting fork
> and scarcely had the meat been well smoked over the flames than
> it was devoured with eagerness by the half famished soldiery.
> Some contrived to procure earthen vessels from a small village
> not far distant but we were not able to procure any salt
> nevertheless it proved a most welcome repast. Among the spoil
> were three pipes of brandy, but our General (Ponsonby) fearing
> they might have been poisoned ordered them to be destroyed.[20]

It was not the first time, nor would it be the last, that William
intervened to protect his men, even though his decision may have been
unpopular.

Chapter 7

Fighting in the Peninsula Part 3: Madrid, Burgos and the Great Retreat

The pursuit continued one more day and was then stopped at Flores de Avila as Wellington's troops were exhausted. So frantic had the pursuit been, that when Le Marchant's body was buried on 24 July the military honours usual for burying a general could not be followed, and the only persons of note who attended were his son, his servant, a medical officer in charge of the wounded and Major Onslow of the 5th Dragoon Guards, whom William had left in charge to ensure the wounded were taken to Salamanca and looked after.[1] William had to write home. His letter to his brother Frederick was typically self effacing:

Flores de Avila
July 25th 1812
My Dear Frederick
You will see in the Gazette a much better account of the complete victory which we have gained near Salamanca than I can possibly give. I will only say that it was gained by one of those prompt vigorous and masterly manoeuvres on the part of Lord Wellington which had he never done anything before would be sufficient to stamp his character as a first rate officer – a manoeuvre as unexpected by Marmont as it was decisive of his ruin. Our brigade of cavalry had the good fortune to act a very prominent and decisive part in it and the deroute of the enemy was beyond anything complete – and had we had another hour's daylight I do not think a thousand of them would have escaped. They have been bullying us for several days particularly on the whole of that day and billets for quarters in Salamanca were

actually found in the pockets of several French officers – but the day closed on the complete discomfiture and precipitate flight of Marmont and his army. We had the misfortune to lose General Le Marchant who was killed by a musket shot. I lament him sincerely though in a worldly sense which by the bye I do not think you much understand. I benefit by it Lord Wellington having without any application on my part, appointed me to the staff as Colonel and given me the command of certainly as fine a brigade of cavalry as can easily be found. My own regiment forming one of it. The doctrine you have always maintained as to Lord Wellington's qualities as an officer will I think not lose ground by this battle or rather victory the most complete and decisive since the days of Henry 5th – and I will venture to say a victory in which chance has less to do and in which generalship was more exclusively the acting cause than any other upon record. Pray give my love to my mother I suppose she has gone to England and you with her but I send this to Georgiana who will forward it to you. My dear Frederick I cannot tell you how sincerely gratified I feel to you for your kindness in going now and then to stay with Georgiana when I am absent. I feel this sort of kindness a thousand fold particularly as I know it gives the greatest gratification possible to her and I assure you she is as grateful for it as I can possibly be
Believe me ever most affect yours
W Ponsonby[2]

William was unstinting in the praise he gave his men.

Camp near Flores de Avila
25th July 1812
REGIMENTAL ORDERS
His Excellency the commander of the forces having been pleased to appoint Colonel Ponsonby to the staff of this army and to the distinguished honour of commanding this brigade, Major Prescott will be pleased to take upon himself the command of the regiment.

The 5th Dragoon Guards well know how highly Colonel Ponsonby has always prized the honour of commanding them and if the pride he has long felt in command of a regiment deservedly of such high character admitted of augmentation its most gallant and glorious achievements in the field as well as its soldier like conduct in quarters since its arrival in this country could not fail to enhance it. He assures the officers and men of the regiment that it is now with considerable regret he takes his leave of them as their regimental commanding officer, although in the course of professional promotion; and he requests Major Prescott the officers, non commissioned officers and the whole of the regiment will accept his warm and sincere thanks for the past as well as his heartfelt and anxious good wishes for the future. May the 5th Dragoon Guards long continue to be ranked as second to none in his Majesty's Service.[3]

Despite his promotion William did not give up his lieutenant colonelcy in the 5th Dragoon Guards – indeed sources still refer to him as colonel – but his responsibilities had obviously greatly increased, so he needed Major Prescott to run the regiment, which Prescott did well. William was now responsible for three regiments totalling approximately 1,000 men, compared to the 330 men he had been responsible for previously. Also he could not rely on help from Le Marchant's brigade major, a role today known as adjutant with responsibility for planning the details of the operations of the brigade. This was because Captain Smith, who had fulfilled this role, had been killed beside Le Marchant in the battle of Salamanca. Nor could William rely on guidance from the overall cavalry commander Stapleton Cotton, as Cotton had been shot by mistake by troopers on piquet duty on the evening of 22 July. Although the wound was not mortal it was sufficient for Stapleton Cotton to have to return to England. Wellington entrusted overall command of the cavalry to Major General von Bock, who was as inexperienced in this position as William was at brigade level. Thus a lot of the organisation as well as strategy fell on William's shoulders. The wounded men and horses had to be taken to Salamanca and the remainder of the brigade had to resume its advance, because Wellington had determined to reap the political as well as the military advantages of seizing Spain's capital, Madrid.

Wellington did have a choice. He could have continued to pursue the remnants of the shattered army heading north and he did this for a time. He entered Valladolid on 30 July, capturing Marmont's supply base and allowing him to replenish his ammunition supplies. But he picked up information that Joseph and the Royal Army had left Madrid in an attempt to reinforce Marmont. In fact Joseph had heard of Marmont's defeat on the 25th and returned to Madrid. He recognised that his force was too small to oppose Wellington and that Suchet and Soult were too far away to help. He therefore decided to evacuate the court from Madrid and move to eastern Spain and Valencia, which was safely in French hands and which he reached on 31 August.[4] Wellington saw the opportunity to seize the Spanish capital and provoke a major rebellion against French rule throughout Spain. If he captured King Joseph as well it would be a bonus. He therefore turned south.

William's brigade was at the front of Wellington's advance, with a duty not only to protect and support the infantry, but also to see off any French cavalry that might challenge Wellington's advancing army. The army progressed towards Madrid via the royal palace of San Ildefonso, with its celebrated gardens. The roads were well paved and the mountain passes 'easy of defence and requiring but a small force were abandoned without a musket shot being fired for their protection.'[5] Everyone must have thought that it was going to be an uninterrupted progress right into Madrid. But Joseph and his generals had other ideas.

On 11 August Wellington's vanguard approached Majalahonda, a village one day's march from Madrid. The vanguard of the army was made up of D'Urban's Portuguese cavalry, King's German Legion dragoons and a battalion of infantry as well as a troop of Royal Horse Artillery. For twenty-four hours there had been manoeuvring between them and a strong French cavalry force of dragoons and lancers commanded by the enterprising General Trelliard. It was evening. The KGL cavalry were making their meal, and the RHA horses were being stabled when the French advanced. The Portuguese cavalry, outnumbered three to one, advanced to charge but then fled and were pursued into the KGL camp.

As Maxwell described in his *Peninsular Sketches*:

> The Portuguese dragoons fled at the first onset, without waiting to exchange one sabre cut with the French; and so rapid was their flight for they rode through the village where the reserve of Germans were posted to support them, that not more than half of the Germans were mounted. Many brave men fell before they could defend themselves, and their colonel was cut down while in the act of shaving himself... Up to this point the combat was one scene of desperation. An irregular and furious crowd might be seen mixed together, fighting without order or regularity; and from the confusion that prevailed, it was not possible to see

distinctly to which side the victory belonged; but at a distance far from the scene of action, the burnished helmets of the Portuguese troopers were distinguishable as they fled from the post they had deserted, and from their braver companions, the Germans who they left to be massacred. The din of arms, the clashing of swords and the fire of the cannon, mingled with shouts from every side completed the confusion. In the hurry of the moment, some tents belonging to the 74th regiment took fire, the flames soon communicated with those of the next regiment and the camp was enveloped with smoke. But this was soon overcome; and by the time we approached the French cavalry had been driven off the field, but not before many of the Germans had fallen. Three guns of Macdonald's brigade had also been taken, and upon the whole it was one of the most disgraceful and unlooked for events that had taken place during the campaign.[6]

In less than an hour Trelliard and his cavalry killed or wounded 200 men, captured three guns, the commander of the KGL brigade and two of the five regimental commanders. The French cavalry losses were one officer killed and fifteen wounded.

Although the KGL fought back, it was only following the arrival of Ponsonby's brigade and the forward elements of the 7th Division accompanied by Wellington himself that the French retired and the guns were recaptured.[7] Wellington referred to it as 'a devil of an affair'. William Stephenson, a private in the 3rd Dragoons, records in his diary that 'the brigade was called to the front in the evening and remained in that position all night.'[8] But the recapture of the guns was another feather in William's cap. Sadly the whole area is now covered by apartment blocks and is a suburb of Madrid, so it is impossible to pinpoint where the engagement took place with any degree of accuracy.[9]

After Majalahonda, Wellington pushed on to Madrid. He entered the city on 12 August at the head of William's brigade of cavalry, a brigade of horse artillery and infantry. Madrid was then surrounded by an earthen wall punctured by great gates in the classical style. Wellington approached along the River Manzanarez and he, William Ponsonby, the heavy cavalry and the rest of the army entered via the gate in the San Vicente bastion, which still exists although it has been resited and positioned facing the opposite direction since 1812.

All involved in the victorious entry into Madrid were overwhelmed by their reception. The 5th Dragoon Guards trooper wrote:

As we approached the city we were met by immense crowds of people of both sexes and of all ranks who evinced the liveliest demonstrations of joy and hailed us as the deliverers of their country.[10]

Bands played, officers and men were 'embraced indiscriminately with fondness and affection'. Streets were strewn with flowers and tree branches, embroidered silks were hung from balconies, doors and windows, and nosegays were thrown into the ranks.

In short this was one of the brightest moments of my existence, all hardships and sufferings were forgotten in the spirit striving scene around us and as our horses proudly stepped over the ground we rose in our own estimation to the rank of heroes.[11]

With fireworks and public fêtes and such rejoicing no wonder everyone remembered Madrid. Bragge, the great snob of the 3rd Dragoons, referred to it as 'the most Delighted Metropolis in the world and certainly the best calculated for the Town Residence of a Gentleman as there is in no Part of it those dreadful Nuisances which necessarily accompany many of our trades in London and elsewhere'.[12]

During the army's time in Madrid there were more balls and celebrations, a celebrated bull-fight and a six-month supply of claret was drunk in three nights. While all this was going on, Wellington held negotiations with the city leaders on how the capital could be governed now the French were no longer there. However, this did not prevent him from writing, the day after his arrival in Madrid, to Cotton:

If Elley is recovered I wish you would desire him to have an eye to the sick and wounded horses and men of the cavalry particularly Ponsonby's brigade which are at Salamanca. The 5th Dragoon Guards are very weak. I have written to England about horses but I am sadly apprehensive that our horses will fall off terribly before the campaign will be over... the wear and tear in these constant marches and skirmishes must wear them out.[13]

The need for forage and water prevailed as much in the city as they did in the country. The cavalry were placed by the river within sight of the royal palace. Archaeological work undertaken prior to 2010, at the time of the construction of the new river embankments, revealed both

French and British cavalry equipment from this period. William would probably alternate his time between his brigade and the palace where the staff were quartered.

Meanwhile, the news of the great victory at Salamanca and William's part in it had reached home.

> Lady Spencer to Lady Bessborough
> Holywell, Aug 17 1812
> Immediately after the news came in yesterday my dear Harriet your brother who was most anxious to get information about dear Fred, went down to the pier where he and Mr Greville got into a little sailing wherry and went over to Portsmouth where he saw a vessel was coming and from which he had the satisfaction of hearing that both Ponsonbys were safe and the one near Lord Wellington had distinguished himself much. This we suppose to be Fred but Lord Ponsonby to whom your brother sent the intelligence wrote word that Fred had already obtained such a character that he wanted no addition – that he hoped the one described was not him.[14]

Certainly William's prospering military career stood him in good stead. He was successful in his second attempt to gain one of the County Londonderry seats to the English Parliament, being returned for Londonderry unopposed *in absentia*. Obviously he could not attend Parliament, and would not be able to until 1814, but no doubt, like other army officers who were also MPs, he would receive correspondence from his constituents to deal with while he was in Spain.

William's brigade was resident in Madrid for less than a week. The remains of Marmont's shattered army, now under the command of General Clausel, recovered quickly. They evicted the Spanish troops from Valladolid and threatened Salamanca, where the wounded from the battle were quartered. The expected general uprising against the French and the junction of the Spanish armies did not occur, which removed Wellington's need to personally remain in Madrid. King Joseph and Soult, for their part, seemed in no rush to recapture Madrid and so, leaving Hill in charge with 36,000 men, Wellington decided to organise a move northwards. He took with him the 1st, 5th and 7th divisions, two Portuguese brigades and the KGL heavy cavalry, as well as William's cavalry brigade: in all 23,000 men. He left the more experienced 3rd and Light divisions in Madrid.

On 18 August the 5th Dragoon Guards left Madrid, with the 3rd Dragoons following on the 19th. On 31 August Wellington too left Madrid. The debacle that would be Burgos was about to unfold.

Wellington's plan was to first remove the threat to Salamanca and then push Clausel and his troops back beyond the River Ebro, thus liberating most of Spain. This would mean that the only areas under French control, apart from certain garrisons, would be north-eastern Spain and the regions of Murcia and Valencia in the south-east and Galicia and Asturias in the north-west.

Wellington moved on Valladolid with William's brigade and some light cavalry. The intention was to attack the French in front of Valladolid on 6 September, but Wellington did not have artillery so the attack had to be postponed. Clausel abandoned Valladolid that night and was pursued by William's brigade.[15] He nevertheless managed to cross the River Pisuerga and destroyed the bridge after him to slow down Wellington's troops. Over the next week, by choosing good defensive positions, Clausel moved slowly back, only allowing Wellington's army to move at the rate of two leagues (six miles) a day. By 16 September Clausel had reached Burgos and offered battle but, seeing that Wellington had received 11,000 Spanish reinforcements, he marched through Burgos and took up a position further north. During the time that he had fought his delaying action the castle of Burgos had been placed in a state of defence. It now had a garrison of 1,800 infantry plus artillery and an enterprising governor, General Dubreton.

Burgos had at one time been the capital of one of the major Spanish kingdoms. The medieval castle was ideally sited and dominated the town and the major roads. As D'Urban noted in his diary, the French had added to the defences.

> Besides the old Castle well repaired with its keep, there are two fortified Lines round it and a Horn-work upon the contiguous hills. The two lines of defence of the castle have ditches paled. The horn-work has a good ditch but the fencing is not complete.[16]

Burgos Castle was important because it commanded the junction of three major roads. First there was the road to the south-west, leading to Valladolid, up which Wellington had advanced. Due south was a major road to Madrid and north-east was the road to Vitoria, the Pyrenees and France. Wellington had three options:

• to bypass the castle and continue pursuing Clausel. If he did this the garrison could attack him from the rear and cut off his supplies.

• to put a light watching force in place so that the garrison could not leave the castle to harass him and continue his pursuit of Clausel.

• to attempt to take the castle before continuing the pursuit, though this would expose him to being attacked by any French forces sent to relieve the garrison.

Wellington took the third option and laid siege to the fortress from 19 September to 21 October. The odds were not in his favour. The French commander Dubreton was very enterprising and he organised a skilful determined defence. William Stephenson recorded that on their arrival on 17 September even the cavalry brigade had been 'cannonaded by the enemy but with very little loss.'[17] Wellington's infantry were drawn from different divisions from those that had been used successfully before in this type of operation. The engineers claimed that the infantry did not follow instructions and the infantry claimed the same of the engineers. In addition Wellington's artillery was inadequate, the weather was bad and many troops were sick. Five assaults were made; the hornwork was taken but the garrison in the castle held on and Wellington's losses mounted. Many years later he said:

> it was my own entire fault; I had got with small means into the forts near Salamanca. The castle was not unlike a hill-fort in India and I had got into a good many of those. I could get into this and I very nearly did it but it was defended by a very clever fellow.[18]

During the siege William's brigade formed part of the covering army, with its main aim being to prevent the French from relieving the fortress. Although the French had pulled back from Burgos they were only twenty-four miles away – slightly over a day's march. The British cavalry headquarters were at Villamar. Apart from being watchful of any French movements, there was not much that could be done. As Bragge wrote, 'We have had a field day, a review and two false alarms since we came to this village. I find by referring to a Journal that this is the only instance of our having remained three weeks in the same place since January.'[19] He also commented:

Burgos is one of the worst large Towns I have seen in Spain and the country round it extremely dreary although abounding with corn. The people are horridly ugly and what is rather remarkable for Spaniards excessively dirty, therefore I have no wish to go farther North except to embark.[20]

Sickness was a problem among men and officers. This was exacerbated by the weather: ceaseless rain and occasional high winds.

Meanwhile, the French had established a relieving force of 44,000 good troops, including cavalry and detachments from the Young Guard, all ready to relieve Burgos.[21] On 13 October the French started to attack the British outposts and continued to do this until 18 October, when all the French troops had joined and were able to put pressure on Wellington's line. On 18 October William wrote from Villamar to the senior member of the family, Lord Bessborough, to report that Lord Bessborough's son Frederick, lieutenant colonel in the 12th Light Dragoons and William's second cousin, had been wounded in the engagement on 13 October.

As you will necessarily hear from various quarters that your son Frederick has been wounded I have thought that it would be satisfactory to you and might prevent much uneasiness on your part as well as on Lady Bessborough's to be assured from me that no serious consequence is at all to be apprehended from his wound. On Wednesday morning last in a skirmish at the advanced posts he received a musket shot in the thigh which however was immediately extracted. The bone is certainly not injured nor has there been any inflammation or fever so that there is every reason to hope that he will be very shortly on his legs again.

We are still before this abominable castle which I fear from our scanty means of offence may yet give us much trouble and cost some time and blood. However the enemy in our front has shown no disposition to molest us in our operations and those in the south are not supposed now to have any intention of advancing towards Madrid. It is therefore only from the weather which has been and continues very bad indeed that we have to apprehend interruption.

I hope everything goes on to your satisfaction in the county of Kilkenny. I beg to be remembered most kindly to Lady Bessborough.[22]

The letter tempted fate, for on the very next day, 19 October, the French attempted to relieve the castle and captured the village of Quintanapalla. William was ordered to collaborate with infantry to retake the village, but the French withdrew on his approach.

Bragge had written to his father on the journey to Burgos:

> I am happy to say that we marched in rear of the whole Army and had consequently nothing to do the whole journey which was upon the whole the most unpleasant we have had, it being extremely cold and the nights very wet.[23]

The retreat, apart from the weather, was going to be a very different story.

On 20 October the French concentrated their forces thirteen miles beyond Burgos. General Clausel had been replaced by General Southam, who now commanded 44,000 men with a potential further reinforcement due any time of another 11,000. They were greatly superior in both cavalry and infantry to the 21,000 Anglo-Portuguese and 11,000 Spanish troops Wellington had around Burgos and this, together with news that Soult was about to move on Hill at Madrid, in overwhelming strength of 60,000 men, together with the fact that no progress was being made in taking the castle, made Wellington decide to raise the siege. It had cost him 2,000 casualties.

On the night of 21 October the retreat began. The distance to be covered was approximately 130 miles before Wellington was able to pause at Salamanca in early November. Then there was another 70 miles to Ciudad Rodrigo and safety, which was finally achieved on 19 November. In this one-month period the army came close to collapse and veterans stated the retreat was worse than that from Corunna in 1808–09. During the retreat William's brigade played a key role, as the Allied cavalry had to prevent the French cavalry from catching the British infantry strung out on the march and cutting them to pieces.

Wellington had his troops divided into two main columns, which would move south on either side of the Arlanzon river. Ponsonby's brigade and a handful of Spanish cavalry had to protect the column made up of the 5th Division (1st, 4th, 9th, 30th, 38th, 44th Foot) and Spanish infantry. They skirted the northern side of the city while the other column, protected by Anson and Bock's brigades, skirted the southern side.

The movement was a complete success and later on in the morning of the 22nd the two columns joined without being attacked by the

French. The troops in what had been the northern column, protected by William's brigade, now headed the army. The southern column followed with the rearguard formed of Anson, Bock's and some Spanish irregular cavalry – some 2,300 horsemen in total – with Royal Horse artillery and KGL infantry in support. That William's brigade was kept close to the 5th Division near the head of the column may seem strange, but the French attack could actually come from a number of directions. Besides the potential to attack from the rear, the French could also attack the British troops from the side if they could cross over the bridges that spanned the rivers on the army's retreat. So William's next objective was to stop the French from crossing the rivers.

Although we are discovering more about Anson's and Bock's actions on the retreat – they had to fight several sharp rearguard actions against the pursuing French at Venta del Pozo and Villamuriel de Cerrato – we only gain tantalising glimpses of Ponsonby's actions in what was independent command. Stapleton Cotton had rejoined the army following recovery from his wound, but he was in command of the rearguard.

The main bulk of the army marched 26 miles on 23 October and stopped around Torquemada. However, sometime during the day the newly appointed but incompetent quartermaster general, Sir Willoughby Gordon, gave incorrect instructions to Ponsonby as to where his brigade should go. Stanhope wrote:

> 23rd the army moved before daylight, the 1st Division in the rear and Halkett's light German battalions the rear guard. Our quarter master general sent Ponsonby's brigade, the only strong one we had, by a mountain road where they were no use.[24]

Stephenson wrote in his diary for the 23rd that the brigade was 'closely pursued by advance guard of the enemy and had but little loss except baggage.'[25]

Bragge, writing once safely back in Portugal in late November 1812, reported:

> During the late operations our usual good luck has attended me and the brigade I belong to; the Brigade… escaping annihilation in the late march to Valladolid when completely cut off from the rest of the army by 5,000 French cavalry with a river in our rear, through which we accidentally found a ford in the night.'[26]

The 24th saw the army cross the Carrion River by the bridges of Palencia, Villamuriel and Duenas. Wellington aimed to form a defensive position to allow the infantry to progress unimpeded to Valladolid, which was nearly halfway between Burgos and Salamanca, where he was hoping to be joined by Hill and his army from Madrid. To establish his position Wellington needed to destroy five bridges: Palencia, Villamuriel and San Isidro on the Carrion River and Duenas and Tiriego on the Pisuerga River.

The bridges at Villa Muriel and San Isidro were successfully blown. Tiriego was damaged but not destroyed, and the French managed to establish an outpost and discovered a ford on the Carrion River. However, much more important was what happened at Palencia, not least because it involved William and his brigade.

George Burroughs, a cavalry surgeon, described the countryside around Palencia as:

fine and diversified with trees for hitherto from Burgos the land is barren and there is a chain of hills running northward in the course of the river to Palencia. The river Carrion itself is narrow and fordable in some places for cavalry and here and there the branches of the willow, dangled in its stream.[27]

John Douglas of the Royal Scots wrote:

Palencia is a beautiful town situated at the foot of a mountain. A dry canal ran nearly parallel with the river, to near the town. A dilapidated bridge over the canal led to a beautiful green ere you reached the town, where a noble bridge crossed the river leading into it.[28]

The town of Palencia was on the enemy side of the river and the Spanish commander decided to hold it, although its ruinous medieval wall made the town indefensible. The Spanish commander gave orders that the bridge should be blown by the British troops only after his Spanish troops had been driven out of the town and recrossed the river.

William detached two squadrons of the 5th Dragoon Guards and 3rd Dragoons to cover the working parties mining the bridges at Palencia. They were soon badly needed. The French, commanded by Foy, caught the Spanish cavalry by surprise and stormed the town. The Spanish could not hold them and fell back in such haste that the British engineers failed to fire the mine; the fuse malfunctioned. The British infantry of the Royal Scots fell back and William's squadrons had to protect the fleeing Spanish troops from the pursuing French, who by crossing the bridge were now on Wellington's side of the river.[29] This may be the event referred to by Stephenson in his diary for the 24th:

> Marched and returned to camp near Duenas the right squadron escaped very narrowly from all being taken prisoner had one man killed but no prisoners. Distance travelled one league.[30]

By crossing the river at Palencia the French had succeeded in turning Wellington's defensive line and he had to fall back on Valladolid using Ponsonby's brigade to hold off the pursuing French.

On 25 October Stephenson wrote that the brigade retreated to camp near Valladolid and halted for a few days in sight of the enemy lines.[31] Wellington now had chance to rest his troops as he blew up more bridges in the area to the south of Valladolid, particularly those spanning the River Douro, which was a much broader and faster river with fewer fords. All boats that could be used to cross the river were also seized. These actions cost the French time, as they had to find fords or bridges that had not been blown up. In one action the 7th Division blew up the bridge at Simancas, south of Valladolid, just as the French arrived to take it.

On 29 October the army crossed the Douro and Wellington took steps to hold that river line. On 30 October he had the bridge over the Douro at Toro and other bridges destroyed. Stephenson records how William's brigade had to blow up the wooden bridge at Ponte Douro near Tordesillas, over which the army had marched the previous day. But some French troops managed to swim across the Douro at Tordesillas and hold out, giving sufficient time for the blown bridge to be repaired so the French could start to cross. This meant that Wellington's position had been turned a second time, and he moved to oppose this new threat with part of his army. At this moment, fortunately for Wellington, the French commander Souham lost 10,000 of his troops, particularly a strong cavalry brigade, who had to return north as the Spanish had seized the important city of Bilbao. At a stroke Souham's forces were reduced to 40,000 men and, as he had received instructions from King Joseph to avoid a general action until the king's forces came up from the south, he decided to stay put.

There was a standoff for two days. Wellington continued to hold his position to allow Hill time to join him from Madrid. On the 30th William's brigade marched into the town of Rueda, where Wellington had his headquarters, and 'halted for a few days to watch the movements of the enemy'.[32] By this time the weather had worsened. It was foggy and the roads became heavy from the pouring rain.

Wellington held his position on the Douro until 5 November. By that time the French had repaired the bridge at Toro, so they could now cross the River Douro at two places. Also Wellington knew that Hill was being pursued by 60,000 troops, commanded by Soult and King Joseph. He made the decision to pull back from the River Douro and join up with Hill at Salamanca. This did not happen until 8 November. So at one o'clock in the morning of 5 November, Wellington wrote to Hill:

> I sent the 5th division of infantry and General Ponsonby's brigade of cavalry to Alaejos this morning the enemy having appeared in that quarter from Toro and I propose to move tomorrow to Nava del Rey. If your troops at Arevalo should have marched ...we shall be tolerably well connected.[33]

On 6 November the rest of the army began its withdrawal. The troops fell back in easy stages to Salamanca, which all had reached by 8 November. There had been no effective French pursuit, but the weather was still very cold and rainy and although some troops were able to be quartered in the villages many had to bivouac out in the open and dysentery and rheumatism became common. Hill joined Wellington on 8 November and there was the prospect of a second battle being fought in the area of Salamanca. Wellington held the strong position of San Christobal, which he had held earlier in the year and had made stronger by redoubts. He positioned William's and some light cavalry brigades far out to the front to give advance notice of any enemy movements.

The River Tormes had been swollen by the rains, making the fords impassable, but when the river levels fell there was every possibility that the combined French armies, with superior cavalry, could cross the river in many places. This would be difficult for Hill and Wellington to counter. However, even though their army now numbered 90,000 the French commanders could not face the possibility of another loss like Salamanca, so instead they adopted a flanking movement and, by threatening to cut the road to Ciudad Rodrigo, forced Wellington to leave Salamanca and fall back to Portugal on 15 November.

For many this was the worst part of the retreat. Poor staff work led to a breakdown in cavalry support and food supplies. The French cavalry picked off stragglers at will and captured Wellington's new second in command, Sir Edward Paget. The weather turned worse. The rain fell in torrents and the marshy plains over which the army marched exhausted the soldiers' strength.

During this part of the retreat Willoughby Gordon's incompetence again showed itself. He sent all the food on a road 20 miles to the north of the three roads that the troops were following. So for three crucial days, on 16, 17 and 18 November, the army was without food. As Bragge wrote to his father:

> You will already have seen a circumstantial account of our late retreats which have really been very disastrous. and from want of a little better arrangement in the Commissariat and other departments rendered more terrible than a sanguinary action, as besides the inclemency of the weather we had the worst of all enemies to contend with, proving fatal to hundreds namely Hunger and want of spirituous liquour, no rations being given to the troops for four – and in many instances six – days. The weather was very rainy, intensely cold and the country we had to retreat over much like part of Oxfordshire being very deep and intersected by numberless brooks and rivers …Our Spring Wagons and mules went by one road and the Troops by another so that every knocked up and wounded man fell into the enemies hands and all the cavalry went with the same column of infantry, leaving two others completely uncovered.[34]

Just to rub salt into Wellington's wounds, Willoughby Gordon had been sending reports to Charles Grey, for the use of the Opposition in Parliament, complaining about Wellington's handling of the Burgos debacle![35]

On 15 November William's brigade had to turn and face the enemy again. Stephenson wrote: 'The enemy advanced with a very heavy cannonade which caused us to turn and march to the front after which we encamped near the village of Lostores.'[36]

Then the brigade resumed its march. The French, although accustomed to living off the land, found it impossible to maintain an army of 90,000 in the field, so 40,000 were left at Salamanca and Soult's army of 50,000 pursued the Allies, knowing full well that if Wellington turned they would be greatly outnumbered. Thus Soult's strategy became one of ensuring that Wellington evacuated Spain, picking off the numerous stragglers and making hit and run raids if the opportunity presented itself. On 17 November Willoughby Gordon left Wellington's central column without cavalry support and the central column was attacked at San Munoz. However, the attack was repulsed and the end of the ordeal was in sight. On the morning of the 19th Soult moved his troops eastwards and in the evening Wellington's army reached safety and was able to move into winter quarters in Portugal. William's brigade had one final duty – to ensure any stragglers made it safely into the camps – before they too went into winter quarters.

During the winter the regiments moved from area to area depending on the supply of forage, but by Christmas most of William's brigade was in the area of Coimbra, where the weather was more temperate. Given the troops' weakened state they were prone to outbreaks of disease. Hunger was followed by a serious outbreak of typhus and dysentery.

The retreat had cost casualties of at least 6,000 men (20 per cent of the army) and returns showed 36 per cent of the British troops were registered as sick.[37] The inhabitants of Madrid and Salamanca had been abandoned, but Wellington still held the four border fortresses. The French had been driven out of Andalucia, Extremadura and the Asturias. Not all the great gains of 1812 had been lost. Nevertheless, it could all have ended much more positively.

It has been calculated that in 1812 the 5th Dragoon Guards marched 2,000 miles in ten months.[38] Given that horseshoes needed replacing every few weeks, and providing for men and horses was not easy, this was a major achievement requiring great leadership and teamwork. William's was the only brigade to accompany Wellington throughout his 1812 campaign.

Now the brigade, both men and horses, could regain its strength. Wellington, smarting from the retreat from Burgos, was planning a master stroke for 1813.

Chapter 8

Fighting in the Peninsula
Part 4: The Battle of Vitoria

Wellington's plan for 1813 was totally different from that of 1812. Instead of invading Spain using the 1812 route from Salamanca to Burgos, he planned to take his army on a different route so he could constantly outflank the blocking French armies, forcing them to constantly fall back and cede Spanish territory without bloodshed. Once he knew the true scale of the French debacle in Russia, he realised that he could drive the French up to the Pyrenees and from February 1813 this was his aim. It would prove to be a masterstroke of genius but was not without its difficulties.

The army Wellington commanded in 1813 was considerably larger than the one he had commanded in 1812. It totalled 104,000 officers and men, comprising:

12,300 British, Portuguese and Spanish cavalry
55,700 British infantry
10,000 Portuguese infantry
21,500 Spanish infantry
5,000 artillery and specialist troops

Moving such a large army was complicated.

The army was a mixture of experienced troops and those without any experience of fighting in the Peninsula. In the cavalry alone, fresh from England, was a whole Hussar brigade of 1,600 men and a heavy cavalry brigade of 900 Life Guards and Horse Guards without combat experience. They would need to be prepared for operational conditions, including day-to-day tasks as well as fighting.

Wellington also needed to deceive the French to ensure they did not suspect the route he would be using. He had to plan the invasion route in great detail as the terrain was inhospitable and the route had not been used before. Wellington had the area surveyed by his intelligence officers.

The winter of 1812–13 had been long and hard. One of the biggest problems for Wellington was that in order to advance his army he needed to be able to guarantee supplies. In particular for the cavalry this meant forage. Because of the severe winter the grass was buried under snow, a problem exacerbated by the route he had decided to take, which ran through the mountains where the snow cover persisted longer than on lower ground.

The delay in setting out gave additional time for William's brigade to regain its strength. On 7 February 1813 William Bragge of the 3rd Dragoons had written to his father 'the Regiment is extremely sickly and I believe I might say the same of the whole army.'[1]

On 25 January the 3rd Dragoons had ninety-four men sick and in the whole British army 17,500 men were ill. There were also problems with the horses. Many had contracted a disease called glanders, brought about by the conditions experienced during the retreat. Bragge wrote 'as you well know it is unavoidable and cannot by any precautions be guarded against where the horses have been so continually exposed.'[2]

Stephenson wrote on 14 February:

Marched to Soure and Adjaciento where we halted for some time. The regiment very sickly and the horses in low condition, a great number of men and horses died while we remained at this place but the quarters very good.[3]

However, by March conditions had dramatically improved. The regiments were benefitting from areas of better forage. Large drafts of men and horses arrived from England to make up the shortages of both in the cavalry. Bizarrely, this was also the time that there were changes in the uniform for the cavalry. New drafts no longer had the old cocked hat. Instead they arrived wearing the new classical helmet with horse-hair tail. By the time the new campaign season started all the 5th Dragoon Guards had been issued with a helmet made

of black japanned leather or metal with a broad peak set on at an angle and bound with brass. The lower part of the headpiece was bound with three layers of brass plates, one above the other, and a highly ornamented brass crest was fixed on the top, tapering gradually towards the back. The crest was surmounted by a long black horse-hair tail commencing in front and hanging well below the back of the helmet as a protection to the neck. At the front end of the crest a black horse-hair thistle shaped plume was fixed pointing towards the front. The crest was ornamented by a series of narrow raised panels down each side and with a head of Medusa in front and brass cheek scales with roses at the top, were provided for fastening under the chin. In front of the helmet a large brass plate was fitted, having the double Royal cipher surmounted by a crown in the centre with an ornamental border.[4]

William, as he was on the staff, would retain his cocked hat. Of more benefit were small tin camp kettles, which allowed food to be cooked more quickly than the old cooking pots. Tents were also introduced for the first time.

On 24 March Bragge could write:

Should we be allowed three weeks more, the cavalry will in every respect be more effective than they were last year and much better appointed. Our brigade will muster upwards of 50 files a squadron which for service is very strong although the establishment is 85 horses a troop.[5]

In May the returns showed that William's brigade numbered 1,400 men.

Meanwhile, the French were having major difficulties. Joseph, Jourdan and Soult had distributed their armies into winter quarters before they had heard of the scale of the Russian disaster. Joseph did not find out until he received dispatches in February, including a letter from one of his ADCs who had been in Russia. Soult was recalled to help Napoleon in Germany, there were to be no more reinforcements for Spain, and up to 25 per cent of the troops currently in Spain were to be sent back for Napoleon's use. This still left six French armies comprising 200,000 men in the Peninsula. Joseph was also ordered to move his capital to Valladolid and hold Madrid as his furthest southern point. Napoleon stated that Joseph's main aim should be to pacify northern Spain. By 23 March Joseph had moved his headquarters to Valladolid. He had no idea of what Wellington's plans would be for 1813. Rumours and misinformation were rife, including of another thrust on Madrid, and Joseph decided to wait and see what Wellington would do and then counter. He appreciated that it would take at least a week to concentrate sufficient forces to counter any of Wellington's moves, and that this could involve giving up territory, but at least he would have certainty.

However, Napoleon now started to interfere directly in the conduct of the war in the Peninsula. He started making changes to the troop dispositions in the Peninsula based on intelligence that was at best out of date and at worst erroneous. Nor did he keep Joseph informed of these changes. The most impactful of these was assuming that Wellington's losses were so great from the Burgos campaign that only the French armies of the south and the centre, numbering 52,000 troops, were needed to contain his operations. This was a wild miscalculation, as Wellington now commanded double this number of Anglo-Portuguese and Spanish troops. Napoleon gave orders that the Army of Portugal of 17,000 men was to be used to assist the French Army in northern Spain, where the guerrilla bands had become larger and better organised. The guerrillas were collaborating with the Spanish regular army, and the British Royal Navy and Spanish civilian governments were operating in all the major towns. In other words there was a full-blown insurrection of the type that Wellington had hoped to encourage when he was in Madrid in August 1812.

In April the army began to move into position. William's brigade was part of General Graham's force, comprising six divisions. Graham's force formed the left wing of the army while General Hill was on the right. Wellington's plan was for Graham's brigade to cross the Douro well inside Portugal and then surprise and outflank the French, who would be misled into thinking that the main attack would be directed by Wellington himself, with Hill and the right column, which moved on Salamanca: this was to be a feint. As Napoleon had ordered Joseph to hold Salamanca and Valladolid, a threat to one of these would mean that the French would be unlikely to suspect a main attack from elsewhere.

William's brigade started moving from winter quarters on 17 April, heading to Oporto via Coimbra. Quarters were good and forage was plentiful until they reached Oporto. Then it began to get more difficult. From Oporto they moved to the city of Braga. Then there was a delay until the staff officers were certain there would be adequate forage for the cavalry to proceed. The route was through the province of Tras os Montes. This was very arduous for the cavalry, as there were no high roads running east and west, only north and south. William Graham, the newly appointed commissariat officer to the 4th Dragoons, recorded:

We remained here until the 13th of May when we moved forward to Fafe, 14 miles, over the most awful mountains I had ever yet seen. We were at one time literally above the clouds, at one time almost immersed in the valleys. One third of our horses dropped their shoes, the roads were so bad. We were often going up and down such deep declivities that we shuddered to look after or before us, for fear of getting dizzy from the horrors of the immense gulphs [sic] below and the overhanging crags above.[6]

Bragge wrote from Braganza on 23 May:

Our brigade arrived yesterday in as good order as could be expected after having crossed the Province of Tras os Montes by a route never before attempted by British cavalry and which never ought to have been marched. We were two hours getting up one hill and for three days never got the regiment out of single files scrambling over rocks, mountains and precipices for eight hours every day.[7]

In spite of Bragge's customary complaints, this was a marvellous achievement of staff work given the numbers involved and the nature of the terrain. On 25 May the brigade continued its advance and on 26 May it crossed the Spanish border.

On crossing into Spain the terrain changed. William Graham commented:

As we entered Spain it was curious to see the difference of the roads. From scaling the frightful cliffs we now fell into as level a country as any. The roads were finely sanded and even as a bowling green, but there was hardly a tree to be seen; the whole country for a tract of forty or fifty miles shewing [sic] one continued field of barley, rye, wheat etc.[8]

The French high command finally began to receive information to enable it to make decisions: the thrust was to be from Salamanca. On 24 May Joseph and his chief of staff Jourdan gave orders to concentrate to the north-east of Salamanca. They could not afford to engage Wellington as they did not have sufficient numbers and had to wait until a strong column of troops escorting the baggage of the remaining French sympathisers from Madrid arrived. This was unlikely before the beginning of June. In the meantime events at Salamanca seemed to prove that their suspicions were correct. On 26 May Hill's troops drove the French out of Salamanca itself and he took up the usual defensive position north-east of the city, implying that the next move would be to Valladolid along the Burgos road.

On 29 May Graham's column was joined by Wellington himself, who had ridden over from Salamanca while Hill progressed northwards in parallel to Graham. Between 25 May and 24 June William's brigade was in motion every day except one and on that day, 9 June, the brigade was inspected by Wellington himself.

On 31 May Graham's troops crossed the Esla river, which was in full flood after the winter snow and rain. Graham, the commissariat officer, writing after the event, recorded:

> Our brigade under Sir William Ponsonby now moved off and about three o'clock came up with the infantry who were passing the river on a bridge of pontoons while the baggage passed over on another. Here was a scene of jolly confusion, the cavalry forded the river and the commissariat bullocks swimming over by their side. I got over on one of the pontoons very luckily. The German infantry floated higher up but many unfortunately lost their lives in the attempt. About eight o'clock I reached our encampment having this day marched forty miles and we were twenty hours on horseback. We took a French piquet of fifty men who were surprised, not expecting us over in the way we crossed.[9]

There is a reference by Green of the Durham Light Infantry to the heavy dragoons positioning their horses in the river to serve as a buffer to allow those infantry who could not use the pontoon bridge to cross more easily and not be swept away by the turbulent waters.[10]

The journey was relentless but the benefits were great. By crossing the Esla on 31 May Wellington was now also beyond the River Douro. He had therefore turned the French main defensive position without any bloodshed, even before the French had concentrated there. The small numbers of French troops kept falling back, unable to do anything.

On 1 June William Graham recorded: 'Kept advancing and the French retreating: the roads were delightful but all the towns lay nearly in ruins as the French had destroyed them.'[11] At Morales on 2 June the Hussar brigade attacked some French cavalry and drove them off.

Wellington, by being on the north bank of the Douro, was able to repair the bridge at Toro to allow Hill, marching from Salamanca, to join him. By the night of 3 June Wellington's whole striking force of 80,000 men was north of the Douro.

The French commanders had only started to suspect that the thrust on Salamanca was a feint on 30 May, and they weren't sure of it until 1 June, when a local French commander reported the British had crossed the Esla in great force. By 2 June Joseph had 40,000 infantry and 10,000 cavalry, which could be concentrated in a day in the area of the River Douro. But with Wellington now beyond the Douro and probably outnumbering him, Joseph decided to vacate Valladolid and fall back on Burgos, which gave more opportunities for defence than the rivers in between. All the baggage containing the possessions of the court and the treasures looted from Spain was sent off towards Burgos. The bridges were blown and the army moved up the road towards Palencia, halting for two days in the hope that Clausel and the Army of Portugal would join them from Navarre. When this did not happen, and having an inkling that Wellington was advancing northwards and preparing to turn his left flank, Joseph began his retreat again on 7 June.

Wellington had no intention of simply following Joseph. He kept his main force on its outflanking movement. This would allow him to outflank any of the defensive positions the French might be preparing around Burgos, but he did send the Light Division, Grant's Hussars and William's heavy cavalry to pursue Joseph's rearguard, to give Joseph the impression this was a simple pursuit.[12] Graham records that the brigade covered between 13 and 21 miles a day. He recalled seeing a convent that the French had destroyed because it had been unable to pay its taxes, where everything had been looted. At one village, Aranillas, 'some of the inhabitants lay dead in the streets who had been shot by the French in their way through'.[13]

On 12 June the pursuit came up against the French rearguard, commanded by Reille on the heights of Estepar and Hormillas, commanding the Hormaza River. Wellington determined to attack them on both the front (with Portuguese and Spanish troops) and the flank (with Grant and Ponsonby's cavalry). When Reille discovered that he was being outflanked by the cavalry he broke off the action and retired to where there were more French troops already positioned. Wellington gave orders for the cavalry to break off the action because he had no intention of throwing them against well-positioned infantry. Stephenson recorded in his diary:

12th June: marched to camp near Orvilliers near to that place we charged the rearguard of the enemy and took one piece of ordnance and several prisoners. We had one captain wounded and several men besides a number of horses wounded.[14]

It is probably this engagement that William Graham referred to mistakenly as occurring on 13 June:

We moved forward. On our advancing to the edge of these hills we found a body of thirteen thousand French before us, who never expected us in this point. Only Major Bull's troop of artillery had come up, with the light brigade of infantry, and most of the cavalry. Another brigade of artillery soon arrived, when the two brigades opened up on the French, who were passing the bridge over the Pisuergo. The French moved as leisurely along the road, to cross the bridge, as if they had been on the parade. Our heavy brigade of cavalry were too near when the French fired a volley at them and wounded Captain Chitivell of the xx dragoons and four men. Of the French about sixty were killed before they could clear the bridge. They got over a brigade of artillery which formed and they began to fire away at us but every shot missed.[15]

This action, as well as Jourdan's discovery that the new defence works were incomplete and the governor's claim that he had neither enough food nor ammunition to supply the army, made Joseph decide on a rapid retreat and to evacuate Burgos. On 13 June the French detonated mines to blow up the fortifications and all eye-witnesses record the noise it made. Woodberry, of the 18th Hussars in Grant's brigade, recalled:

The ground really appeared to shake for the moment and we were struck dumb and motionless with the horrid roar. Not only were many houses in the city injured, all the glass blown out of the splendid cathedral, but a hail of shells fell all over the surrounding quarter and killed 100 men who were halted in the square and a few dragoons who were crossing the bridge. There were casualties also, of course, among the unfortunate citizens.[16]

No doubt the French hoped to take advantage of the terrain and take up more defensive positions long before they got to Vitoria. But again

Wellington kept up the remorseless pressure, maintaining the north-westward march with the aim of turning the next obvious French position, which would be along the Ebro. Ignoring the rugged terrain through which the French thought it was impossible to bring guns and wagons, he continually outflanked the French army without having to attack their rearguard and, for four crucial days, the French did not know where he was. William's brigade covered 127 miles in seven days. On 16 June the French crossed the River Ebro and took up a position. Joseph had been joined by the divisions of the Army of Portugal that had been operating in the north, so he now had 50,000 infantry and 10,000 cavalry. But on 17 June Wellington was north of the Ebro and moving rapidly eastwards by a circuitous route, which was not the fastest way but would take him to Vitoria and would not be the route the French expected. Wellington would approach Vitoria from the south and Graham from the north. On the 18th there were two actions at San Milan and Osma and the French relinquished their final strong defensive position on the Ebro River and fell back on Vitoria.

The weather took a turn for the worse. William Graham wrote:

During the last four days march it rained incessantly. The country was one contained field and hill of mud; the dress of our soldiers was hardly distinguishable, and as for the differences of officers and men, it was difficult to say which was which. The French army by this time had united and, in their march, destroyed every village: nothing was to be seen but one picture of universal havoc and desolation.[17]

The French retired on Vitoria and took position in the Zadora valley to the west of the town. This was a plain six miles wide and eleven miles deep, bounded by mountains with the River Zadora running through the valley. The river was crossed by ten bridges, none of which had been blown up by the French, and numerous fords. Vitoria was at the eastern end of the valley at the junction of five key roads, the most important leading to Bayonne, Bilbao and Pamplona. The massive baggage train of plunder, as well as the carriages, contained Spaniards who had thrown in their lot with the French. All had to get to France by the Bayonne road. One convoy left Vitoria on the 19th; another, escorted by a French division of 3,000 men, left at 3am on the 21st, but many more were still waiting for safe passage from Vitoria. This would take time, and Wellington would need to be delayed or defeated first. The initial French strategy seemed to be defence in depth in three lines, the first based on natural heights above the river, and using the French superiority in artillery. Although the French had 60,000 men compared to Wellington's 78,000, they had 153 guns to Wellington's ninety-six. The French plan was amended when reports were received of Allied troops to the north, which caused the bulk of the third line to take position to the north of Vitoria.

The French forces were reasonably close together. Wellington's, however, were going to approach in a number of different columns and he had to coordinate their separate attacks which, given the rugged nature of the terrain, was not easy. Nevertheless, if executed as planned, it would prove to be a telling blow. Sir Thomas Graham would approach from the north and cut off the main line of retreat for the French along the Great Road to Bayonne. Sir Rowland Hill would attack the French left. Wellington would then attack the centre with two columns and together he and Hill would push the French back to the town of Vitoria and capture them and the baggage convoy. He had to execute the plan quickly because, unlike Joseph, he knew that Clausel was marching with reinforcements from Pamplona. The earliest Clausel could arrive at Vitoria was 22 June, so Wellington needed to attack before then.

William's brigade was part of Wellington's first central column. This comprised the 3rd and 4th Divisions and three brigades of heavy cavalry under William, Henry Fane and Robert Hill, as well as D'Urban's experienced Portuguese. Hill's brigade consisted of the Lifeguards and the Blues; newly out of England and untried. Fane's brigade, however, consisted of the 1st Dragoons and 3rd Dragoon Guards, who had been serving in Hill's independent command in southern Spain and were very experienced.

The battle began about 8am on 21 June. It was very much an infantry battle. For the bulk of the battle the cavalry was not deployed, although it is doubtful if Wellington originally intended this to be the case. It seems that his original plan was for this column to advance to the Zadorra River, wait for Hill's division to take possession of the heights and then to cross the river and assault the French centre. Hill did manage to gain a position on the heights, but he couldn't turn the French flank, which Wellington needed to happen before he released the 3rd and 4th Divisions and the heavy cavalry. Wellington's central column under Dalhousie/Picton and the northern column under Graham had been delayed, but at about 11.30am Graham's troops arrived and a bitter contest began for the villages commanding the bridges to the north of Vitoria. In the early afternoon Picton's division appeared, seized the bridge at Mendoza and stormed across the river. The French fell back a mile to a position closer to Vitoria, but Picton's division attacked this and the French fell back to a new position. Orders were sent to recall the troops opposing Hill so they would not be cut off.

Up to this time the heavy cavalry had not been deployed and for the officers and men who had experienced the charge at Salamanca this must have been a frustrating experience. The unknown trooper from the 5th Dragoon Guards wrote:

> The brigade to which I belonged personally was dismounted on the elevated spot in the centre of our position which afforded us a commanding view of both armies. As we gazed attentively on the movements of the different columns and could distinctively hear the words of command and perceive our infantry advancing to the charge our men animated with the enthusiasm of British soldiers were impatient at remaining any longer inactive and frequently demanded to be led on to take part in the fight, but the opportunity was not yet arrived and we were compelled to await our orders in silence.[18]

Now, with the French falling back, there was an opportunity. Cole led his 4th division across the bridge at Nanclares as part of the attack on the centre, and Napier records how the heavy cavalry followed: 'a splendid body also passing the river galloped up squadron after squadron into the plain ground between Cole's right and Hill's left.'[19]

Ponsonby's brigade was sent to support Picton and again waited for the breakthrough. This was intended to occur after Wellington had assembled a grand battery at about 4pm, to smash the French line. The French artillery responded. But then four events happened very quickly. First Hill started to turn the new French left position. Then a divisional commander, Leval, made an error in withdrawing his troops, creating a gap in the centre which put pressure from a different direction on Gazan, the commander of the French left. Gazan decided to retreat eastwards, leaving his fellow commanders in the lurch. Finally, and most dangerously, a rumour spread that the Great Road had been cut and the army was about to be attacked from behind.[20]

At about 5.30pm Joseph ordered a general retreat. Some troops, such as those of Reille, fell back in good order, but for the rest it was very much 'every man for himself'.

Wellington could have committed his cavalry to pursue the fleeing infantry, but apart from sending the Hussar brigade into Vitoria he chose not to. Some of his divisional commanders did deploy the cavalry attached to them, but only against the French cavalry who were positioned in the rear of the French army.

There were two reasons for Wellington not committing the cavalry. Firstly, the ground was unfavourable, as the French had realised when they chose to place most of their cavalry regiments in the rear. Bragge wrote:

> ... the Ground was so intersected with woods and inclosures that the cavalry could not act against their infantry and their cavalry took care to keep out of the way which accounts for our not having taken more prisoners... our cavalry had little to do during the day except support the infantry which we did the whole day and once wheeled into line to charge the cavalry but upon seeing us advance they dashed into a wood and escaped.[21]

The 5th Dragoon Guards trooper, like Bragge, refers to the 'unevenness of the ground which was in many places rough and broken and full of deep ditches, rocks and clumps of trees.'[22]

Secondly, Wellington kept tight control of his heavy cavalry. He did not support brigade commanders acting on their own initiative. With Stapleton Cotton still absent there was no overall cavalry commander. True, Bock of the KGL had that nominal title, but he was with Graham's corps engaged in the attack from the north during the battle and was nowhere near the heavy cavalry. So the only person who was going to order the heavy cavalry into action was Wellington, and he would only do this if he needed to. And at the moment he was busily engaged in the final stages of what had been primarily an infantry battle and needed to bring the action to a conclusion.

Thus William's role during the Battle of Vitoria turned out to be one of supporting the infantry. This was crucial, but obviously not as glorious as the role he had played at Salamanca. The brigade suffered minor casualties. The 3rd Dragoons lost one trooper and one officer wounded and eight horses. The 5th Dragoon Guards had one man wounded.

However, the day was not yet over. There was still an opportunity to pursue the French, who were taking the road to Pamplona. Wellington used William Ponsonby and his brigade in the pursuit, and would later reward them for their efforts by allowing them to display the word 'Vitoria' on their standards and presenting the commanders with gold medals.

Chapter 9

Fighting in the Peninsula
Part 5: The Final Engagements

When the French broke about 5pm they fled in a number of directions, but mainly flooded along the road to Salvatierra and Pamplona, protected by the French Army of Portugal, which kept its order. Grant's Hussar brigade had been ordered to pursue, but got sidetracked by coming across the French baggage train of 2,000 carts and carriages. Many of the 18th Hussars in particular dishonoured themselves by getting drunk and joining in the plunder; officers as well as men. Such behaviour disgusted Wellington, who would later punish the Hussars severely. He broke up the brigade and ensured they did not bear the battle honour 'Vitoria' on their standards. He was also conscious that with the hussars and infantry plundering the baggage train, which was just outside Vitoria, there was a danger that Vitoria itself could be sacked.

Wellington now turned to his heavy cavalry, who were much more disciplined. Firstly he detached Robert Hill's brigade of household cavalry to guard the town, and they did not let him down. Secondly, he himself led William and his brigade, with infantry support, in pursuit of the fleeing French in the direction of Pamplona. This little-known action was hampered by the lateness in starting, as well as a combination of broken ground unsuitable for cavalry, torrential rain and darkness, which brought the pursuit to a halt after five miles. Wellington returned to Vitoria frustrated.

As the Hon. James Stanhope, one of Wellington's ADCs, wrote:

Had the ground been of a nature that our cavalry might have acted, I believe nothing would have escaped, but the numerous woods in which were enemy infantry instantly checked our cavalry till infantry could come up and their columns throwing away arms had the start and speed of our men who had marched so far.[1]

Nevertheless, the short evening pursuit led to a legend, told by Fortescue, that gives us an indication of the discipline William had instilled in his brigade and his concern for his men's well being.

> General Ponsonby's brigade of cavalry passed by a heap of dollars scattered on the road and not a man attempted to touch them whereupon the General left a sergeant major behind who brought in as many of the coins as his horse could carry, thus enabling a distribution to be made of 5 dollars a piece to everyone of the 1300 men. In the night there was a regular fair at which 8 or 9 dollars was offered for a guinea.[2]

This was a perfect demonstration of William's concern that all his brigade should benefit equally from the bounty, regardless of rank – but not at the expense of the strategic objective to pursue the enemy. Wellington very much approved of his approach, which was totally different from the actions of the hussar regiments in the aftermath of the battle. William himself did obtain King Joseph's silver gilt dinner and dessert service, but purchased it in an auction after the day's events were over.[3]

Next day Wellington restarted the pursuit. The French had maintained their flight until midnight, jettisoning more baggage and arms on the way and succeeding in putting some distance between themselves and their pursuers. King Joseph ended the day at Salvatierra, sixteen miles from the battlefield. The French increased the gap from their pursuers by starting at dawn the next day. Wellington, however, did not recommence the pursuit until 10am. The reasons for this delay are not clear. He might have needed to make plans and ensure discipline in his army, as many of the troops had returned to the battlefield under cover of darkness to search for plunder. Further bounty could be found on the road so the scavenging troops would have become spread out, and it probably took a long time to pull the army together.

William Graham, the commissary of the 4th Dragoons, spent the night of the battle away from the regiment and managed to rejoin it at 2.30pm the next day. He records going around Vitoria, seeing the captured French artillery and then heading off to join William's brigade, which he found twelve miles beyond Vitoria – the brigade had only covered seven miles since the previous evening.

> The road now wound through mountains, with a very wintry look, well covered, however, with wood of the pine order. The roads

were very dirty. We arrived about half past two at the regiment, encamped in a wood. In this camp Lord Wellington wrote his dispatches in a poor village called Salvatierra. Next morning commenced the pursuit of the fugitives, along the Royal Road or Carminha Rea, to Pampeluna. The road wound through almost inaccessible mountains and the weather came on very wet.[4]

Wellington was well aware that the pressure had to be maintained. But two other factors had to be considered. Firstly, General Foy, with additional troops, had been advancing southwards towards Vitoria to assist Joseph when he received news of the French defeat. He turned back towards France and there was a chance that his force could be defeated. Secondly, there was General Clausel's army. As Oman comments,[5] there was a possibility that Wellington might be able to defeat this French army as it approached Vitoria. Clausel's Army of the North, comprising 20,000 men, had been marching to join the French army at Vitoria and was still a day's march away when the battle was fought. Clausel was advancing from the direction of Pamplona.

Wellington therefore first had to ensure he had sufficient forces to defend Vitoria. Then he detached Graham to continue to pursue Foy and the other French units that were heading north. Finally he made plans to deal with Clausel who, he correctly surmised, had not heard of the French defeat and was still heading unknowingly towards Wellington.

Wellington assembled an army of pursuit consisting of four divisions of infantry, Grant's Hussars and William's brigade of heavy cavalry. It was probably the organising of the infantry that delayed the pursuit on the 22nd. Between 22 and 26 June inclusive, Ponsonby's brigade covered 57 miles, including one day when it rested 'as we were all much fatigued with constant wet and marching.'[6]

Clausel only heard of the French defeat on 22 June. He had got very close to Vitoria, approaching it from the south. What he did not yet know was the scale of the defeat and, as there was the possibility that Joseph might regroup his forces around Pamplona, he decided to retreat south-eastwards along the River Ebro in the hope that he could swing north and join the French forces. However, he started to pick up reports that Spanish guerrillas and British troops were seeking him out. There is a story that one of the reports came from a Spanish magistrate who was a French sympathiser. Thus Clausel resumed his march to join up with Suchet at Saragossa. What he did not realise was that by 26 June Wellington had arrived on the outskirts of Pamplona and could now swing south and cut him off. In order to be successful, Wellington's plan needed Clausel to remain unaware of his movements and not attempt to increase the marching speed of his troops on the way to Saragossa.

To accomplish Wellington's plan Ponsonby's brigade swung southwards. On 27th his brigade marched to Olite via Tafalla, a distance of 35 miles. They were now 25 miles from Clausel, but the Allied infantry support was 10 miles further back. William Graham remembered that 'The day was dreadfully hot and the baggage of all the cavalry so crowded the road, that the dust thrown up by it was ready to choke us.'[7]

On 28 June William's brigade camped at the convent of Caparrosa. Two of the three regiments of the brigade and the staff were quartered in the grounds of the convent. William Graham described it:

> It seemed to be an old gloomy monkish pile. All the interior of the chapel in the ancient Gothic style; the apartments small and filthy and the convent nearly surrounded by a wood in which we had however plenty of game, and curious to say, many wild pigs. These last had become really wild, though of the domestic kind. The original cause we could not find out. Some few were killed but the gallant and noble General Ponsonby published a prohibition as they might still be private property.[8]

William's action in prohibiting the shooting of the pigs, although no doubt unpopular, was in accordance with Wellington's orders to not antagonise the local population.

From Caparossa the cavalry were ordered to progress to Caseda. But on the 29th Wellington received reports that Clausel had marched his troops so quickly over the last few days that they were now too far ahead for his attempt at capturing them to be successful. Clausel reached Saragossa on 30 June. With Clausel gone, and Wellington's infantry dropping in numbers through stragglers searching for plunder, the cavalry was ordered to retrace its steps towards Pamplona to ensure the French garrison there was not relieved.

Many Peninsula accounts concentrate on the siege of San Sebastian, to the detriment of that of Pamplona, perhaps because after a while the actual task of besieging Pamplona was handed over to the Spanish infantry so that the British infantry could concentrate on San Sebastian. However, both fortresses had to fall to allow Wellington to feel confident enough to invade France. Pamplona was a very hard nut to crack. It had

Vaubanesque fortifications, was garrisoned by 3,000 French troops and had the reputation of being one of the strongest fortresses in Europe. It seems clear that Wellington's strategy was to starve the garrison into submission rather than storm the city. To do this he had to stop any French attempts to defeat the besiegers and raise the siege. He also had to prevent supplies from getting into the city. Pamplona was surrounded by cornfields and there were tales of the French bribing the besieging Spanish troops to allow them to bring corn into the city. As Pamplona was situated on a plain, cavalry were also needed to prevent the French from breaking the siege, and from June until the city's capitulation in October 1813 this is how William's brigade was employed.

William Graham described Pamplona as follows:

> Pampelona stands on a rising ground with a small descent from it on every side. The fortifications are so constructed as to command every hill within range of cannon shot. The hills about it are not high but numerous in every direction, the whole being hills and valleys for about three miles , when the cliffs of the Pyrenees begin to rise, each tier mounting higher and higher till lost in the clouds.[9]

William's brigade was quartered in the area around Pamplona at Tafalla. As before regiments were moved when forage for the horses ran scarce. Again the brigade could not bring hay or corn with them, and the horses had to feed on what the cavalry could find. Sometimes the Spanish offered forage helpfully. On other occasions they hid it for their own use. Graham again:

> Our horses fared the worst as we could not bring hay and corn with us. These were obliged to live upon the barley, oats and wheat, all green in the ear, which we found in the fields, but were obliged to cut down for the purpose. Sometimes the inhabitants would furnish plenty of oats and barley, the latter of which they only use for forage and for these we paid in gold.[10]

For the troopers the villages provided bread. For meat William Graham had provided live bullocks all the way from Portugal, as well as rum, although this was not used much as there was plenty of wine in the neighbourhood.

Those of the brigade who kept diaries or wrote letters home approved of Tafalla. It was a large town with well-built stone houses and red tiled roofs. There was a market for woollen goods. Fruit and ice cream were plentiful. Sir Stapleton Cotton, newly returned to the army, gave many balls for the army and the local inhabitants and the local townspeople reciprocated. On 4 July William and the heavy cavalry gave a 'grand ball and supper for the towns folk and other regiments'.[11]

However, this peaceful existence was interrupted on the night of 26 July when the brigade was ordered to march for Pamplona, which it was ready to do by 4am the next day. Marshal Soult, the new French commander, had started to implement an audacious plan to relieve the besieged town.

In July Soult had been appointed by Napoleon to restore the morale of the French army, replacing the discredited King Joseph and Marshal Jourdan. Within a fortnight he had assembled a force of 55,000 infantry and two cavalry divisions. He launched a surprise attack on 25 July, through the Pyrenean passes of Maya and Roncesvalles, in order to relieve the garrison at Pamplona. British forces guarding the passes were forced to retreat and Soult advanced to Sorauren, only five miles from Pamplona. Here Picton and Cole had established a forward position on the Heights of Oricain, overlooking Sorauren. Behind it, closer to Pamplona, were the Heights of San Cristobal, held by Spanish troops blockading Pamplona from the north. Picton placed his third division at the end of the Spanish position, extending the line; William's brigade and the Household cavalry, the Hussars and D'Urban's Portuguese were ordered to protect Picton's flank. Facing them were Foy's troops of infantry and cavalry. Graham wrote:

> Our orders were quite unexpected, and we lay at our ease waiting till Pamplona would surrender it being Lord Wellington's intention to blockade and starve it out. But the French army, having received strong reinforcements, attacked us and drove us back till they came in the neighbourhood of Pampelona.[12]

The first Battle of Sorauren was fought on 28 July. The French infantry attacks were beaten back. The cavalry had not much to do. The French cavalry commander, Pierre Soult (brother of the Marshal), showed no intention of doing anything more than skirmishing and keeping Picton at bay. Stapleton Cotton had been told by Wellington that his cavalry was to be used for flank protection and not for taking the offensive.

Two days later, on 30 July, the Second Battle of Sorauren took place. The French garrison received a signal ordering them to leave the city and join the attacking French. Graham records:

> The signal was answered by firing a gun from the citadel and immediately after they issued out in a body from the gate on the road leading to France. I saw them all out and formed when our cavalry and the Spanish army advanced down on them and immediately a very heavy skirmishing commenced.[13]

Eventually the Spaniards, who outnumbered the French ten to one, forced them to retreat into the city. Soult's attempt at relieving the Pamplona garrison had been defeated and was not repeated.

Wellington's attention now moved to capturing San Sebastian and invading France through the Pyrenees. The terrain was mountainous and there was no need for heavy cavalry. On 31 August San Sebastian fell and on 7 October Wellington crossed the Bidassoa, thereby invading France. On 25 October Pamplona finally surrendered. On 10 November Wellington defeated Soult at the battle of the Nivelle, thereby securing the passes of the French Pyrenees and the plains beyond. Soult withdrew his forces to the area around the strongly defended town of Bayonne, which was the main depot of the French army, protected by Vauban's fortifications. Wellington decided to tighten his grip and, dividing his force, approached from both the south and the south-east. Soult, having numerical superiority, attacked but was defeated at the Battle of the Nive, fought from 9–13 December. Soult then strengthened the garrison in Bayonne and moved eastwards, while Wellington's troops settled into winter quarters close to Bayonne.

All the area fought over after Vitoria, with the exception of the plain around Pamplona, was mountainous country and unsuitable for heavy cavalry. As a result William's brigade remained in Spain. From August 1813 to the ending of the siege of Pamplona, William and his brigade remained near Pamplona, moving as the demands of procuring forage required. The officers joined the locals in balls and boar hunts and there were horse races and general hunting. On Sundays there were church parades. From October to 27 December the brigade was based around the city of Estella, where William also established his headquarters. Graham wrote:

> Estrella is a very fine town surrounded nearly by mountains. This place was General Ponsonby's headquarters. There were several

convents here some of which were nearly in ruins... In this town are many fine houses. There is an excellent market here for vegetables, fruit, meat etc. Fowls are in great plenty and wine is sold in several houses.[14]

The brigade stayed in the area until supplies of forage were exhausted in December. Then it moved back to the area close to Vitoria, where it remained until the spring of 1814, scattered among various villages.

In the meantime William had received further recognition. On Saturday 5 June, two weeks before the battle of Vitoria, the *Caledonian Mercury* recorded, among a long list of promotions:

War Office June 1 1813
His Royal Highness the Prince Regent has been pleased in the name and on behalf of his Majesty to appoint the following officers to take rank by brevet as under mentioned their commissions to be dated 4th June 1813
Colonels
Honourable William Ponsonby of 5th dragoon guards to be Major General in the army[15]

On 28 March 1814 the *London Gazette* carried the following announcement from Horse Guards:

The Prince Regent has been graciously pleased in the name and on behalf of his Majesty to command that in commemoration of the brilliant victory obtained over the enemy by the army under the orders of the Marquis of Wellington in the battle of Vitoria on the 21st June 1813 the under mentioned officers present upon that memorable occasion shall enjoy the privilege of bearing badges of distinction in conformity to the regulations published on the 7th October last
Major Generals
Honourable William Ponsonby

By command of his Royal Highness the Prince Regent. Frederick Commander in Chief
H Torrens Military Secretary[16]

Between January and April 1814 William took his first leave for three years. This was unusual for a general, as many of his contemporaries had estates to run and went on leave a number of times during the war. Perhaps William believed that as the winter of 1813–14 was bad, Wellington would not need the heavy cavalry's services until spring, as had been the case twelve months before. However, in February Wellington went on the offensive. The heavy cavalry was summoned from Navarre on 25 February and marched up the Great Road from Vitoria to St Jean du Luz, and on to the front, which they reached by 10 March, thus missing the Battle of Orthes where Soult was again defeated.

The brigade had benefitted from the autumn and winter recuperation and numbered 'upwards of 1,000 horses in the finest condition imaginable.'[17] It was commanded in William's absence by Lieutenant Colonel Lord Charles Manners of the 3rd Dragoons, who was the second son of the 4th Duke of Rutland and had served at Corunna and as an ADC to Wellington. He had commanded the 3rd Dragoons since August 1812. On 10 April the brigade took part in the Battle of Toulouse, which was the final main battle of the war and indeed unnecessary, as on 6 April Napoleon had abdicated, bringing the war to an end. The news had not reached either Soult or Wellington.

William arrived to resume command of his brigade in April. Celebrations of the end of the war and the restoration of the Bourbon monarchy continued. On 27 April William, along with 300 of the more senior officers of the Allied armies, wearing their least-worn uniforms and displaying the Bourbon white cockade, accompanied Wellington in riding out to welcome the Bourbon Prince the Duc d'Angoulême and his entourage to Toulouse.[18] A ball was held in his honour and he responded by holding another ball and inviting the senior Allied officers.[19]

Gradually the celebrations tailed off and the senior officers now faced a different problem: getting their regiments home. Stapleton Cotton, in overall command of the cavalry, had already returned to England after the Battle of Toulouse, so a lot of the overall organisation work fell on the brigade commanders. Throughout May the infantry were moved from their cantonments around Toulouse and moved westwards towards Bordeaux and the Garonne estuary. It was decided that the infantry would sail home from Bordeaux – although some regiments had to send a battalion to help fight the war in America against the United States.

The cavalry posed a bigger problem – what was to be done with the horses? As early as 19 April Wellington wrote to Earl Bathurst:

Some, probably half of each regiment might be disposed of in this country or in Spain or to the Spanish or Portuguese cavalry with advantage; but I calculate that there will be not less than 9,000 horses belonging to the cavalry, the artillery and the staff and field officers of the infantry to be embarked. It might be possible to march the cavalry, at least across France with the permission of the French Government which I beg leave to suggest for your Lordship's consideration.[20]

Bathurst communicated the idea to the Foreign Secretary, Lord Castlereagh, who gained the agreement of the French government. The number of horses had increased to 12,000 and the idea was to use two points of embarkation: Boulogne and Calais. It was reckoned that it would take six weeks to reach the Channel ports. Final details were worked out between the French government and the quartermaster general, Sir George Murray. Care was taken to ensure there would be adequate supplies and quarters for the troops and the cavalry were to be joined by twenty-one battalions of infantry. The Hussar brigade, the Household Brigade and the heavy cavalry were to set off at 24-hourly intervals starting on 2 June, on a route that would take them to, among other places, Montauban, Souillac, Limoges, Argentan, Orléans and Mantes, which they hoped to reach by 1 July.[21]

William and his regimental commanders had to get their troops ready and this included sending any dismounted men and heavy baggage to Bordeaux, from where they could be shipped home.

The journey across France was comparatively uneventful, although the troops were not always hospitably received, depending on whether or not the town through which they rode was pro-Bourbon or pro-Napoleon. French troops were also making their way home from the army, or from imprisonment in England, and it was important that there was no conflict. Unfortunately the Life Guards quarrelled with some locals and fought with them, killing several.[22]

From 24 June officers were allowed to visit Paris and William may have taken the opportunity to visit the capital, which had been closed to English visitors since 1802. He would have gone to the Opera and the theatres, looked at the palaces and the Louvre and seen some of the Napoleonic buildings, including the unfinished Arc de Triomphe.

From Mantes William's brigade marched to Boulogne and waited its turn for the transports to take them to England. At Boulogne William's brigade was reviewed by Major General Sir Henry Fane, another heavy cavalry commander who had been present at Vitoria. He expressed much gratification at its condition after so long a march. There was a drawback in being in good condition, however, as Sir Henry selected a number of horses from the brigade to be given to the French government as part of a consignment of 150 of the best cavalry horses to serve as mounts for the royal guard of the newly restored French king, Louis XVIII.

Just before the brigade embarked William expressed to his men, in brigade orders, his approval not only of what they had done in three years, but also of their conduct, commenting on 'the high sense he entertained of their uniformly excellent conduct both in quarters and in the field', adding:

> it is a gratifying circumstance that during the whole period of service they have, in no instance, individually or collectively, occurred animadversion in general orders; that no individual of the brigade has been brought before a general court martial; and that not one instance has occurred (to the major general's knowledge) of interior disagreement in the brigade. With equal truth the major general can assert that upon every occasion which has presented itself to them, whether regimentally or in brigade, of acting against the enemy they have nobly maintained the superiority of the British cavalry and fully justified the high opinion so repeatedly expressed with regard to them by his Grace the Duke of Wellington. It is certainly a matter of regret that the nature of the country which was latterly the scene of operations, was so little calculated to afford the Cavalry a scope for brilliant or decisive achievements, such as that of the ever memorable 22nd of July 1812 and the three regiments will ever have to congratulate themselves on its having fallen to their lot to be the brigade employed in that glorious and effectual charge which contributed in so eminent a degree to decide the fate of the day and to secure the signal and complete defeat of the French army. The Major General conceiving it to be highly desirable that the three regiments should possess some permanent badge in commemoration of the day to which they must ever look back with feelings of pride and exultation: conceiving also the strength and justice of their claims to this honourable distinction to be indisputable, has some time since preferred on application, as to the success of which he has every reason to feel most sanguine; having for its object to obtain His Royal Highness The Prince

Regent's gracious permission that the 5th Dragoon Guards and the 3rd and 4th Dragoons may bear inscribed on their standards the word 'Salamanca', and assume the appellation of 'Salamanca Regiments'.

It only remains for the major general to declare his heartfelt satisfaction at the exemplary conduct of every part of the brigade during the march through France and to congratulate the regiments upon the entire approbation expressed by Major General Fane of the excellent condition and effective state of their horses, as well as of the general appearance of the Brigade. Major General Ponsonby concludes by requesting that Lieutenant Colonel Lord Charles Manners, Lieutenant Colonel Prescott and Major Hugonin will themselves accept and have the goodness to communicate to the regiments under their respective commands, his best and warmest thanks for their zealous and steady services during the time he has had the honour of commanding them in brigade together with his earnest and sincere good wishes for their future welfare. He also requests Brigade Major Hill will accept his best thanks for the zeal and assiduous attention with which he has discharged the duties of his situation.

W Ponsonby Maj General[23]

The brigade embarked at Boulogne as separate regiments and had to wait for both a high tide and a favourable wind for the crossing. The 5th Dragoon Guards embarked on 17 and 18 July, and landed at Dover on 19 and 20 July respectively. The 3rd Dragoons disembarked at Dover on 20 and 21 July.

The 5th Dragoon Guards then marched to Woodbridge barracks in Suffolk and remained in the Suffolk area, taking up their old role of maintaining the peace. As at the end of so many wars there were reductions in headcount. However, for the troopers and for William it was a chance to catch up with friends and loved ones they had not seen for many months.

Chapter 10

A Brief Interlude at Home

William arrived back in England in the summer of 1814. Apart from a few months' leave at the beginning of that year he had been away from England since July 1811. In that time social conditions had changed. The war had brought inflation and economic distress. There were threats of class war between the Luddites, as they were called, and factory owners seeking to introduce new efficient machinery into their premises as the Industrial Revolution gathered pace. There was a new morality, with evangelical preachers addressing mass meetings and writing pamphlets. The logical thought processes of the Age of Reason were being replaced in music, art, architecture and poetry by Romanticism. Mozart had been replaced by Beethoven, Goldsmith by Byron, Chiswick Villa by the Brighton Pavilion.

The return to peacetime normality was slow. The Treaty of Ghent to bring the war with America to an end was signed on Christmas Eve 1814 and even then there would be one major battle to be fought at New Orleans before the news reached the combatants. Farmers who had made profits from high corn prices insisted on the imposition of higher tariffs on cheaper imported corn in an attempt to control the market. There were riots in London and the army was called out. People expected Income Tax to be repealed, but instead more taxes were introduced to pay the large National Debt. The government cut the manpower in the army and navy to reduce costs. The euphoria that had greeted the end of the war evaporated as reality kicked in.

But against this background at least families were reunited. William was now able to spend time with Georgiana and his young family. The Borthwick Institute at York University has a series of letters written by him to his mother during the months of December 1814 and January 1815 and another set sent to his sister Mary by concerned friends after his death. From them we can assemble a picture of how he spent his time.

We know he and Georgiana went on holiday to Margate.[1] One of the side-effects of the Napoleonic Wars and the Prince Regent establishing his court at Brighton was the start of the British preoccupation with the seaside. The wars had prevented the well-to-do from visiting Europe, and this meant that apart from being in London for the season and spending the rest of their time on their country estates, or at Bath, they had nowhere else to go. However, the example set by the Prince Regent, the so-called 'First Gentleman of Europe', of spending time by the sea had provided an alternative, and had encouraged the growth of other seaside towns. One of these was Margate. The artist-engraver William Daniell commented:

Margate, in the course of little more than half a century, has risen into a well-frequented, if not a fashionable, watering place. Being situated at a convenient distance from the metropolis, and adapted to the expenses of the intermediate rather than of opulent classes of society, it has become the resort of a great number of citizens and their families.[2]

Apart from holidaying at Margate and visiting friends and relations in London, the family also visited Ireland.

Domestic life seemed to appeal to William, but it was not without its difficulties. As he wrote to his mother:

Living almost entirely here – seldom seeing anybody I know as little what is going forward as if I was 200 miles off. We have now no coachman or carriage or horses so that Georgiana except one morning to take Louisa to a dentist's has never been in town since our return from Ireland. Georgiana is now quite well again. I fancy the swimming in her head and headaches are owing to some accumulation of bile. All the children are quite well. Tell Frederick I have just received his letter and will execute his commission. I enclose a letter from Georgiana. My love to Mary and believe me ever most affectionately yours WP.[3]

However, William could not shut himself away from public affairs entirely. He had returned from the Peninsula with a great reputation as a fighting soldier. The *History of the 5th Dragoon Guards*, published in 1835, referred to him as the 'regiment's favourite commanding officer'. He is always referred to as 'gallant', but also modest and not someone who courted celebrity status. However, as a major general he was expected to play his part in the outpourings of public thanksgiving. He had been with his brigade in France in July and therefore missed the great Thanksgiving ceremony in St Paul's Cathedral and the visit of the European monarchs. But there were still dinners to attend. Francis Horner, an able young Whig politician, wrote a letter to his mother on 4 July 1815 saying;

> The person I knew best among those who have fallen was Sir William Ponsonby, one of the mildest and gentlest of human beings; but in the field always flaming with enterprise. One of the last times I saw him, and his cousin Frederick Ponsonby…it was at a dress dinner; they were both covered with orders and medals won in the battles of Spain.[4]

For the Whig Party, who had resolutely opposed the war, William's success in the Peninsula was a godsend. The great Whig spokesman Henry Brougham had predicted Wellington's defeat and retreat from the Peninsula before Christmas 1813. Willoughby Gordon, a Whig, had disgraced himself by his incompetence as quartermaster general in the Peninsula. Samuel Whitbread, a great Whig orator, seeing how much the public mind had changed, had forced through Parliament an increased grant of money to Wellington on the basis that the Tory government's original amount was not large enough! Now, with William back, the Whig Party could feel less isolated in having a hero of their own, whose uncle was leader of the Whig Opposition in the House of Commons and whose best friend was Whig leader in the House of Lords.

While he was away in Spain William had been elected *in absentia* as MP for the County of Londonderry, and this of course brought obligations to attend Parliament and look after the interests of his electorate. We know that he frequently attended Parliament. He voted against the return of Genoa in February 1815, but there is no record of him making a speech. He interested himself greatly in politics and used his mother, who was staying with the Greys, to try to influence his brother-in-law.

> My uncle in a note which I had from him this morning enquires very anxious whether I have heard any thing from you about coming up to town and whether Charles intends being in his place in the House of Lords on the 9th February. I can give him no

information as you do not mention a word on the subject – It is certainly a time when his attendance would appear almost indispensable. I doubt whether there has ever occurred an occasion when it was of so much importance. God Bless you my Dearest Mother. Georgiana and the children are all well – and send their love. Adieu. Believe me ever affectionately yours
W Ponsonby.[5]

One burning issue was how the war with America would be brought to an end. On 3 December William wrote to his mother:

With respect to politicks I can add little to what you read in the newspapers – people begin to be very sanguine of the negotiation at Ghent and make themselves sure of immediate peace – God send it may be so. Though I apprehend it can only be obtained by a total retraction of all the ill judged and unwarranted demands which in the usual strain of absurdity they expected to enforce. However in my opinion any peace which does not compromise our maritime rights or our honour must be good – you cannot have an idea of the ludicrously deplorable figure cut by the Treasury Bench and on the last night even more so than before – Horner made a most clear and powerful statement full of facts which they did not attempt to deny, any one of which ought to be sufficient to damn any ministry.[6]

There were also military matters to attend to. William had not forgotten his old brigade or his own regiment. The granting of battle honours in those days only occurred when the regiment's commander lobbied for them and William had continued to press for this on his return. This was not straightforward. First of all he had to get his commander, Stapleton Cotton (now Lord Combermere), to agree. Then Lord Combermere had to get Wellington's agreement. Wellington had to persuade Sir Henry Torrens of Horse Guards to persuade the Duke of York as Commander in Chief. But this is what William did and so we find recorded in Wellington's Dispatches a letter written by Wellington to Major General Sir Henry Torrens on 12 July 1814:

Sir, I have the honour to enclose the extract of a letter from Lieutenant General Lord Combermere containing a request from Major General the Honourable William Ponsonby that the brigade of cavalry consisting of the 5th Dragoon Guards, the 3rd and 4th Dragoons to the command of which he succeeded in the battle of Salamanca on the death of Major General Le Marchant should be permitted to bear the word 'Salamanca' on their standards.

I beg you to lay this application before the Commander in Chief and take that opportunity of informing His Royal Highness that nothing could exceed the good conduct of these corps on the occasion for which the distinction is claimed.[7]

William's persistence had paid off and it was announced in the *London Gazette* on 16 November that:

His Royal Highness The Prince Regent having been graciously pleased, in the name, and on behalf of his Majesty, to approve of the 5th or Princess Charlotte of Wales' Dragoon Guards being permitted to bear on their Colours and Appointments (in addition to any other badges or devices heretofore permitted to be borne by that regiment) the word Salamanca in commemoration of the distinguished gallantry displayed by that regiment in the Battle fought on the plains of Salamanca on the 22nd day of July 1812.[8]

This was followed on 6 April 1815 by another order:

His Royal Highness the Prince Regent was pleased in the name and on the behalf of His Majesty, to approve of the Fifth or Princess Charlotte of Wales regiment of Dragoon Guards being permitted to bear on its standards and appointments (in addition to any other badges or devices which may have been heretofore granted to the regiment) the word PENINSULA in commemoration of its services during the late war in Portugal, Spain and France under command of Field Marshal the Duke of Wellington.[9]

In addition William sent to the 5th Dragoon Guards the drum major's staff of the 66th French Regiment de Ligne, captured at Salamanca, which he had ornamented at his own expense with the desire that it be carried by the trumpet major on all occasions of parade. In November 1814 the officers of the 5th Dragoon Guards responded by presenting him with a valuable sword, which they had voted him in 1813 as 'a mark of gratitude for the care and attention which he had paid to their interests.'[10] The drum major's staff is still with the regiment and the sword is in the regimental museum at York.

William had to consider what he was going to do now that peace had been established. He did not belong to the most affluent branch of the Ponsonby family and he needed to earn an income to support his family. But with the war against Napoleon ostensibly finished, there were few opportunities for a newly appointed major general of cavalry. The only active area of operations was America. The war with the United States was unlikely to last much longer and anyway very little cavalry had been employed during the conflict. In England there was still no police force and so the army was still used to suppress discontent. At the same time the government was reducing the numbers in the army in order to achieve a reduction in costs. Everything pointed to William resuming his role of lieutenant colonel of the 5th Dragoon Guards, to be posted around the United Kingdom just as before the war. After the excitement and promotions of Spain, it is unclear what his feelings about his prospects were.

However, a more ghastly spectre than unfulfilling work soon arose, in the form of financial difficulties. In a set of letters, the first dating from 3 December 1814, it is clear that William's mother, living with his sister at the Grey residence in Northumberland, had tasked him with sorting out the family's finances. William's father had died with large landed estates that he had shared among his family. But he also had sizeable debts. This situation had been exacerbated by the wilful extravagance of William's elder brother John, who had borrowed more. Indeed John's indebtedness was so bad that he had spent several years abroad, hiding from his creditors. Unless the creditors were repaid the Ponsonby family (who had annuities based on the revenues from the estates) could not receive the benefits. This situation particularly affected William's mother and his younger brother Frederick. William and his other brothers all had income from their occupations and William's sister, Mary, had the Grey family fortune to protect her.

One of the problems was that no one really knew the extent of the family indebtedness and whether anyone was pressing for payment. The level of income from the estates was also uncertain, as the lands were administered for the family by agents. It is quite clear that the agents had not been collecting the rents.

By December William had established that John had borrowed £20,000 (£1.2 million in today's terms) from Jewish moneylenders who were charging 18 per cent interest and were likely to seek legal redress if payments were not made. This meant that if John ever returned to England and could not repay his creditors, he was liable to be thrown into a debtor's prison. The payment of the interest alone exceeded the income from John's estates by £2,000 a year. William suggested to his mother that they should approach their wealthy relations, the Bessboroughs and the Cavendishes, to advance £23,000 to pay off the moneylenders and sign a Trust Deed to repay the money. The advantage of this approach was that the family would be protected from legal action and the amount of repayments would be less than that required by the moneylenders.

> Do you think any of our rich and kind relations could be induced amongst them to advance a sum of money (suppose £23,000) to enable us to pay off these annuities? I acknowledge it would be a most unpleasant and mortifying proposal to make but things are in that desperate predicament that I am afraid if we mean to make any effort to save John from total ruin and utter disgrace we must determine to overcome all reluctance arising from those feelings or even perhaps from what I might call delicacy.[11]

William's mother was not keen to approach relatives. None of her letters survive, so we can only guess at the reason. Perhaps her reluctance was due to a concern for family honour and her not wanting the embarrassment of disclosing the level of indebtedness. However, perhaps she also knew that the Bessboroughs themselves were financially embarrassed due to massive gambling debts, a fact she did not communicate to William.

An alternative solution was to sell some of John's lands. William started correspondence with the Irish agents with this in mind. In an economic downturn it was not a good time to achieve a high price. Offers were made (£70,000) much lower than the asking price (£87,000) and then withdrawn. John did nothing to help sort out the situation and in fact delayed his return to England so William was left to manage the affairs.

The more William investigated the situation the more serious he found it to be. John's pressing creditors grew in numbers and amounts. Within a few days the amount to be repaid was £30,000. By 16 December it was £40,000. Early in December William referred to the fact that John was facing 'irretrievable ruin'.[12]

William was greatly concerned.

I cannot describe to you my dearest Mother how very much all this most unpleasant business has worried and annoyed me – and I am in addition in dread every day of hearing of John's being in some most serious difficulty at Paris – as I know not where he is to look for the means of paying his expenses there – If the sum of money above mentioned could be got it would I think enable us to make a start towards putting the matter in train of arrangement. Without it the difficulties are so numerous and insurmountable that I despair of ever being able to establish the trust which John is anxious to make – I shall make no excuse for plaguing you with so long, so disagreeable and, I am afraid, so perplexed, a statement – I only lament the necessity and the pain which the facts must inflict upon you. Pray let me know as soon as possible your ideas and opinions on the subject.[13]

By 12 December William had more melancholy news to impart. He was himself embroiled in John's financial problems. The situation was also causing his mother great distress.

December 12th

My Dearest Mother

It really made me quite miserable to receive your most melancholy letter today. I feel very sorry not to have it in my power to answer it by this post. But I was obliged to go to London before the post came in and did not return till after it was gone out (it goes out from here at 4 o'clock). In what you say of yourself describing yourself as an incumbrance upon John etc I do assure you even if it was possible such a feeling could exist anywhere but in your own most anxious maternal mind, that the fact is quite otherwise, as on the contrary the only means he can, I am afraid look to, to live on, is your jointure which you are so kind as to forego in his favour and which is out of the reach of the creditors.

But time presses very much indeed as the annuitants will certainly proceed at law and not only occasion enormous expense but probably totally defeat any possible arrangement. I find I am personally most deeply concerned in this matter in addition to the interest I could not but have in John's distresses – I find that some annuities to a large amount for which I joined in security for John he assuring me that he was so pressed at the

moment that he must be ruined if he failed in raising the money but that the very first money he could obtain by loan should be appropriated to pay off these annuities – now I find they have not been paid off as I had hoped – and if we fail now in getting money to pay them off I and my wife and children will be in the most distressed state possible. I do not accuse John of breach of confidence on this occasion but I believe the truth to have been that he continued afterwards to constantly be set with difficulties that he never had it in his power to redeem them. It is now four years since the transaction. This I am sure will be an additional motive with you, if any additional inducement can exist for you to consider how this dreadful calamity may be averted. Have you ever consulted C Grey on all these disagreeable matters? – You will probably have heard from John from Dover – I hope he will lose no time in coming up to town. God bless you my dearest mother
Believe me ever most affectionately yours
W Ponsonby[14]

In another letter he clarified the amount involved:

I do not recollect whether I mentioned to you the amount of the annuities for which I am joined in security with John. It is a most serious sum and could not but involve me in total ruin – it is something above 12,000 at annuity interest of about 15%. He says he has never had it in his power to pay them off. It is to me however a most heartbreaking case. If I had no wife and children I should care but little – but I do not know the day these annuitants may pounce upon me and perhaps attack me by execution on my house. I am disposed to give John credit for not having been himself at all aware of the extent of his difficulties or of his means being unequal to the payments of all his debts – But it has been thoughtlessness exceeding anything one could conceive possible.[15]

So William had established that he was in fact guarantor of some of John's debts, and that his despicable elder brother had reneged on his promise to repay the sums borrowed and cancel William's liability as surety. William decided to consult his Uncle George, the leader of the Opposition, who was also a lawyer by profession.

Major General The Hon. Sir William Ponsonby, KCB. Produced as a print from the engraving by G. Maile, it depicts Sir William as he may have appeared at the Duchess of Richmond's Ball on 15 June 1815. It was typical for such prints to be produced as mementos for relations and friends of the deceased.

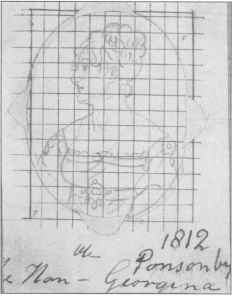

Sketch of Georgiana by the painter Henry Bone for a pair of miniatures. The sketch was made in 1812 when Sir William was in the Peninsula. (By kind permission of the National Portrait Gallery, London.)

Enamel miniature of Sir William by W. Essex, produced in 1840, the twenty-fifth anniversary of his death, according to family tradition for his daughter Charlotte and worn on her arm. The miniature is in fact a locket containing strands of Sir William's hair. Essex used Bone's original sketch of William, made in 1807, to produce the miniature. (By kind permission of Andrew Talbot-Ponsonby.)

William's mother Louisa, née Molesworth, died 1824.

William's father William Brabazon Ponsonby, 1st Lord Ponsonby of Imokilly, 1744–1806, by Thomas Laurence. Painted in around 1800.

John Ponsonby, William's elder brother. Sketched by the painter Henry Bone, possibly after Sir Thomas Lawrence. (By kind permission of the National Portrait Gallery, London.)

1812 *Lord Ponsonby for after Lawrence*

George Ponsonby,
William's uncle.
(Author's collection)

Bishopscourt, County Kildare, Sir William's childhood home. (Author's collection)

Curzon Street, Mayfair, London. Both George (William's uncle) and John (William's brother) lived in this street. This is George's house at 19 Curzon Street. (Author's photograph)

The cavalry barracks at Canterbury, the 5th Dragoon Guards' depot during the Peninsular War. The picture gives a good idea of a cavalry barracks. (By kind permission of Robert Thompson.)

Royal Cavalry Barracks, Canterbury

A print of an officer of the 5th (Princess Charlotte of Wales') Dragoon Guards, 1800. The uniform is that which William would have worn. (Author's collection)

The Battle of Salamanca; Wellington giving orders during the battle. Drawing by W. Heath, engraved by J. Clarke and M. Dubourg from 'Great Britain and her Allies'. The heavy cavalry with bicorne hats on the right are William Ponsonby's 5th Dragoon Guards. (Author's collection)

The Salamanca battlefield today – photographed by the author from the Greater Arapile. Renowned historian and battlefield tour guide Ian Fletcher points out the direction of Le Marchant's decisive cavalry charge. (Author's photograph)

Madrid: the ornate gateway through the San Vicente bastion, by which William and the Duke of Wellington entered the city in 1812. (Author's photograph)

The modern bridge across the Douro at Tordesillas, showing the width of the river and the importance of holding any bridges to protect Wellington's retreating army in autumn 1812. (Author's photograph)

Sir William's small gold medal for Salamanca.

Sir William's large gold medal for Vitoria, with clasp for Salamanca. (Medals courtesy of Spink and Son Ltd)

The uniforms of the Union Brigade as they appeared in 1815.

A trooper of the 2nd North British Dragoons or Scots Greys. His bearskin is protected from rain by a leather covering. Contrary to depictions by many modern artists we know from first-hand accounts that some of the Scots Greys wore their bearskins without the waterproof covering on 18 June. (Author's collection)

A cornet of the 1st (Royal) Dragoons with the regimental standard or guidon. Contrary to depictions by many artists (including Lady Butler) the guidons were not carried into action at Waterloo. (Author's collection)

A trooper of the 6th (Inniskilling) Dragoons. Although the 1st and 6th had very similar uniforms, particularly the helmets, the Royals had blue facings and the Inniskillings yellow. (Author's collection)

The Norbertine (Premonstratensian) Abbey of Ninove, the location of the cavalry headquarters of Lord Uxbridge, 3km from Denderhoutem. The painting shows how the monastery was intended to look on completion. In fact the south range was never completed and the meal after the great cavalry review was held on the upper floor of the western range of the cloister. (Author's photograph, courtesy of Ann de Bruyne, Head of Tourism at Ninove.)

The baroque abbey church at Ninove today. (Author's photograph)

The site of the great cavalry review on 29 May 1815 at Schendelbeke. (Author's photograph)

Gateway to the abbey at Ninove, through which Blucher, Wellington and Sir William rode after the cavalry review on 29 May 1815, as it is today. (Author's photograph)

The Duchess of Richmond's ball, 15/16 June 1815. This is a still from the film *Waterloo* (1970), directed by Sergei Bondarchuk and produced by Dino de Laurentiis. From left to right: Jack Hawkins as Lieutenant General Sir Thomas Picton, Terence Alexander as Lieutenant General Henry Paget, 2nd Earl of Uxbridge, Michael Wilding as Major General the Honourable Sir William Ponsonby and Rupert Davies as Colonel Alexander Gordon, 4th Duke of Gordon. (Author's collection)

Genappe: the narrow but great obstacle over the River Dyle. Sir William and his brigade passed over the ancient bridge (since replaced), crossing the Dyle on 17 June 1815. (Author's photograph)

Waterloo

Wellington's ridgeline, on his left facing the French. The paved way is the Chemin de Ohain, which has changed little since 1815. Unfortunately, the banks and hedges no longer exist. The front regiments of a number of d'Erlon's divisions crossed the paved way.

The ridge of Mont St Jean, on which the French were attempting to deploy when struck by the Union Brigade. The building in the distance is the convent of Frischermont, which was built after 1815. On 18 June it was where Best's Hanoverian brigade was situated. (Author's photograph)

The advance of the Union Brigade up the reverse slope, showing the steepness of the slope and how hidden the Union Brigade were from the French.

The ridge facing the Lion Mound, down which the Union Brigade charged. The paved road is the Chemin de Ohain, minus its banks and hedges and therefore less of an obstacle now than to the armies in 1815. (Author's photograph)

The area of the French counterattack and Sir William's death, as seen from the Allied ridgeline. Colonel Bro launched his devastating attack to the left of the wood situated on the right. From the Allied ridgeline they were to the left of the wood. The wood appears in both the Ferraris and the Craan maps of 1774 and 1816. Local tradition has it that some trees were planted in the wood as a memorial to Sir William, and traces of formal planting were revealed by a geophysics survey in 2015. I am indebted to the wonderful tour guide Alasdair White for this information. (Author's photograph)

Depictions of Sir William's death

The Fall of Major General Sir William Ponsonby, KCB by George Jones Esq., RA, 1817. It is a good depiction of the hand-to-hand fighting, but the artist has mistakenly given the 4th Lancers czapskas. (Author's collection)

Coloured aquatint by M. Dubourg after Manskirch, published by Edward Orme in 1817. Although wearing green tunics, the 4th Lancers actually wore brass helmets and it is clear only Orban killed Sir William. (Author's collection)

Print by A. Martinet, officier des chevaux-legers Français, 4e Regiment. Colonel Bro would have worn a uniform similar to this when he led the 4th Lancers in the attack on Sir William and the Union Brigade. The 4th Lancers wore a green uniform with red facings and brass helmets.

Print by A. Martinet, a lancer. François Orban would have looked like this when he killed Sir William.

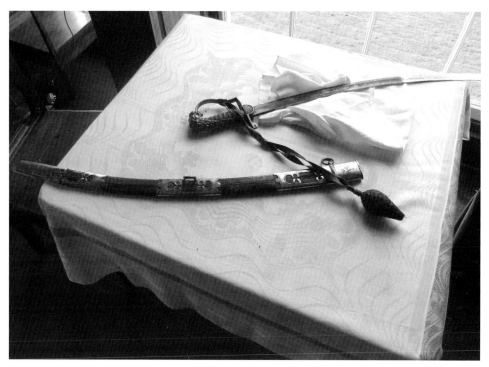

Sir William's sword, with scabbard, taken by marechal de logis Orban after the battle and returned to the family by M. Barbet de Vaux.

The wonderful decoration on the top of the blade of Sir William's sword, including the ironic 'Long live the Emperor' in Spanish! (Author's photograph, by kind permission of Elizabeth Phipps and the Ponsonby family.)

The scabbard of Sir William's sword.

The Georgian church at Kensington before it was replaced by the current church in the Victorian Gothic style. Sir William was buried in the Molesworth family vault (his mother's family). There is no record of a memorial being erected. (Author's collection)

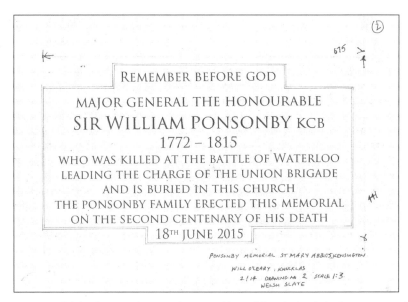

The new memorial in St Mary's Kensington, Sir William's burial place, erected by the Ponsonby family in 2015. Designed by Will O'Leary and carved by his wife Charlotte O'Leary, a direct descendant of Sir William. (Courtesy Caroline Pilkington, also a direct descendant of Sir William.)

Hampstead December 16th

My Dearest Mother

...My uncle George at my request met me the day before yesterday at Richards' where we went into the state of John's affairs as far as our information enabled us and my uncle took notes for the purpose of drawing up a statement of things and a plan for putting them in some train of arrangement which I trust he will complete in one day or two – great difficulties we must expect but if a loan can be obtained of about £40,000 and for which I think we can contrive satisfactory security it will still be in our power I trust to make an arrangement but without a loan I see no hope. I am going to Richards' again today – indeed I have hardly had 10 quiet days since I returned home in consequence of John's business.

God bless you my dearest mother

Believe me ever most affectionately yours

W Ponsonby[16]

December 17th

My Dearest Mother

In my letter of the day before yesterday I dwelt on the several points which I find in your letter I received yesterday. I am very sorry that you seem to have so little hope of success from our 'Rich Kindred'. If they are not induced to come forward on this most desperate occasion I am afraid all is lost. I cannot help feeling sanguine that they will be induced to make an effort to save us. Tell Fred I received his letter yesterday, that I am exceedingly sorry for his disappointment, and I will write to him on Thursday. For myself I really feel in such a state of nervousness and consternation I am quite bewildered. I propose going over to Richmond tomorrow morning to see my uncle. I told you he had promised to draw up a statement of the case and I hope to prevail on him to open the matter to some of our friends.

Ever affectionately yours

W Ponsonby[17]

It is clear that William's uncle believed, like him, that an approach to influential family connections was what was needed. In particular he decided to approach Lord Fitzwilliam, the former Lord Lieutenant of Ireland, who was probably the wealthiest Whig landowner in England.

Despite opposition from William's mother and Charles Grey, George Ponsonby, using his legal knowledge, drew up a scheme to rescue the family and sent off a letter to Lord Fitzwilliam.

Hampstead December 23rd 1814
My Dearest Mother
... I am sorry you and Charles are so decidedly averse to the applying to our rich kindred. I agree with you both that the objections are as strong as possible and that it is a most uncomfortable and most unknown measure only to be resorted to in a case of desperate necessity – this necessity I fear does prevail in full force and I am of opinion no other measure can afford any choice of warding off total ruin both from John and from me. However the die is cast, my uncle's letter to Lord Fitzwilliam is gone – I heard from him this morning to that effect and we must only now in trembling hope await the answer. I am glad at all events that since the measure has been adopted tho' in itself contrary to your opinions yet that the application has been made by the person you considered most proper. As soon as I hear the results I will let you know. I am really in a most dreadful state of anxiety – and as for poor John his situation is lamentable.
Believe me ever most affectionately yours
W Ponsonby[18]

It must have been a miserable Christmas, particularly when, as feared, one of John's creditors actually demanded William repay one of the amounts under the terms of the surety. William had also determined to keep the news of his indebtedness away from Georgiana so she would not worry. In his most bitter letter on the subject, William wrote to his mother on Boxing Day:

December 26th
My Dearest Mother
I have just now received your letters of the 22nd and 23rd – I am quite certain of the pain which you have felt at the extent to which I am involved in John's bankruptcy. I do pity him sincerely – even more for the impression which this matter when known cannot but make upon the minds of his friends and the world than for the privations he must submit to for the rest of his life. Thoughtlessness I am afraid will not be considered

as a sufficient justification – when the interests, almost the existence, of others was involved – but no more of this –, I have not yet heard from my uncle since he wrote – but I enclose a letter which I have received from Lord Fitzwilliam. Knowing that my uncle had written and considering the kindness with which Lord Fitzwilliam had always so markedly shown me and being myself so deeply involved in John's affairs and so wholly interested in their arrangement that I really felt it a sort of duty to be myself the person to communicate to him my severe part in these disasters. I accordingly on Saturday did write to him to state my part of the case. Uncle will give the answer coming as it does from Lord Fitzwilliam. It is hardly necessary to enclose it. I feel quite overpowered and can hardly write. Richards was obliged to pay £120 for me suddenly on Saturday to one of John's annuitants to prevent an immediate execution on my house and I received Saturday morning another demand for £450. I try but is it possible to divest one's mind of all feeling of reprehension and resentment towards a person who could expose his brother to such calamitous distresses – the feeling of resentment I will conquer but over my opinion I have no control – I have not yet heard from my uncle – I will enclose to him your letter respecting Fisher. I think he will be able to induce xx to act.

I am very glad to hear Charles' spasm went off so well and he has had no return. Adieu my dearest mother I cannot say merry Christmas to you. To me tho the first I have been at home since 1810 it has been far, far indeed the contrary. Poor Georgiana to whom these troubles and my dreadful anxieties and apprehensions are, thank God, as yet unknown; has been enjoying the circumstance of my being at home. I can hardly refrain from tears when I look at my poor little children unconscious as they are of the misfortunes to which their father's imprudent perhaps criminal conduct may have exposed them.

God bless you my dearest mother
WP

Don't forget to send me back Lord Fitzwilliam's letter I hope you will not disapprove of my having written to him. Do not mention the matter to anybody unless it be in strict confidence to Charles.[19]

However, after Christmas there was better news. Lord Fitzwilliam had agreed to help and it was expected others would as well.

Hampstead December 29th
My Dearest Mother
I saw my uncle yesterday – nothing could exceed the kindness of Lord Fitzwilliam's answer and if two or three others can be induced to take a similar part we may indulge sanguine hopes of ultimate success. The substance of Lord Fitzwilliam's answer is that provided a list of friends can be found to come forward and that an arrangement can be made which may be effectual for the purpose he will exert himself to advance £10,000 this is certainly most friendly and most generous – it is Lord Fitz himself – my uncle will speak to Lord George – I hope he will help us also.[20]

The good news continued in the New Year with the Cavendish family offering their help:

January 2nd 9 o'clock
As I am setting out to Colnbrook to see a very cheap house I have only time to write a line to say that my uncle has seen Lord George who received him most kindly and 'follows Lord F's example though not quite to the same amount and says the Duke will do so also' – these are the words of my Uncle's note – certainly nothing can exceed the kindest and most handsome assistance of these our friends and I trust they may be the means of saving us from otherwise inevitable ruin. God Bless you my Dearest Mother. Ever affectionately yours
Wm Ponsonby

If Lord Jersey can or will give us a help towards our loan – though the sum will not be as great as we could wish yet I think we shall be able to manage. It would certainly be much better if we could at once pay off all the annuities but I do not know where we can look for assistance beyond those above mentioned.[21]

To take his mind off the financial woes there was some welcome news for William. Along with other military leaders he was going to receive a knighthood.

Caledonian Mercury: Monday Jan 9th 1815
Supplement to the *London Gazette* of 3rd January
Wednesday Jan 4th 1815
(continued from our last)
15th. His Royal Highness the Prince Regent acting in the name and on behalf of his Majesty has been graciously pleased to appoint and nominate the under mentioned officers of his Majesty's Naval and Military forces to be Knights Commanders of the Most Honourable Military Order of the Bath viz:
78. Major General the Honourable William Ponsonby[22]

Hampstead January 10th
My Dearest Mother
Your letter of the 5th reached me yesterday evening on my return from London. I have seen Lord Rosslyn who is exactly what I expected –ready to make every exertion in his power in our present difficulties and will most cheerfully undertake to be one of the trustees should we succeed which I trust we shall in establishing a trust. I am to meet him today at Mr Richards', whom I was in hopes my uncle would also have met, but I have just heard from him, saying he was obliged to be at the Secretary of State's office. However we shall be able to make some progress I hope. I can perfectly well understand your feelings as to the Duke of D and your delicacy about writing to him. The fact is that he has not been applied to by my Uncle on this occasion. My uncle spoke to Lord George who after stating what he was ready to do himself added that *the Duke would do the like.* To that I apprehend Lord George had previously had some conversation with His Grace on the subject. He has written to John in the kindest terms offering him Chiswick, and inviting him to Chatsworth – John I believe is likely to be in town today or tomorrow – Lord Rosslyn wrote yesterday to offer his home in St James' Square. Lord Jersey I know is disposed and anxious to assist as far as it may be found in his power – but I am afraid at the present moment his own embarrassments are very considerable – however he comes to town I believe on purpose Thursday next – I will write again tomorrow – tell Frederick I secured his letter with Fisher's enclosure – as to the confirming the intentions of my father with respect to Dick's children there can be no hesitation. But under the present circumstances it

appeared to me that it would be better to postpone the arrangements, until the general arrangement in contemplation should be determined on and of which this would of course form a part. I therefore enclosed it to my uncle for his opinion. Who decidedly agreed with me – he has not yet returned Mr. Fisher's letter as I requested which has prevented my hitherto forwarding it to George –

Georgiana is entirely unacquainted with my part of these dreadful difficulties and has only a knowledge of John's so far as that his affairs are embarrassed but without an idea of the extent of his embarrassment. God bless you my dearest mother. My love to Charles, Mary etc. Ever affectionately yours
W Ponsonby[23]

Hampstead January 12th
My Dearest Mother
I received yesterday evening your letter of the 8th having gone to town in the morning. It was too late to answer it when I returned as the post goes out at 4 so that I always when I go to town lose a day – I am very sorry to hear of Charles' two attacks of pain. I hope he has had no further return of it – and that you are right in your opinion that they are not dangerous. I have had two interviews with Lord Rosslyn, who told me he would write to you himself – and I have no doubts he has explained to you his view of the case – it is indeed a melancholy one – one from which nothing but the most full and disinterested assistance of our most excellent friends can possibly relieve him or me. John was to be in town yesterday early, I called with Lord Rosslyn at past 5 in St James' Square but he was not then arrived – nor have I heard from or of him by this morning's post – which if he had arrived before 8 I certainly should have done – as Lord Rosslyn promised to write by the two penny post. My dearest mother it is unnecessary for me to say how very much I lament the inconvenience you suffer from the non payment of your interest and I lament it the more from the apprehension that there is really no substance to pay it at the present moment. Messrs Pack having been freed to accept bills for the Jewish annuitants to the amount of £30,000 as the only means of preventing them seizing upon the estate and which if not paid these bills will not fail to proceed to extremities instantly. The demands on the estate in the shape of interest,

annuities etc exceed at present the annual income by about £300 so that till the annuities are got rid of it is impossible that anything can be done – I have just heard from John that he has arrived. God bless you my dearest mother, ever affectionately yours W Ponsonby

You enquire as to my new title – it is Sir Wm P KCB (Knight Commander of the Bath) what does C think of this measure?[24]

By 24th January William was hoping the worst was over:

Hampstead – January 24th 1815
I fully appreciate my Dearest Mother your anxiety on my account. I do feel sanguine hopes that I shall ultimately be extricated from my most uncomfortable situation at least so far as regards the annuities. At the same time I am afraid I should very far overstep the mark did I consider myself as safe. – However I endeavour as far as possible to put the whole matter out of my head. Whatever lay with me to do I have exerted myself to do and nothing remains but to submit to my fate or perhaps I should more properly say, to resign myself as cheerfully as I can to the dispensation of providence.[25]

William, through his dedication, and with the help of his uncle and the 'rich kindred', had weathered the storm. Subsequent papers in John Ponsonby's archives at the University of Durham show that his unscrupulous elder brother did not learn his lessons. He left the running of the estate to his younger brother Frederick, who managed temporarily in the 1830s to bring income and expenditure under control. But John did not honour the terms of the agreement that William and his uncle had devised. Sadly Bishopscourt had to be sold in 1838 to the 3rd Earl of Clonmell. By that time William, his mother and his uncle had been dead for many years.

Chapter 11

The Trumpets Call

For Sir William, as he now was, the world was going to change yet again. On 26 February Napoleon escaped from Elba and began his audacious attempt to regain the French throne. On 1 March he landed near Frejus on the Mediterranean coast with 1,100 men. By 20 March he was restored as the ruler of France in Paris and Louis XVIII had fled ignominiously into exile. The *coup d'état* happened with astonishing speed, as regiment after regiment of dissatisfied soldiers rallied to the imperial banner. The rapidly changing situation was captured in the French newspaper *Le Moniteur*.

'The cannibal has left his den.'
'The Corsican wolf has landed in the bay of San Juan.'
'The tiger has arrived at Gay.'
'The wretch spent the night at Grenoble.'
'The tyrant has arrived at Lyons.'
'The usurper has been seen within 50 miles of Paris.'
'Bonaparte is advancing with great rapidity but he will not set
his boot inside the walls of Paris.'
'Tomorrow Napoleon will be at our gates!'
'The emperor has arrived at Fontainebleau.'
'His Imperial Majesty Napoleon entered Paris yesterday
surrounded by his loyal subjects.'[1]

The Great Powers, busy squabbling over what the European landscape should look like post-Napoleon, now found they had Napoleon to deal with again. On 13 March they declared war against him, using the argument that he was an enemy of humanity. However, actually getting rid of him was a very different matter. True, there was a royalist insurrection in the Vendée and certain of his old officers and marshals refused to join him, but these factors were not going to bring about his overthrow. That would only result from concerted military action by the Great Powers of Austria, England, Prussia and Russia.

The Allies' strategy was to overwhelm Napoleon by sheer weight of numbers, as they had in 1814. There was already an Anglo-Dutch army in Belgium, which had as its core 15,000 British troops, many of whom had originally been deployed in 1814 in the unsuccessful attempt to take the fortified town of Bergen-op-Zoom. There were also Belgian and Dutch troops which had previously been part of Napoleon's army and whose loyalty, if deployed against him, was unknown. To increase these numbers more regiments were provided from England and Ireland as they became available. The Anglo-Dutch army was placed under the command of the Duke of Wellington. In addition to this Allied army there were 130,000 Prussians and Saxons in the same area under Marshal Blucher, with whom Wellington could collaborate. Blucher and Wellington's forces combined therefore totalled 242,000 men. However, total assurance of victory would only come once the vast armies of Austria and Russia were deployed. These totalled over 500,000 men. Austrian and Bavarian troops would march through the Ardennes. Russian troops would move through Germany. The Allies would therefore have 740,000 troops against an expected French army of 230,000 men spread along the northern, eastern and southern frontiers of France and also engaged in suppressing a revolt in the Vendée. But this overwhelming Allied force would take months to reach the frontiers of France. The earliest date they were expected to arrive was the end of June or the beginning of July. The Allied powers decided not to begin offensive operations until all the invading forces were in position. In the meantime more British troops would be sent to Belgium, the troops trained and the Duke of Wellington would transfer from his role as British envoy at the Council of Vienna to become commander of the Allied forces in Belgium. Wellington left Vienna on 29 March.

The British troops already stationed in Belgium comprised fifteen battalions of infantry. But to be part of an international invasion force, cavalry and artillery were needed. As in most post-war periods the numbers of troops had already been reduced, and there had been no apparent need for those cavalry units that had fought so well in the Peninsula to train up their replacement horses. This meant that the regiments that comprised Sir William's Peninsular brigade would not be ready in time to play a part in the ensuing conflict. Indeed, the 5th Dragoon Guards were specifically informed that they could not be sent abroad because of the large number of untrained horses they now had.

To compound the problem, as the English government had not immediately called out the militia when Napoleon returned to Paris, many units of the regular army were unable to hand over their garrison, anti-insurrection and coastguarding duties so that they could travel overseas.

Nevertheless numbers increased impressively. By the start of June, in addition to Belgian and Dutch troops, Wellington had under his command thirty-nine British and King's German Legion infantry battalions, twenty-one British and King's German Legion cavalry regiments and artillery and Royal Horse artillery. To command them Wellington started to assemble a team of capable senior commanders, many of whom had served with him in the Peninsula. One of these was Sir William Ponsonby.

On 3 April Sir William was recalled, but without a brief. There were as yet no heavy cavalry among the British army in Belgium. Indeed, it was not until 5 April that the first heavy cavalry regiment, the Scots Greys, received orders to hold themselves in readiness for foreign service. Certainly Sir William remained in England, attending Parliament, but as April drew to a close he knew that he was heading to Belgium. A letter to his sister Mary, which she kept, shows that he must have been preparing to leave. You can sense his haste in writing it:

To the Countess Grey Portman Square London
Hampstead April 26th 1815

My Dearest Mary
I was very sorry indeed not to be able to call and take leave of you and the girls yesterday but my Mother will tell you how hurried I was about indispensable matters. I am much disappointed at not having seen and got aquainted with your boys. I just saw Charles in the House of Lords but could not get to speak to him. God bless you Dearest Mary
Ever affectionately yours
W Ponsonby
Georgiana sends her love.[2]

William never had the chance to say goodbye to his sister or his great friend. He was in Belgium by 30 April. In a memo written by Wellington to the Prince of Orange, the Earl of Uxbridge, Lord Hill and Delancey on that day he referred to Sir William Ponsonby's brigade.[3] On 4 May Braithwaite Christie, who had been his ADC in the Peninsula, was appointed his ADC in Belgium. On 5 May William was formally appointed to command the Union Brigade, and on 9 May he actually inspected one of his regiments in the Dender valley.

> General Order
> May 4th Brussels
> Lieutenant Braithwaite Christie of the 5th Dragoon Guards is appointed ADC to Major General Sir William Ponsonby from the date of the Major General's appointment on 3rd April 1815
> E Barnes[4]

> Bruxelles
> 5th May
> No7. Major General the Honourable Sir William Ponsonby is to command the brigade of cavalry consisting of the Royal, 2nd and 6th Dragoons.[5]

This brigade is usually referred to as the the 2nd Heavy Cavalry Brigade, but has passed into immortality as the Union Brigade, as it represented three countries: the Royals representing England, the 2nd Royal North British Dragoons (popularly called the Scots Greys) representing Scotland and the 6th (or Inniskilling) Dragoons representing Ireland.

However, this brigade was very different from Sir William's brigade in the Peninsula, as only the Royals had seen active military service since 1795. The other two regiments had been engaged in peacetime activities and this presented their colonels, and Sir William as brigade commander, with major challenges: no one knew how the units would behave in action. As Sir William had not commanded any of the regiments before, he did not know the officers or men. Nor had all three regiments yet arrived in Belgium. The Royals would only arrive on 27 May, so Sir William had only twenty days to lick his brigade into shape. This was not long enough to prepare, if the Union Brigade was going to face the French heavy cavalry, which had a superior training system.[6]

Of the three regiments that would gain immortality on 18 June, the weakest in terms of active military experience were the Scots Greys.

The Scots Greys

The Scots Greys had not served in the Peninsular War. Indeed their last military service had been in 1794, when they had charged and broken a French square at Willems in the Netherlands. Before that their most recent military experience had been in 1760 during the Seven Years War, when the regiment had charged at the Battle of Warburg. Since then they had been quartered in most parts of the United Kingdom, undertaking, like most cavalry regiments, duties ranging from coast patrols in Sussex to quelling riots in Ludlow. However, they had been much admired by King George III, who used them to provide a Royal Guard at Buckingham Palace. Unfortunately this meant they had become a 'fashionable regiment', attracting a rich set of officers who might have been fearless foxhunters but had no military experience.

Cornet Kinchant, who would later die at Waterloo, wrote in 1815:

> I don't think there is a private in it under 5 foot 11 inches and the officers are a fine gentlemanly set of fellows. There are only three Scotchmen among the officers but the privates are in general Scotch. The horses are all grey and in excellent condition.

To give an idea of their social status he wrote: 'Our dress altogether is extremely rich and consequently costs a lot of money. The court dress coat alone is forty guineas. It is covered with lace from head to foot.'[7]

The commander of the regiment was James Inglis Hamilton, the adopted son of General James Inglis Hamilton, but whose true father was Sergeant Major Anderson of the 21st Foot, who had served under the general in America. The general had adopted James as his heir and secured his promotion through the ranks of the Scots Greys from cornet in 1793 to lieutenant colonel in 1807 and then full colonel in 1814. He had served in the Flanders campaign as a lieutenant and therefore in a junior capacity. Apart from Colonel Hamilton there were very few officers left in the regiment who had seen active service, and even that was over twenty years ago. Of the six troop captains and eleven lieutenants, three captains and six lieutenants had been appointed in 1815. The Scots Greys might look good at review, but there were potential problems when engaged in action due to their officers' lack of battlefield experience.

On 5th April the Scots Greys were ordered to hold themselves in readiness for foreign service. The next day a more detailed set of orders arrived instructing them to embark at Northfleet for Belgium. It took seven days to reach Northfleet via Bristol, Chippenham, Marlborough, Newbury, Reading, Staines, Camberwell and Gravesend. However, although they embarked on 14 April the winds were unfavourable and they didn't arrive at Ostend until the 20th. This must have been awful for the horses, which were kept in their stalls on the transports. On the 20th the regiment disembarked and progressed to the Dender valley via Ghent. On 1 May Hamilton was told his regiment would be part of the 2nd Heavy Cavalry Brigade. By 6 May the regiment had established its headquarters at Denderhoutem.

The Inniskilling Dragoons
Like the Scots Greys the Inniskillings had last seen active service in the Netherlands in 1794. After that they were engaged on home service and from 1809–14 had been in Ireland. In Ireland they avoided the problems associated with being a 'fashionable regiment'. All six captains had been appointed into post before 1811 and of the eight lieutenants all but two had been appointed before 1814. The lieutenant colonel was Joseph Muter, who had been in command of the regiment since June 1813. He seems to have been very unpopular with his officers. Lieutenant Johnston wrote to his mother that none of the officers 'wished to be a moment in Muter's society'.[8] Nevertheless, Sir William trusted him more than he did Hamilton. At Waterloo it would be Muter whom William confided in to put the brigade in motion, despite the fact, as Muter wrote to Siborne years later, 'Colonel Hamilton of the Greys stood above me, but somehow, neither Sir William Ponsonby or myself, adverted to it'.[9]

On 6 April the Inniskillings started their march to Gravesend from Mansfield via Northampton, Romford, and Greenwich. It took them sixteen days. The regiment sailed in two groups, presumably due to a lack of sufficient transports. One group sailed on 25 April; the other on the 29th. The regiment was quartered near Ghent, but moved to the Dender valley, being quartered in six little villages around the regimental headquarters at Herzele from 11 May.

The Royals
Unlike the other two regiments, the Royals did have Peninsular War experience. They had arrived in the Peninsula in 1809 and had been praised by Wellington: 'I think I have never seen a finer regiment. They are very strong, the horses in very good condition and the regiment apparently in high order.' They had distinguished themselves in the

skirmishing on the withdrawal from Bussaco and at Fuentes de Onoro, and Wellington had always regarded them highly. All four captains at Waterloo had been appointed before 1813 and only three of the nine lieutenants had been appointed in 1815, the other six having been appointed before 1812. Their lieutenant colonel Arthur Clifton had commanded the Royals in the Peninsula since 1810. Referred to in the defamatory informal regimental *Journal* as 'the Ruler', and not popular, he was nevertheless judged to be 'a good officer and competent to do his duty', and he certainly maintained discipline.

After the war in Spain ended the Royals had been based in the south-west, in various towns including Dorchester, engaged in suppressing smuggling. After the regiment's long service in the Peninsula this return to peacetime duties disheartened many of the officers and men. We are told in the regimental *Journal* that Colonel Clifton repeatedly wrote to Horse Guards begging for the regiment to be allowed to serve. Finally, on 21 April he got a favourable response and was ordered to take the regiment to Canterbury. Again the regiment crossed in two groups. On 13 May two squadrons embarked at Ramsgate. They had a good crossing and landed on the 14th. The rest of the regiment embarked at Dover on 16 May and landed at Ostend on the 17th. On 27 May they were ordered to establish their regimental headquarters at Ninove.

Sir William not only had new regiments in his brigade, but he also had a new commanding officer. On 15 April Henry Paget, Lord Uxbridge, had been appointed to command the cavalry. Uxbridge had been an inspirational cavalry commander during Sir John Moore's Corunna campaign, but he and Sir William had not met, as Uxbridge had not served under Wellington in the Peninsular War – he had run off with the wife of Wellington's younger brother! Wellington had wanted Stapleton Cotton appointed to the cavalry command in Belgium, but he had blotted his copybook by leaking the story of one of the Prince Regent's love affairs. The Prince Regent responded by blocking his appointment to command. Historians point out how well Uxbridge and Wellington got on, but there must have been some tension or Wellington would not have sought to have Cotton appointed. Comments that Wellington made, such as calling Uxbridge an 'adulterous rogue' and his response when reminded that Uxbridge had run off with his sister-in-law 'I don't care as long as he doesn't try to run off with me', show Uxbridge was not forgiven.

Nevertheless there is no doubting the energy that Uxbridge brought to his command. He and some of his staff arrived at Ostend on 25 April.

What followed was a series of inspections of the various cavalry units. In these reviews the cavalry would execute manoeuvres chosen by their lieutenant colonel. When these were not occurring, the energies of the officers and men had to be channelled away from idleness. So Uxbridge instituted weekly horse races in the area surrounding Grammont and cricket matches at Enghien.

Another key cavalry figure was Lord Edward Somerset who, like Sir William, had commanded a regiment under Le Marchant and had served under Sir William after Salamanca as commander of the 4th Dragoons. He was also handling a new command. The 1st Cavalry Brigade consisted of the Life Guards and Royal Horse Guards that had arrived in the Peninsula in 1813 and had seen action in the final battles of the war. Joined to them were the 1st Dragoon Guards, who had not served in the Peninsula. Lord Edward and Sir William seem to have been good friends.

Other generals with Peninsula experience included Sir Hussey Vivian, who had been the first to arrive in Belgium on 16 April, taking command of the 6th British Cavalry Brigade comprising the 10th and 18th Hussars, as well the 1st Hussars of the King's German Legion, 1,500 men in all. Sir Ormsby Vandeleur took command of the 11th, 12th and 16th Light Dragoons. The 12th Light Dragoons had Sir William's second cousin Frederick as their lieutenant colonel.

All the cavalry were quartered in the Dender valley to the west of Brussels. Because of their large numbers the main problems were forage and supplies of water. To meet these needs the Dender valley was ideal. The land was good and carefully and extensively cultivated. To provide the required fertiliser cattle were housed in stalls close to the farmhouses. Besides cultivated land there were extensive woods. The River Dender flowed through the valley and provided the horses with the water they needed. As it was navigable if food or hay ran out, more could be brought in on flat-bottom barges. Mercer refers to the Dender as:

> holding its course through extensive flat meadows covered with luxuriant crops of hay or affording pasturage to herds of fine cattle. Beyond the river valley the country assumed a different aspect: long and less abrupt slopes, a total absence of hedges.[10]

There were three main towns. Furthest north was Dendermonde, which, as its name implies, was where the Dender met the Scheldt. It had a well-developed harbour. The population was between 5,000 and

6,000, with some of its inhabitants engaged in linen manufacture. Mercer describes it as 'mean and gloomy'.[11] South of Dendermonde was Alost, with its canal harbour, which Mercer describes as being 'full of boats laden with corn and hay for our cavalry, the contractors having established here their grand depot.'[12] Further south was Ninove, with 3,000 inhabitants, dominated by its great Baroque Premonstratensian monastery. The three completed sides of the monastery's cloister were occupied by Lord Uxbridge, his staff and the commissariat, and became the headquarters of the cavalry. 'All the surrounding area was full of cavalry or horse artillery.'[13]

Mercer described the countryside:

> Villages and large farms appeared in all directions, intermingled with extensive woods; the fields exhibited the exuberance of crops- wheat, rye, hops, buckwheat etc with their lighter tints relieving the more sombre tomes of the woodlands. Here the spire of a village church, there the conical roofs and quaint architecture of a chateau, peered across the foliage of the woods and increased the interest of the scene...I thought I had never seen anything half so rich as the fine landscape spread before me.[14]

Dotted throughout the valley were numerous farms, and it was here that the troops were quartered. The horses grazed in the orchards with the men sleeping beside them or in the farmhouses. Mercer describes the farmhouses:

> These farming establishments were very much alike, generally speaking, embosomed in orchards which in their turn are surrounded by lofty elms. The dwelling house is usually of brick only one floor, a high roof under which are the dormitories with garret windows, sometimes two tiers of them. On the ground floor the windows are large and open in the French style, outside shutters almost invariably green. Commonly there are only two rooms on this floor, one on each side of the passage, the door of which opens on the yards as do the windows. One of these rooms is the kitchen or ordinary residence of the family, the other is a salle de ceremonie. In the first is the usual display of brass pans, kettles crockery etc which with some common benches and a large table or two constitute its furniture. As everywhere throughout this country the most perfect cleanliness prevails...The salle exhibits a collection of stiff old fashioned chairs

with rush bottoms and high upright carved backs, ponderous oaken tables snow white window curtains and a series of very common prints in as common frames suspended from the walls. These usually represent saints etc. The barns, stables, cow houses and other out offices form the other three sides of a square of which the front of the dwelling is the fourth. A rough pavement of about ten or twelve feet wide runs all around in front of the building; the remainder of the area is one vast dung-hill having a reservoir in the centre to receive its drainings, whilst it receives those of the cow houses stables and dwellings by means of gutters constructed for the purpose. This precious fluid is the great dependence of the Flemish agriculturist as the principal fertiliser of his fields.[15]

This combination of woods and cultivated fields and an absence of pastureland, except around the River Dender itself, did cause one problem for the cavalry: where could they practice their deployments? Mercer records 'At length and I cannot remember how we found a piece of scrubby common of some acres in extent near the village of Denderhout(em). Thither we repaired occasionally to practise ourselves and prevent our people forgetting entirely their drills.'[16] Denderhoutem was the village Sir William chose as the headquarters of his brigade.

Denderhoutem today, like all the villages in the Dender, has expanded. More homes have been built for people who work in Aalst (French 'Alost'), which has now outgrown both Dendermonde and Ninove. Nevertheless, you can still sense Denderhoutem's early nineteenth-century role as a small hub for a fundamentally agricultural area. A stream feeding into the River Dender can still be traced running through the village. The large medieval church in the village centre hints at the wealth of the neighbourhood. There are two squares and outside traffic still stops as sheep cross the road and tractors turn. None of the accounts mention chateaux in the vicinity and, as we have two letters from Sir William written from Denderhoutem, we can assume that he stayed in one of the houses in the village. It would need to have been large enough to house the staff comprising the Scots Greys Regimental HQ as well as his own staff, so he may have stayed in one of the coaching inns or larger dwellings around the market square.

Cornet Francis Kinchant of the Scots Greys was not impressed with Denderhoutem, referring to it as

a miserable small village not large enough to contain one troop, the remainder, officers and men are quartered at cottages in the neighbourhood. A pig sty in England is a palace to my quarters, hosts of lice, bugs fleas and filth of every description abound in an extraordinary degree in all the habitations of these dirty vagabonds. To counteract however as much as possible the unpleasant effects of sleeping in the duty hut, I have pitched my tent.[17]

By basing his headquarters at Denderhoutem Sir William was acting pragmatically. Less than two miles to the south was Uxbridge's cavalry headquarters at Ninove, which was where Sir William's third regiment, the Royals, would be garrisoned when they arrived on 26 May. Three miles to the west was the village of Herzele, the headquarters of the Inniskilling Dragoons, who arrived on 11 May and were quartered in six small villages in its vicinity. At Denderhoutem was his most inexperienced regiment, the Scots Greys, so Sir William could keep an eye on them. The Scots Greys received two more troops on 15 May.

Given the number of cavalry regiments situated in the Dender valley, accommodation was at a premium. Lieutenant Johnson of the Inniskillings wrote to his mother that Captain Holbech, Cornet Dames and he were housed:

at one wretched farmhouse with one room and a closet to do everything, we cook our own dinner in our own mess kettles which we had brought from England with us and use our own canteen just as if we were in camp. Holbech sleeps on a table, Dames on six chairs and I in a closet where there is a bedstead which Holbech would not take for fear of bugs…Still we are very happy and perfectly convinced of our being rather well off than otherwise, as some of the other officers have three Dutch officers sleeping in the room with them which must be very disagreeable.[18]

The events of May 1815 were a mixture of formal inspections and activities to keep the troops occupied, although well-heeled officers could easily ride into Brussels and see the sights of the city and visit friends or, like Kinchant, visit the brothels. For others there was the chance to socialise. On 13 May the Scots Greys celebrated their increase in troop numbers:

This jovial meeting took place in an orchard, a quarter of a mile from the village, the table was formed with planks extending about 40 yards along the middle of the orchard, and a sumptuous dinner laid out which every man partook of to his satisfaction. The dinner being over and daylight taking leave of us very soon, candles, lamps etc were hung upon the impending fruit trees which formed a spacious bower, all kinds of fruit growing over our heads and the brandy and wine were plentifully circulated. In this manner we spent the night drinking the health of King George, the Prince Regent, the Duke of Wellington and his army etc etc and at daybreak in the morning all cares were drowned with flowing bumpers.[19]

On Friday 5 May Uxbridge and Vivian visited Sir William at Denderhoutem. The next day they all inspected the Scots Greys. On Tuesday 9 May Sir William again inspected the Scots Greys. Sergeant Johnston stated that he 'was much pleased with the regiment's appearance and declared it to be the best body of men and horses he ever saw.'[20]

On 15 May Sir William inspected the Inniskillings. On 22 May Uxbridge reviewed the Scots Greys and on Wednesday 24 May all heavy cavalry regiments were reviewed by the Prince of Orange. Afterwards there was a dinner at Ninove. On 16, 23 and 30 May there was horse racing at Grammont, where the officers raced each other. On Wednesday 17 May there was a cricket match at Enghien.

On 28 May William replied to a letter he had received from Lieutenant General Sir Henry Fane. Fane had commanded another heavy cavalry brigade at Vitoria, which had included the Royals that had just joined William's Union Brigade. The Fane family were also related to the Ponsonbys through marriage.

Denderhoutem
28 May

My Dear Fane
We know no more than you do in England what passes in France or what the real state of mind there is to Bonaparte, the Bourbons etc etc. Reports upon all these topicks (sic) are in great abundance, but coming as they do from persons hostile to Bonaparte and themselves deeply interested, little regard is to be paid to them. The British cavalry are all cantoned in the villages near Ninove, where Lord Uxbridge has his headquarters. It is in the highest possible order, forage having hitherto been abundant.

The whole of the British cavalry and horse artillery are to be reviewed tomorrow by the Duke of Wellington in a great meadow on the banks of the Dender. Blucher and God knows who else is to be present. We shall have 46 squadrons and six troops of horse artillery, it will be a grand sight, the Greys and the Inniskillings are very fine regiments and in excellent order. The Royals (my other regiment) only came up the night before last to cantonments about six miles from hence. I am told they also are in very high trim; so that I have reason to be highly satisfied with my brigade. We have no guess when we are likely to commence upon operations, we suppose it must be pretty soon. The weather is uncommonly fine and almost as hot as Spain.

Believe me my dear Fane, yours very sincerely, Ponsonby[21]

The review that Sir William alluded to and that everyone remembered was the great cavalry review on Monday 29 May at Grammont. It actually happened outside Grammont itself, between Schendelbeke and Iedeghem on a meadow by the Dender just beyond a bridge from the village of Schendelbeke. The review involved 6,000 troops: fifteen regiments of British cavalry (including the Union Brigade) and six troops of horse artillery. The weather was bright and hot with a gentle breeze. Wellington arrived at 1pm along with Blucher and others and was greeted with a salute of nineteen guns. It was very much a public affair, as there were thousands of spectators present, civilian as well as military. Mercer, who was involved in the review, left us this account.

We were formed in three lines. The first near the banks of the river was composed of hussars in squadrons with wide intervals between them and a battery of horse artillery (6 pounders) on either flank. The second line – composed or with only the usual squadron intervals – was composed of heavy dragoons having two batteries… in the front of centre and a battery of nine pounders on either flank. The third was a compact line like the second but entirely of light dragoons supported on either flank by a battery of nine pounders.[22]

It was a splendid spectacle. The scattered line of hussars in their fanciful yet picturesque costume, the more sober, but far more imposing line of heavy dragoons, like a wall of red brick, and again the serviceable and active appearance of the third line in their blue uniforms with broad lapels of white, buff, red, yellow and orange- the whole backed by the dark wood of the declivity already mentioned formed indeed a fine picture.[23]

Of course Sir William was there in command of his brigade. As Sergeant Johnston of the Scots Greys commented:

His Grace the Duke of Wellington seemed much gratified with the appearance of the men and horses and Prince Blucher appeared quite transported with the sight often remarking to the Duke that it excelled all he ever saw. After this the lines were ordered to break into open column of half squadrons right in front, and pass His Grace in this manner, after which the lines were formed when the Duke put the whole through various movements and formed us in our original position; we then fed our horses and filed off to our respective quarters.[24]

The review lasted from 1pm to 6pm. The cavalry had had nothing to eat or drink and it had been so hot a day that a number of troopers fainted. After the review finished there was a banquet for the officers at Uxbridge's headquarters at Ninove. Colonel Sir Augustus Frazer, who had been present at the review in the afternoon and commanded the Royal Horse Artillery, wrote a letter to his wife the next day:

Lord Uxbridge's headquarters are at Ninove, some six miles from the ground of review. His lordship gave a dinner to the Duke, Blucher and all the generals and commanding officers of corps. Dinner was laid out for about one hundred. Never was any thing better arranged. His lordship lives in an abbey, the large rooms of which were well calculated for the princely feast… Before dinner the party met in a fine hall. Dinner was served about five: it was princely, consisting of many courses all served on plate. An excellent dessert followed, and the finest wines of every kind flowed in such profusion that 'tis well if I can this morning write of anything but pink champagne. The moment dinner was over, folding doors behind the Duke opened, and a band struck up 'God save the King'. The Prince Regent's and the Duke of York's healths followed that of their royal father; and then Lord Uxbridge gave the Duke, which was drunk with three times three. By this time, all the doors of the hall being open, the ladies and gentry of the place came to look at the feast. The Duke gave Blucher's health and success to the arms of Prussia, three times three again. Blucher, in a neat speech, gave the Cavalry and Horse Artillery of England, the Prince of Orange and the House of Nassau, the Duke of Brunswick, with three times three. The Allied Sovereigns; preceded by the health of the Emperor Alexander; and last with louder cheers than ever, the Navy of Great Britain... Coffee was then brought in for the Duke and Princes, and we rose and returned to the former hall, the lofty passages to which were lined with well dressed people, eager to show their respect to the Duke... A triumphal arch had been erected at Ninove in the morning, with very flattering devices; the whole town, adorned with branches of trees, looked like a grove, and our troops, wearing the oak bough of the 29th May, gave to the whole additional gaiety. After remaining some little time in the hall, during which coffee was served, the different carriages drove up, and the party separated. A guard of honour of the Life Guards was ready to receive the Duke as he came out. We left Ninove about eight o'clock, highly pleased with a day such as cannot often, and may never, be seen again.[25]

Although the wonderful abbey church is still in existence and beautifully restored, the room where the meal took place is no longer there. In the nineteenth century there was a disastrous fire in the monastery buildings. The Norbertine order of canons decided not to rebuild and the stones from the conventual buildings were sold off for building materials. A railway line was constructed through the site. But the gatehouse through which Blucher, Uxbridge, Ponsonby, Wellington and others rode still stands and nowadays is the entrance to a residential area.

The month of June saw activities very much like May's. Horse races took place at Grammont on 1, 6, 11, 12 and 13 June. On 12 June the prize was a gold cup donated by Lord Uxbridge. On Saturday 3 June there was an inspection of cavalry equipment and on Friday 9 June William put his brigade through a brigade field day. After this, according to Sergeant Johnston, he expressed himself as follows:

They are the finest body of men and horses I ever saw and I feel it a great honour conferred upon me, in being appointed to the command of a brigade which have eminently distinguished themselves on many former occasions, and I doubt not but that victory will be ours whenever we meet the enemy.[26]

Besides getting his brigade into shape Sir William had a role to play as a senior commander and a member of high society. Balls were held in Brussels to provide social diversions for the officers and the large number of members of English society who were visiting Brussels for the first time now that the Continent was open for travel. It also gave the senior military officers a chance to meet each other. A range of social events were held, some of which Sir William attended.

On Monday 1 May there was a rout at the Duke and Duchess of Richmond's, followed the next day by a concert. On 27 May there was a Grand Ball in honour of Blucher and on 3 June Wellington gave a ball, which he repeated on 7 June and followed with a 'grand party' on the 8th. Other celebrities followed his lead. Sir Charles Stewart, the British Ambassador to the Hague, gave a ball on Monday 5 June. On Wednesday 14 June Lady Conyngham (the former lover of John, Sir William's elder brother, and a mistress of both the Tsar's brother Nicholas and the Prince Regent) gave a ball. And of course on Thursday 15 June there was the celebrated Duchess of Richmond's ball.

We know from a letter written by the Marchioness of Conyngham that William was in Brussels often. On 6 August she wrote:

… on the Sunday before (the battle) he had begged of Lord C and myself to come and see his brigade which he said he would have out for us and of which he seemed very proud. We saw a great deal of him he came over to Brussels very often.[27]

And why not? There was no suspicion that Napoleon would take the offensive. Wellington had written a secret memorandum on 30 April following news that the Imperial Guard would move from Paris to Beauvais and that Bonaparte would visit the northern frontier. The Duke had laid down what should be done if Napoleon attacked: 'General Sir William Ponsonby's, Sir John Vandeleur's and Sir Hussey Vivian's brigades of cavalry will move upon Hal.'[28]

On 2 May Wellington was of the belief that Bonaparte would attack the Bavarians, who had crossed the Rhine.[29] On 11 May he thought that the French were waiting for him to attack them: 'My opinion is that they have placed their army in its present position with a view to a defensive.'[30] On 12 May he wrote 'I do not believe that Napoleon is on the frontier.'[31] On 2 June Wellington wrote to his brother Sir Henry Wellesley:

> The whole of Schwartzenberg's army will not be collected on the upper Rhine till towards the 16th at about which time I hope we shall begin. I shall enter France with between 70,000 and 80,000 men. The Prussians near me with twice as many. There is certainly a serious insurrection in La Vendée and the French have already moved some of their forces from the frontier.[32]

No doubt the Bourbon court now exiled at Ghent wanted to stress that Bonaparte was facing opposition in France. The exaggerated reports of opposition in the Vendée helped fuel the belief that Napoleon could not attack and the initiative would lie with the Allied armies, who would attack in overwhelming numbers. More British troops were arriving and the Austrians and Russians were on their way, with the expectation that they would be at Metz by 24 June. The timetable to invade France at the end of June/beginning of July was on schedule and on 13 June Wellington wrote to his former Peninsula subordinate, Lord Lynedoch:

> There is nothing new here. We have reports of Bonaparte joining the army and attacking us but I have accounts from Paris of the 10th on which day he was still there and I judge from his speech to the Legislature that his departure was not likely to be immediate. I think we are now too strong for him here.[33]

On 4 June William wrote to his elder brother from Brussels:

My Dear John

I enclose a letter which I found in the military post office here, hoping it will reach you. I made it to the care of Sir John Doyle Guernsey – as my mother informs me you are expected there. I shall be very glad of your safe arrival there as I am afraid the state of France is such as to make it, if not dangerous, at least very uncomfortable to the English. I conclude the letter which I wrote to you from hence about a month ago never reached you. I alluded in it to Antonio, saying that if you wished to get rid of him I should willingly take him again – however considering the uncertainty of communication also the distance at which we were etc etc I have found it necessary to provide myself with a person

in his capacity who suits me perfectly and as the odds are strongly that we shall have commenced, perhaps nearly finished our operations before he could reach me (supposing you wished to part with him etc) I have given up all thought of him. It is generally believed here that the great majority of the people of France are adverse to Bonaparte and that great dissatisfaction and considerable ferment prevails in all parts of the country. You however having been so lately in the short list know the real state of the case. But it appears to me that Bonaparte will require the universal and cordial support of every arm and every heart to enable him to resist successfully the enormous force which is about to attack him on every side and such support I conceive he has little chance of obtaining. It being uncertain when or where this letter may reach you I shall conclude with my love to Fanny – believe me affectionately yours
W Ponsonby[34]

On 11 June William wrote to his mother. She later wrote on the letter:

'The last letter written to me by my beloved son 7 days before the fatal battle'.

Denderhoutem June 11 1815

My Dearest Mother
I have to thank you for your kind and comfortable letter which was a great pleasure to me. I am always delighted to hear you like and approve of our little girls and do hope they will grow up what we could wish – little Lou in a letter which I received from her yesterday gave me an account of the visit of G Mama and Aunt Mary. I am very happy to hear that Charles spoke so very well (though I should consider his doing so but a matter of course).

There seems to be in England a decided feeling for war – a perfect confidence as to the successful result. How far this confidence is well founded a few months will show. Bonaparte will certainly have need of all his extraordinary abilities to resist the immense force about to attack him and I should think it impossible for him to do so unless he is backed by the cordial and near general support of the population of France. Upon this point it is impossible to obtain any information to be depended upon. The accounts given by the people about Louis 18th certainly do not come under this description. He is now said to be at Maubeuge which is not very far away from here and as you know absolutely upon the frontier – his game would be (and it is certainly his manner) to endeavour to strike a decisive blow on this side before the Russians and Austrians come into play – and if he finds himself strong enough to give him any rational prospects of success I have little doubt he will try it.

The Duke of Wellington however considers himself very strong and is very confident. My brother George had written me xx (as well as Richards) of Lord Fitzwilliam's most kind and handsome proceedings respecting the arrears. I quite agree with you that he is a person quite by himself... – I have not heard what or whether any arrangement has since been made respecting the principal of the annuities – it was very good of you to give me so comfortable an account of Georgiana. I am glad she has gone to town now and then and to two or three parties, her life at Hampstead must be very solitary and dull and stands much in need of some relief.

I hope John has got safe away from France by this time – the state of the country is to render the residence of an Englishman there by no means comfortable. How particularly unfortunate he has been, I wish he had fixed upon some town in Germany rather than France as he certainly cannot afford the expense of travelling from place to place.

We are told here that the insurrection in la Vendée is very extensive and formidable and I believe it is so but there is too much reason to apprehend that Bonaparte will be able to crush it before the grand attack commences. It is understood here that he was at Maubeuge yesterday and has been at Valenciennes. His game would appear to be (and certainly it is his manner) to strike a blow here before the Austrians and Russians come into play and I am surprised at his not having already attempted it. However we understand that the roads communicating with Belgium have been completely broken up, the bridges broken and every possible obstacle contrived which of course must place difficulties in the way of an attack on his part in the same proportions as of our advance so that one must suppose that it is not his intention to make an attack – I think your resolution will hardly hold out against Charles' attacks and indeed I should think it the best and most agreeable plan for you.

I see that the catholics have lost ground considerably not only in the number but also in the zeal and tone of their suppositions, the necessary consequence of their interference unreasonable and most ungrateful conduct. Unless they alter very much their mode of proceeding they never can have any chance of obtaining a decision in their favour. I enclose a little note for Frederick. Give my love to Mary and her girls, Charles etc and believe me my dearest mother ever your affectionate WP.

I send this through Major General Sir Willoughby Gordon Quarter Master General who will I am sure forward to me any letter etc you may wish at any time to send me, I conclude you know him – he is a friend of C Grey's.[35]

We can see in Sir William's letter that he had accurately gauged Napoleon's plan, but reports from France gave a false sense of security. The possibility of Napoleon launching a pre-emptive strike was discounted on the basis that Napoleon had broken all the bridges. It is true that some had been broken, but not all.

Chapter 12

'Humbugged by God!'
15 and 16 June

Napoleon crossed the border on Thursday 15 June with 123,000 men, brushing aside the Prussian outposts. By the evening of the 15th his left wing under Marshal Ney had established a position at Frasnes and Napoleon himself was at Charleroi with the right wing of his army. He knew from his intelligence network that Blucher's position was well forward of Wellington's and it would take time for Wellington to concentrate his troops and come to Blucher's aid. With this in mind he hoped his rapid advance would encourage the Prussians to retreat to Germany, leaving only Wellington's army to deal with. However, if Blucher did decide to fight, Napoleon intended to defeat one army and then turn and defeat the other. It was irrelevant to him which he fought first, but the defeat of both had to be decisive in order to re-establish his prestige and force the European powers to make peace. This was what the 1815 campaign was about – the capture of Brussels was not Napoleon's main aim.

News of Napoleon's approach had been communicated to Wellington, who was due to attend the Duchess of Richmond's ball, and the organisational process went into overdrive. Lady de Lancey records how her husband started to write out the orders to concentrate the army. De Lacy Evans, who would serve as Sir William's additional ADC, was persuaded to help him. They started drafting the orders between 6 and 7pm. Messages were dispatched using the dragoons of the King's German Legion. As so many senior officers were at the Duchess's ball there was no point giving them the orders, as they would have to ride back to their commands before anything could be organised. So the dragoons were told to take the orders to the divisional headquarters in order that the army could start to be assembled without loss of time. It was decided to assemble the infantry first.

Where was the army to concentrate? The belief at headquarters was that Napoleon would cross the frontier at Mons, approximately 25 miles west of Charleroi. This belief was totally sensible. By crossing at Mons Napoleon could easily march on Brussels, just as he could from Charleroi. But crossing at Mons also allowed Napoleon to cut off Wellington's line of retreat and gave him an opportunity to seize Louis XVIII in Ghent. So headquarters believed that any attack further east must be a feint to persuade Wellington to march his troops eastwards, while Napoleon would invade with the majority of his troops at Mons to the west. Because of this Wellington had positioned most of his troops to the west of Brussels. The cavalry were in the Dender valley with the divisional headquarters at Ninove, 15 miles west of Brussels. Lord Hill, with the second division, was 40 miles west of Brussels between Oudenarde and Tournai, while the Prince of Orange and his troops were closest to Charleroi. Wellington's first set of orders simply instructed his army to concentrate, but at various positions from where he could still march and block any attack that might come via Mons, Nivelles or Charleroi.

Fortunately for Wellington, Prince Bernhard of Saxe-Weimar, commanding a Dutch-Belgian force of 4,700 men and sixteen guns at Quatre Bras, dispatched a report to his superiors that he was under attack by the French and could not hold out much longer. Quatre Bras was 20 miles south of Brussels and 25 miles east of Mons. It was a small hamlet situated at a vital crossroads. One road went from Nivelles through Quatre Bras towards the Prussian positions and Namur. The other road extended to Brussels via Genappe. If Napoleon seized this crossroads he would have blocked any attempt by Wellington to march to Blucher's aid. Prince Bernhard's superior, Baron de Perponcher, and the Prince of Orange's chief of staff, General Constant Rebecque, decided to ignore Wellington's orders to concentrate the Dutch-Belgian troops at Nivelles nine miles to the west and instead to reinforce Prince Bernhard at Quatre Bras. This was just as well, because actually facing Prince Bernhard and his 4,700 men was the entire left wing of the French army. Again, fortunately for Wellington, the French were strung out over a large area as a result of marching that day, and with darkness falling they decided not to make a serious attack on Saxe-Weimar's position but to wait for the morning.

Meanwhile, the dragoons carried Wellington's original orders to concentrate to the divisional headquarters. For the cavalry this meant the orders had to go to Ninove and the instructions were simply for the cavalry to collect there. Twenty-year-old Lieutenant Jackson of the Royal Staff Corps had been assisting de Lancey in writing the orders.

Now, just when he thought he had finished, de Lancey approached him and handed him the orders, saying 'I am told you know the road to Ninove; here is a letter for Colonel Cathcart (later Lord Greenock), be as speedy as possible.'[1]

Ninove was 15 miles from Brussels and Jackson tells us he reached it by a cross-country road:

> As I approached that place I found lights in adjacent villages and men stirring about, indicating that the order for marching had been issued. Colonel Cathcart was the Assistant Quarter Master General to the whole of the cavalry, and an excellent officer, to whom I was well known. 'You may tell Delancey that in an hour or so we shall be on our march to Nivelles, in accordance with the orders received.'[2]

At Ninove Uxbridge's administrative staff wrote out instructions to the brigades. The officer in command of the administration was Colonel Cathcart; apart from him the only other member of staff who had not gone to the Duchess's ball was Captain Thornhill. Cathcart believed he received the orders from Jackson between 11 o'clock and midnight, but it may have been a little later. He and Thornhill then wrote out the orders, one copy for each brigade, and had their orderly dragoons ride with the orders to the respective brigade headquarters.

Many of these orders no longer exist, but we do have the one sent to Sir William's brigade as it was found on the battlefield, either on his body or that of his brigade major, after Waterloo. It seems to have come into the possession of the Duke of Argyll and on 19 September 1842 Lord Greenock wrote to him enquiring about it:

> My Dear Lord Duke,
> I think you mentioned to me some time ago that you had in your possession an order in my handwriting or signed by me which had been picked up on the field of Waterloo and which your Grace had honoured by preserving as a relick of that memorable day. If you should still possess this document and can without inconvenience refer to it Your Grace would confer a great favour upon me if you will have the goodness to cause a copy to be forwarded to me as early as circumstances may permit. I am not aware of the date or the purport of this order but the Duke of Wellington having expressed a desire to me through Colonel

Gurwood to be informed of the precise hour at which certain orders were circulated to the cavalry respecting its movements previously to the battles fought on the 16th, 17th and 18th of June 1815 it is possible that the document in question may throw some light on the subject and be the means of enabling me to satisfy the duke in this particular better than I could do from my own recollection for during the hurry consequent to such operations I had no time to preserve copies of the orders I had to circulate or to make any memoranda respecting them.

If the superscription be preserved it should likewise be copied for probably upon it the hour of the dispatch would have been noted as well as the address of the General or other officer to whom it was transmitted.

With many apologies for giving your Grace this trouble. I remain my dear lord duke
Your grace's faithful and obedient servant GREENOCK[3]

The message referred to read:

Immediate
Major General Sir William Ponsonby
Or officer commanding 2nd brigade
Denderhoutem
Greenock

Immediate
Ninove June 15th 1815
Memorandum
Major General Sir W Ponsonby
Denderhoutem

Major General Sir Wm Ponsonby's brigade will assemble with the utmost possible expedition this night at Ninove where it will receive further orders.

The Regiments had better be formed on the high road leading from Ninove to Voordem near the quarters of part of the Royal Dragoons between Oultre and Ninove.
Greenock Lt Col
Ass Q M General

An orderly officer to be sent to Ninove

The superscription: reads: 'Received at one and ¾ am 16 June'.

Lord Greenock commented to the Duke of Argyll on 7 March 1843:

it is highly interesting to me as shewing the precise hour at which the order for the assembly of the cavalry at Ninove was received at the quarters of Sir William Ponsonby which appears by a memorandum on the cover to have been one and ¾ am on the 16th June as it has been the subject of some controversy it having been imagined by some that the cavalry ought to have been put in motion at an earlier hour.[4]

So by 1.45am the brigade had received its orders. Where was Sir William? We know that he attended the Duchess of Richmond's ball, along with his cousin Frederick. Their names are on the guest list, but we also have Lady Conyngham's account. She wrote on 6 August 1815, from Brussels:

I saw him a few hours before the fateful battle and his countenance, his smile, the place where I saw him still haunt me, we had just asked him to dance a French country dance with Elizabeth (her daughter) when he disappeared and went off to his brigade.[5]

The ball had started at about ten o'clock at the Richmonds' residence on the rue de la Blanchisserie. It is reckoned that 200–210 people attended.[6] Half were civilian and half were military. Two-thirds were men. All were personal guests of the Duchess of Richmond, who decided whom to invite. She chose not to invite Sir William's ADC Braithwaite Christie, or his brigade major Thomas Reignolds.[7] Sir William probably arrived earlier in the day with other military commanders and their servants. He would have dined and changed for the ball somewhere in Brussels. As he had to change, he would probably have travelled in by coach or cabriolet with his servant. There was dancing (a mixture of waltzes, quadrilles and country dances), a display of Highland dancing, a sit-down supper and more dancing, during which officers began to return to their regiments.

At 10pm, just before he departed for the Duchess's ball, Wellington ordered a further set of movement orders, known as 'the After Orders' to be issued. These instructed the troops to continue to move south towards Enghien, although one division of infantry was ordered to move eastwards towards Nivelles. By this stage Wellington had heard that there were no French troops in front of the Allied position at Mons, but he does not seem to have believed it. Lord Uxbridge wrote out the order to his cavalry commanders at 23.45:

June 15th 1815 ¾ past 11pm
General Cavalry orders
1. The cavalry will march immediately from the left to Enghien.
2. Whatever brigade arrives first within a mile of Enghien, will choose a convenient spot near the road, to form in columns of half squadrons at quarter distance.
3. The brigades as they arrive in succession will form in rear of that first forward
4. The baggage will march in the rear of each brigade under a sufficient guard
5. The RHA of the cavalry will also march by troop independently to near Enghien..........
6. An officer of each brigade and an officer per troop from the RHA will meet Lt Genl the Earl of Uxbridge at the Hotel Royal at Enghien
Uxbridge Lt Gen
Such sick as are unable to march, will be sent to Brussels. Horses unable to march with the brigades will be sent to Ninove.[8]

Uxbridge then rode to Ninove with his new cavalry orders. The round trip from Brussels to Ninove and back again took Jackson a maximum of six hours, but he admits he returned at a leisurely pace,[9] so allowing for a round trip of five hours at relative speed, it would take Uxbridge about 2.5 hours to get to Ninove from Brussels. This means he would have arrived at Ninove at about 2.30am if travelling on horseback, perhaps a bit later if travelling by cabriolet. William may have accompanied him, or he may have ridden to Denderhoutem that night. If he did, and the length of time it would have taken does depend on his means of transport, he would probably have got to Denderhoutem at about 3am. Jackson does say that on his way back he 'fell in with several officers of rank making for their troops, having hurried from the Duchess of Richmond's ball and I knowing all the arrangements for the army generally I was able to tell them what roads to take in order to intercept their divisions.'[10]

Paradoxically, because only Sir William was present at the Duchess of Richmond's Ball, no one else from any of his regiments having been invited, the brigade organisation was intact and could function when Greenock's instructions were received. Brigade Major Reignolds acknowledged the orders and then sent out his own orders to the regimental headquarters to mobilise the three regiments. He sent a dragoon to Herzele to raise the Inniskillings and one to Voorde near Ninove to raise the Royals. Then it was up to the regimental headquarters

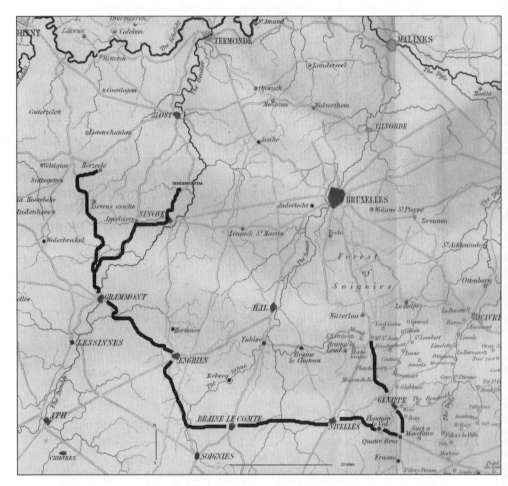

The movement of the Union Brigade from Denderhoutem, Herzele and Ninove to Quatre Bras then Mont St Jean via Genappe on 17 June
The route is superimposed on a map of the area drawn in the 1840s. The extended route covering 50 miles had sections where all the cavalry followed the same road. This meant it was impossible for the cavalry to reach Quatre Bras any sooner than it did in the evening/night of 16 June.

to assemble the troopers, who were scattered in their various farmhouses. This was done by bugle calls sounding the assembly, at prearranged points.

Officers in the Scots Greys who were based at Denderhoutem reported that bugles were blown between 2am and 3am. The Inniskillings received their orders at 3 or 4am, and the Royals at about the same time, which given the relative equal distances of the two headquarters from Denderhoutem is right.[11] The troops had to travel from the scattered farmhouses where they had been quartered to regimental headquarters, be organised into their squadrons and collect all the supporting equipment and supplies that were necessary. This took a great deal of time. Assembling 'this night at Ninove' was optimistic and perhaps, like many head office requests today, was designed to convey a sense of urgency rather than describe the reality.

The first regiment to make the rendezvous was the Royals, as they were already in the vicinity of Ninove. Again they were in various hamlets. So perhaps they were ready at about 6am. The Scots Greys and Inniskillings had further to travel, but the Scots Greys might have arrived quickly as they had received the assembly call first, so they and the Royals could have joined up about 6am. However, the Inniskillings, having received orders at 3 or 4am, had not formed to begin their march from Herzele until 7am. As they had the furthest to travel they might not have arrived at Ninove until between 8am and 9am. To save time it seems that the plan was for the brigade to unite en route. Charles Radclyffe, captain in the Royals, states: 'On the 16th in the morn (4.30am) orders arrived for an immediate march (it was nearly eight before the brigade could assemble) and the whole by different routes marched on Enghien.'[12]

So far the brigade was marching south and was following Uxbridge's after orders to proceed to Enghien. At Enghien they would be due south of Ninove. It was here at the Hotel Royal that Uxbridge received further orders, carried by an officer of the staff corps, to proceed to Braine le Comte. This meant the cavalry would turn to the south-east. From Braine le Comte the cavalry would swing east to Nivelles and on to Quatre Bras.

This may have seemed a convoluted route. Indeed there was a faster route from Ninove to Quatre Bras going via Halle, but of course Uxbridge had to make decisions based on his instructions from Wellington, and Wellington had to adapt his requirements to changing circumstances. It was because Wellington believed that the main attack would come from the direction of Mons rather than Charleroi that he ordered the cavalry to move south. It was only after meeting Blucher and seeing the French dispositions, as well as taking into account the French army in front of him at Quatre Bras, that he could be certain that there would be no attack from Mons and could order Uxbridge to swing his cavalry round and head south-east.

Fortunately for Wellington, Ney did not concentrate his troops as quickly as he should have done and seems to have been told by Napoleon not to seize Quatre Bras until he was ordered to do so. Napoleon did this because he had determined to move against Blucher, who was concentrating three of his four corps around the village of Ligny, about 10 miles north-east of Charleroi. Napoleon dispatched the instructions at 8am from Charleroi and they would have reached Ney by about 10.30am.[13] Because Ney had not taken steps to concentrate his forces, he could not immediately begin the action.

At 10pm on 15 June Wellington had instructed the reserves based around Brussels to march due south to the village of Waterloo, and they started to arrive there from 8am onwards. They were just over 11 miles from Quatre Bras. At about 9.40am Wellington arrived at Genappe and ordered the reserve troops to march on Genappe while he rode on to Quatre Bras to assess the position. He arrived there at 10am. By then Belgian and Dutch reinforcements had increased the number of troops there to 6,500. Wellington, seeing very few French in his front, left Quatre Bras about 1pm and rode on south-east to consult with Blucher, who had concentrated his forces around Ligny. When Wellington arrived at Blucher's headquarters at Brye it was quite clear that there would be a major battle there between the French, who had assembled 68,000 troops and 210 guns, and Blucher's 87,000 Prussians with 224 guns. Having promised to support Blucher provided he was not attacked himself, Wellington left Blucher at 2pm and rode back to Quatre Bras.

At 2pm Ney finally launched his attack. The senior commander at Quatre Bras, the Prince of Orange, had 8,000 infantry, no cavalry and sixteen guns. Ney had managed to concentrate 10,000 infantry, 2,000 cavalry and thirty guns from his total command of 40,000. He planned to make an overwhelming infantry attack, supported by cavalry and artillery, and seize the crossroads to prevent Wellington from moving troops to support Blucher. The first French attack went well. The Allied forward positions in two farms were taken and the Dutch-Belgian forces started to fall back. Fortunately reinforcements started to arrive in the shape of General Picton's reserve troops, the Duke of Brunswick's cavalry and infantry and more Belgian-Dutch troops.

Wellington arrived back at Quatre Bras at about 3pm and, having seen the number of French around Ligny and those now engaged at Quatre Bras, gave orders for his forces to concentrate on Quatre Bras. This of course was easier said than done. The battle would go on until 9pm, but the cavalry would not arrive in time to intervene.

This was not the cavalry's fault. Taking the long route from Ninove to Enghien and having to halt for orders before turning east took time. The roads were bad and all the regiments on the march east were on the same road, so the pace was determined by the slowest regiment. To travel from Ninove to Enghien took Mercer and G Troop five hours and Vandeleur and his light dragoons a little less. Arrival at Enghien for the Union Brigade would be between 1pm and 2pm.

From Enghien onwards progress slowed. Now the orders put all the cavalry on the same road. This led inevitably to bottlenecks. As Mercer mentions 'to the same point various columns of cavalry were converging', and 'all followed the road to Braine le Comte via Steenkerke even though everybody I spoke to denied having any orders yet all kept moving in one and the same direction.'[14]

Mercer reached Braine le Comte by 4pm in the afternoon, having wasted an hour waiting for orders at Enghien. From there the cavalry column marched to Nivelles and from there to Quatre Bras. Clarke-Kennedy, an officer in the Royals in Sir William's Union Brigade, wrote:

'After the direction of our march had been three or four times changed and there had been several halts in the course of the day, the brigade moved towards evening upon Quatre Bras'.[15]

The Royals stated that they arrived at Quatre Bras at 10pm, the Inniskillings at 11pm.

As Major Radclyffe of the Royals summed up, when he wrote up his entry for the 16th in his diary:

A sudden order of marching arrived at 6 o'clock. Major General Sir William Ponsonby's brigade was in motion and continued to the town of Grummove where a momentary halt was made, about a league beyond this place the road became bad and hilly which rendered the line of march, now moreover impeded by several other brigades of cavalry, very slow and tedious so that this long and tedious march of about 56 miles did not come to an end until 11 o'clock at night when the brigade reached the position of Les Quatres Bras.[16]

For the Union Brigade, arriving at Quatre Bras in the darkness, it had obviously been a very frustrating day – a journey of between 50 and 60 miles, very long by cavalry standards, and nothing, as yet, to show for it.

By the time they arrived night had fallen on two battles. At Ligny, despite being outnumbered, Napoleon by 9.30pm had broken the Prussian army in two and it was only darkness that saved them from destruction. Prussian casualties were 19,000 against French losses of 14,000. Napoleon believed that he had also crushed Prussian morale and that Blucher's defeated army would move eastwards out of Belgium to safety in Germany. At Quatre Bras both sides gained reinforcements, but from 4pm the Anglo-Allied army achieved numerical superiority and by 6pm they numbered 28,500 infantry and 2,000 cavalry with sixty-eight guns against Ney's 16,500 infantry 2,800 cavalry and fifty guns.[17] Losses sustained reduced these numbers and the losses had been heavy. It is calculated that the Anglo-Allied army had 4,600 casualties to 4,100 French.[18] The losses had been particularly severe in Picton's division and this would have a major impact at Waterloo. The battle's result had swung one way and then another, but the battle ended with the Allied army having regained its original positions and there was every expectation that the struggle would continue in the morning.

It might appear that the French had the upper hand in the day's fighting, but due to a clash in personalities they had been deprived of the chance of Ligny being a totally decisive victory. Napoleon, finding himself opposed by the bulk of Blucher's forces, had sent Ney instructions at about 3pm requiring him to march down the road Wellington had ridden down earlier in the day and attack the Prussian flank, once he had secured Quatre Bras. This would have led to a total victory. When it became obvious that Ney could not do this, Napoleon had ordered General Comte d'Erlon, who was moving his corps of 20,000 men to support Ney at Quatre Bras, to do so instead. Ney unfortunately countermanded the order and insisted d'Erlon march to support him. D'Erlon, who was 2 miles from Ligny and 7.5 miles from Quatre Bras, did not follow Napoleon's instructions. He divided his force and sent General Durutte's 4,000 infantry and a cavalry force of three regiments under General Jacquinot totalling 1,200 men towards Ligny and turned back to Quatre Bras. Although Durutte did clash with some Prussians he dithered, and a more vigorous approach would certainly have increased Prussian losses. But d'Erlon, if he had acted sensibly by moving his whole corps to Ligny, would have achieved that decisive victory that Napoleon needed. Instead he arrived at Quatre Bras as darkness fell and was unable to make a contribution. However, this did mean that his corps, because of its lack of casualties, could be used to deliver a decisive blow in any subsequent battle. This is what would happen at Waterloo two days later.

There is one more aspect of these two days that deserves attention. Lieutenant Colonel Hamilton of the 30th Foot was severely wounded at Quatre Bras but survived until 1838. In his obituary in the *United Service Journal Part 2* for that year is the following tantalising account:

> There is a circumstance scarcely if at all known connected with the sad fate of General Ponsonby. Colonel Hamilton had a powerful and beautiful charger which he wished to dispose of previous to the battle of Quatre Bras being aware (having lost many horses killed under him during his service) that he would only get £25 allowed him in case of a casualty whereas his charger was worth £100. On the evening of the 15th June 1815 General Ponsonby's ADC came to Colonel Hamilton to treat for the horse, but nothing decisive took place, and from not hearing anything more upon the subject, Colonel Hamilton concluded that the General considered that the animal was overvalued; he therefore lent him to his own Quarter Master much to the subsequent dismay of the venerable officer whose steady old trooper carried the Colonel through the day (at least until he was wounded) – whilst the fiery Bucephalus upon which the worthy Quarter Master was seated terribly disconcerted him putting his equitation to a severe test to the great amusement of the idlers and 'non effectives' in the rear of the army. Had General Ponsonby only sent to Colonel Hamilton to borrow his horse he might have been spared to return to the beloved partner of his bosom, whose memory was occupying the last thoughts of the gallant warrior; for it is a fact well known that General Ponsonby was repeatedly told that his horse was not strong enough for the work he would have to perform.[19]

Sources have always commented that Sir William rode an inferior horse at Waterloo 'a bay hack', stating that his charger could not be found on the day. In fact one modern historian, having confused accounts, said he did this deliberately, for the same reason as Hamilton of the 30th.[20] However, it does seem that the story of the inferior horse is true. William would have had at least two chargers with him, but for some reason as early as the 15th needed to find another one. To send Braithwaite Christie from Denderhoutem to Soignies, where the 30th Foot was based, was a long journey and suggests this was an urgent need. Given the state of Sir William's finances it cannot have been to add an additional horse to his stable. Perhaps his chargers were ill. Braithwaite Christie, on finding out the purchase price, would have to get Sir William's view on whether a deal could be struck, but by the time he got back to Denderhoutem Sir William was already at the Duchess of Richmond's ball. By the time Sir William arrived at Quatre Bras on 16 June Lieutenant Colonel Hamilton was lying wounded in the farm at Quatre Bras and the opportunity to conclude the deal had passed. The implications of this we will see later.[21]

Chapter 13

'The Prettiest Field Day of Cavalry You Ever Saw' 17 June

Everyone expected the French to renew the attack at first light, so Sir William ordered his men to be prepared to go into action at a moment's notice. Clark Kennedy of the 1st Royals recalled:

> The Royals bivouacked for the night in an open field, a little in rear of the houses of Quatre Bras, the horses being linked in column, saddled and bridled, the officers and men lying or standing by them. The night proved a fine one.[1]

However, although both sides' cavalry and infantry pickets fired on each other intermittently from 2am onwards, the French did not renew their attack on the morning of the 17th. Ney's forces had increased to 35,000 men now that d'Erlon had finally joined him. But Wellington's forces had increased with the reinforcements that arrived during the night to between 42,000 and 47,000 men, so it is likely that Ney did not want to renew the action against such a superior force. Also Ney did not know the results of Napoleon's actions at Ligny so he waited for orders. These arrived at about 9am, ordering him to renew the attack and promising that Napoleon would move his troops to Quatre Bras and catch Wellington's forces in the flank. Inexplicably, neither Ney nor Napoleon immediately put the plan into operation. The French troops were allowed to have breakfast. For his part Wellington was informed at about 7.30am that Blucher had been forced to retreat as a result of being defeated at Ligny. Wellington knew that if he did not move he could be crushed by the forces of both Ney and Napoleon, and decided to retreat, but as there was no movement from either French force he also allowed his troops to have breakfast and ordered the retreat to start from 10am. The wounded were moved out first and some of the men from Sir William's brigade were ordered to convey those of the wounded who could sit on a horse to Waterloo. This was done by each man leading his horse by the bridle with a wounded foot soldier lying across the saddle. Clark Kennedy of the 1st Royals wrote:

> My squadron was ordered to the Inn of Quatre Bras to assist in conveying as many of the wounded men to the rear as were able to bear the motion of a horse, and a considerable number were removed in this manner to the rear of the position at Waterloo, though several that were severely wounded were necessarily left behind.[2]

The Inniskilling Dragoons committed as many as three troops to help carry the wounded infantry to Brussels.[3]

Wellington ordered the remaining cavalry to provide a screen so the French would not see that his infantry were retreating. He also left four batteries of horse artillery to protect the cavalry. The cavalry simply moved into the positions vacated by the infantry. The infantry began to retreat just before 10am as planned; the first troops to retreat were the Belgian and Dutch regiments. Some troops followed the main road from Quatre Bras to Brussels; others followed parallel lines of march. By noon all the infantry had left the battlefield, falling back to the ridge of Mont St Jean, which was 13 kilometres (9 miles) from Quatre Bras.

About 1pm, with the infantry having departed, except the light companies of the Guards and the 95th Rifles, who also remained, Uxbridge now concentrated his cavalry. They numbered between 8,000 and 10,000 men. The cavalry deployed in four lines: first the pickets, about 1.5 miles out in front, second the hussars and some light dragoons, third the heavy cavalry and fourth some more light dragoons. The Guards and Rifles were then sent back to take up a defensive position at Genappe to protect the cavalry when it eventually had to move through the town.

Only at midday did Napoleon lead his troops towards Quatre Bras. His cavalry, comprising cuirassiers, lancers and chasseurs, led the way with the infantry following. Napoleon arrived at Quatre Bras at 2pm and prepared to attack the Allied cavalry while Ney at last stirred into action, moved forward his cavalry. Together the French cavalry now numbered 22,000 men. The French cavalry were supported by fifty guns of the horse artillery. Behind them came the infantry of 1st, 2nd and 6th corps and the Imperial Guard and its artillery.[4] Altogether the pursuing French army numbered 66,000 men and 215 cannon.

Major General Vivian commanded the 6th cavalry brigade of hussars. He was deployed in the front and recalled:

We remained quietly on the ground until about two o'clock, when immediately on my left I observed a great dust, and by looking a little nearer I discovered an enormous column of cuirassiers, lancers, hussars etc moving over a hill onto the high road which was on my flank. My pickets were soon engaged and driven in. A brigade of the enemy trotted up the road and formed opposite me, a little ravine separating us.[5]

Captain William Hay of the 12th Light Dragoons observed:

At a great distance in the wood on each side of these roads, clouds of dust began to spread over the trees. The dust appeared thicker and thicker and dead silence pervaded our ranks. I thought even the horses were more still than usual, no champing of bits no clattering of swords. Every eye was directed anxiously to what was passing in front.

In a moment as if by magic, debouched from the dark green foliage, which had hitherto kept them from our sight, by the three roads, the gorgeous uniforms of the French cavalry, composed of the cuirassiers, lancers and brass helmeted dragoons. On they came at a gallop, those from the right hand road forming on the plain to their left, the centre to their front, and the left to their right, until three lines fronting our own were drawn up. There were now in front of us waiting twenty two thousand cavalry – double our number – and these supported by 50 guns of artillery all ready for action.[6]

Wellington ordered Uxbridge to withdraw the cavalry. He then rode back to Mont St Jean, which he had already chosen as the position he would take up that evening. Three routes were used as it was impossible to send all the cavalry through the narrow streets of Genappe. Sir William and Lord Edward Somerset's two brigades of heavy cavalry retired along the main road through Genappe to Waterloo. Dornberg's brigade, comprising the dragoons of the King's German Legion and the

British 23rd Light Dragoons, and Grant's Hussar brigade took a westerly route crossing the River Dyle and then moving on to Mont St Jean. Vivian's brigade of Hussars and Vandeleur's brigade of Light Dragoons moved eastwards and then north, retreating along narrow lanes to Thy where they crossed the Dyle and continued towards Mont St Jean. In the meantime the horse artillery, including Mercer's battery, fired on the advancing French cavalry to buy time for the withdrawal to occur.

Just as the French cavalry moved to attack the heavens opened. As Mercer wrote:

> ....the rain came down as if a waterspout had broken over us. Flash succeeded flash and the peals of thunder were long and tremendous whilst as if in mockery of the elements the French guns still sent forth their feebler glare and now scarcely audible reports- their cavalry dashing on at a headlong pace, adding their shouts to the uproar... The obscurity caused by the splashing of the rain was such that at one period I could not distinguish objects more than a few yards distant... the crashing and rattling of the thunder were most awful and the glare of the lightning blinding. In this state we gained the bridge of Genappe at the moment when the thundercloud having passed over left us in comparatively fine weather, although still raining heavily.[7]

The torrential rain, which lasted for four hours, dramatically affected the pursuit. The distance between Quatre Bras and Genappe is only about 4 miles, which galloping cavalry could cover quickly.[8] But on 17 June 1815 the paved road was awash and the fields were mud. In this part of Belgium the mud has an almost glutinous quality, which makes walking through it on foot or on horseback almost impossible. The French had to keep to the paved road. As the infantry corps had to follow each other, each infantry corps was slowed down by the preceding infantry corps' artillery. The action became one of retreating cavalry with horse artillery being pursued by cavalry with horse artillery, with both sides slowed by the rain and the waterlogged road and fields.

The French divided their cavalry forces to pursue all three retreating columns until Dornberg's and Grant's western column and Vandeleur and Vivian's eastern columns crossed the River Dyle at their respective points. Then the French cavalry regrouped to pursue Sir William and Lord Edward Somerset's heavy cavalry, the Royal Horse Artillery and the Rifles on the main road through Genappe.

Accounts of the retreat usually focus on Mercer's exciting description of his exploits while escaping with his guns. However, there were a number of incidents involving the Union Brigade. An anonymous sergeant of the Scots Greys recalled in a letter to his wife that on the morning of 17 June:

> Our brigade was ordered down to the wood to decoy them (the French) out of it. We had to dismount in a field of rye till about 12 o'clock noon then they came out in great force as if every man would have been killed in a moment, we wheeled about quite cool and they played their cannon upon us for miles all the way the Earl of Uxbridge told us to turn round and wave our swords and huzzah till we came to a village (Genappe).[9]

Sergeant Johnston of the Scots Greys wrote:

> when we had retreated about three miles we formed the line and fronted them. They marched on cock sure of victory until they reached a hill nearly a mile in front of our line, when they opened a most galling cannonade upon us which was chiefly directed against our brigade but more particularly against our regiment.[10]

The village of Genappe, nearly halfway between Quatre Bras and Mont St Jean, had the potential to be a disastrous bottleneck. There was a tiny bridge crossing the River Dyle; so tiny that some sources say the cavalry had to cross in ones or twos. It is difficult today to find the bridge and appreciate its role as a barrier. But the narrowness and steepness of the streets, which would slow down the cavalry, and particularly the horse artillery, can still be seen and appreciated in what has now expanded into a small town.

Mercer described the ride through Genappe as follows:

> The town of Genappe stands on the slope of a hill rising immediately from the little verdant valley through which the Lys flows – here little bigger than a brook. Arrived at the bridge we slackened our pace, and ascended leisurely the narrow winding street, in which not a living soul was visible. The shutters were all closed, and streams of water pouring from the roofs formed a perfect torrent of the gutter running down the middle of it.[11]

At Genappe Uxbridge decided to try to check the French pursuit using the narrow streets to his advantage. He took up a position on the rising ground 600–700 yards beyond the northern entrance to Genappe. Somerset's heavy cavalry were positioned to the left of the road and Sir William's Union brigade to the right. As a result of the torrential rain, once the horses were off the road they sank to their knees and sometimes their girths in the sodden soil in the fields. This would make any manoeuvring very difficult and fast action was impossible unless it was on the road. In front of the heavy cavalry were the 23rd Light Dragoons and a single detachment of the 11th Light Dragoons. In front of the Light Dragoons, about 200 yards from the northern end of Genappe, were the 7th Hussars. They had been deployed to the south of Genappe as a rearguard. Once the skirmishers fell back they had retired through the village and rejoined the rest of the rearguard.

The French cavalry, although preceded by a few drunken horsemen who were soon captured, were led by the 1st and 2nd lancers, and for many of the British cavalry this was the first time they would have seen this elite cavalry force, which could deploy sabres, pistols, carbines or lances at will. The lancers were in a very strong position. Their flanks were protected by the town's buildings and their nine-foot-long lances held off any attacking force. Uxbridge, who was the colonel of the 7th Hussars as well as commander of the British cavalry, ordered the 7th Hussars to attack, possibly aiming to give them an opportunity to gain more recognition, but the chances were not in their favour. Although they fought hard the 7th Hussars could not make any impression on the lancers and, having charged twice, they were beaten back and came under fire from French artillery.

Lieutenant George Simmons of the 95th Rifles recalled: 'the 7th Hussars charged but were sadly mauled. The Life Guards and Oxford Blues made some very fine charges, and literally preserved the 7th from being cut to pieces.'[12] Lieutenant John Banner of the 23rd Light Dragoons stated:

> The artillery which accompanied the French advance guard to Genappe was immediately planted on the left side of the town on the bank of the river which passes through it, from which station the enemy opened a heavy and incessant fire upon our cavalry when ascending from Genappe, by which they were exceedingly galled and sustained some loss; our artillery being all at the period considerably in front, we were without a cannon to return a shot.[13]

Lord Uxbridge recalled the 7th Hussars and ordered the 23rd Light Dragoons to charge. Understandably the 23rd Light Dragoons did not want to suffer as the 7th Hussars had, and did not advance, so Uxbridge turned to Somerset's heavy cavalry and in particular the Life Guards. The Life Guards were mounted on heavier horses but again might have been held off by the lancers if the lancers had maintained their original position.

However, the lancers had moved. This is sometimes accounted for by them being over-eager, or being pushed forward by the mass of troops in their rear trying to get through Genappe. What is frequently ignored is the fact that the lancers had to leave the protection of Genappe and turn at the crossroads on the outskirts of the town so they could maintain the pursuit of the Allied cavalry. The chaussée has an incline and this meant that the lancers were not only more spread out in order to manoeuvre, but also had to advance up the hill. They no longer had buildings to protect their flanks and as they advanced up the road they were charged by the Life Guards, mounted on much heavier horses, who were moving downhill. The lancers gave way. Many of them turned back into the narrow streets and the Life Guards continued their charge, inflicting severe casualties.

> This charge was perhaps one of the most effective ever made by any troop. Although the French sustained the attack with firmness, they were quite unable to stand their ground in such a situation, advancing up the hill against the flower of the British cavalry. The French were overthrown with great slaughter, and were literally rode down in such a manner that the road was covered with men and horses scattered and sprawling in all directions down to the main body of the enemy's advance guard.[14]

Uxbridge then pulled the Life Guards back, leaving Sir William's Union Brigade to the west of the chaussée. Whinyate's troop of Royal Horse Artillery fired some of Congreve's rockets along the chaussée. As Mercer recalls, the effect was amazing:

> Meanwhile the rocketeers had placed a little iron triangle in the road with a rocket lying on it. The order to fire is given – port-fire applied – the fidgety missile begins to sputter out sparks and wriggle its tail for a second or so, and then darts forth straight up the chaussée. A gun stands right in its way, between the wheels of which the shell in the head of the rocket bursts, the gunners

fall right and left, and those of the other guns taking to their heels, the battery is deserted in an instant.[15]

It proved to be a lucky shot which the rocketeers could not repeat, but this, and the effect of the Life Guards' charge, discouraged the French from closing in force on the Union Brigade, which for its part proved it could skirmish as well as light cavalry. Uxbridge recalled much later:

Having thus checked the ardour of the Enemy's advanced guard, the retreat was continued at a slow pace and with the most perfect regularity. Assuredly this sudden effort (i.e. the charge of the Life Guards) had the very best effect, for although there was much cannonading, and a constant appearance of a disposition to charge, they continued at a respectful distance.[16]

This did not mean that Uxbridge's cavalry had nothing to do. Uxbridge had to make sure the French were not given an opportunity to launch another attack, which had more promise of success. This is where cavalry skirmishing came in, which involved facing the advancing enemy, perhaps moving towards them as if about to charge, perhaps firing pistols or carbines, and then withdrawing behind the next line of horsemen. This allowed the other cavalry to progress unhindered on their way and distance themselves further from their pursuers. Light cavalry normally filled this role, but Uxbridge gave this task to Sir William and his brigade and they evidently performed well, showing that the exercises undertaken on the field days in the Dender valley had been very useful.

On 9 December 1815 Uxbridge (now Marquess of Anglesey) wrote an account to a Colonel Allan. In it he refers to Ponsonby's brigade's actions:

The enemy now brought up cannon and deployed. They attempted to move up on our right but this effort was effectually foiled by the well executed movements of Sir William Ponsonby's brigade. There was a great deal of skirmishing and cannonading during the retreat which was effected in perfect order.[17]

Later on, Uxbridge recalled 'The Royals, Inniskillings and Greys manoeuvred beautifully, retiring by alternate squadrons and skirmished in the very best style'.[18]

The unknown Scots Greys sergeant wrote:

still their (the French) object seemed our brigade. We formed on
an open country with [??] in our rear where our artillery were
forming batteries and preparing for action. We had to face them
2 hours to keep them in play, and stop their progress till our
artillery were ready, at that time I did not see one British foot
soldier or artillery man for two hours, indeed none but our three
regiments acted.[19]

Major Radclyffe, in command of a squadron of the Royals, wrote:

I was detached with my squadron to cover the brigade by
skirmishing and Major General Sir William Ponsonby and the
brigade generally were placed to applaud the style in which we
acquitted ourselves. It rained with greater violence than I ever
witnessed before, which I found to my advantage when it was my
turn to skirmish. The enemy had two squadrons of Chasseurs
opposed to me and as they could not overpower us by their fire they
huzzaed and endeavoured to excite each other on with cries of *Vive
l'empereur* and one actually charged towards my skirmishers but
stopped short. I was flattered by the approbation of Sir W Ponsonby
and the admiration of the brigade on the style in which the squadron
under my orders covered the brigade etc.[20]

There was more than one squadron involved, but Radclyffe seems to
have borne the brunt of the effort. Captain Clark Kennedy, also of the
1st Royals, recalled:

The other two squadrons under the command of Lieutenant
Colonel Dorville and Major (afterwards Lieut-Colonel) Radclyffe
remaining and retiring shorty afterwards towards the position,
where they arrived a little before dusk along with the other
cavalry, which had been covering a slow and orderly retreat
during the greater portion of which, from Genappe to Waterloo,
the left squadron under Colonel Radclyffe was warmly engaged
skirmishing with the Enemy's advanced guard of cuirassiers who
pressed them hotly, frequently collecting with the apparent
intention of charging, but never venturing to do so during the
regular and orderly retreat of about five miles.[21]

After a while Uxbridge, seeing his objective achieved, ordered Sir William and his brigade to rejoin the rearguard on the paved road.

> but finding that all the efforts of the Enemy to get upon our right flank were vain, and that by manoeuvring about the plain, which was amazingly deep and heavy from the violent storm of rain, it only uselessly exhausted the horses, I drew these Regiments in upon the chaussée in one column, the guns falling back from position to position, and from these batteries, checking the advance of the enemy. We were received by the Duke of Wellington upon entering the position of Waterloo, having effected the retreat with very trifling loss. Thus ended the prettiest Field Day of Cavalry and Horse Artillery that I ever witnessed.[22]

Uxbridge's cavalry stopped Napoleon from getting to Mont St Jean before Wellington had concentrated his army. This also meant that because the French only arrived on the heights of Rosomme as dusk was falling, they could not concentrate their forces. On the 18th Napoleon would thus lose valuable time assembling his forces, meaning that his attack would begin later than he wanted it to. All this was achieved, according to Siborne, for the loss of 115 men and ninety-eight horses. The greatest losses were among the 7th Hussars. Sir William's brigade only recorded losses among the Royals, which amounted to only one man killed by a cannon ball, two men wounded and two horses killed.[23]

Given the long journey of the day before to get to Quatre Bras, and the fighting retreat of 17 June, the Union Brigade must have reached Mont St Jean exhausted but elated. Little could they have been expected to know what would happen in the next 24 hours and the crucial role they would play.

Chapter 14

Waterloo, 2pm 18 June – the Battle Lost!

William spent his last night in a cottage in the small hamlet of Waterloo.[1] Howarth, in *A Near Run Thing*, wrote that he rode out from Waterloo with Wellington on the morning of 18 June to the ridge of Mont St Jean:

> Wellington rode out along with the Duke of Richmond, Lord William Lennox, Lord Fitzroy Somerset, 8 ADCs, General Muffling, Lord Uxbridge, Lord Edward Somerset and Sir William Ponsonby each with aides, Sir Thomas Picton, Sir James Kempt, the Prince of Orange, Sir Edward Barnes and Sir William de Lancey.[2]

Ponsonby's brigade, like every other regiment in the army, had spent a miserable night. Radclyffe of the Royals recalled:

> we found ourselves in our place in close column behind the second line of infantry, fetlock deep in mud, no baggage for the officers and neither provision nor water for the men, though some stray cattle had been killed and eaten and a small supply of spirits had a short time before been found on the road so that we might be said to go coolly into action for every man was wet to the skin.[3]

Lieutenant Hamilton of the Scots Greys records that:

> In spite of the rain we slept pretty soundly, lying at our horses heads, they being formed in line and linked together, but we were repeatedly awoke during the night by their taking fright at the lightning and thunder, at the same time advancing over us! But no one was hurt! And as the nights in the middle of summer are

short we arose with the day break a miserable looking set of creatures we all were covered with mud from head to foot – our white belts dyed with the red from our jackets.[4]

However, other members of the Union Brigade claimed they spent a jovial night, having raided pig sties, hen roosts and invited the Highlanders to join them, who brought spirits.[5] No doubt troops took what they could find and made the best of it, with some doing a lot better than others.

Lieutenant George Gunning of the 1st Royals wrote:

The heavy black clouds cleared away at 7am and at 8am on Sunday morning, the 18th of June, about three hours before the battle began in earnest I was sent by Sir W Ponsonby with a pass order for the cavalry and horse artillery to feed. I visited each brigade agreeable to that order.[6]

The Union Brigade was initially at the bottom of the reverse slope of the Mont St Jean ridge, to the left of the crossroads made by the Charleroi–Brussels chaussée and the Braine L'Alleud–Ohain road. It was where the remains of the Belgian tram buildings now stand today. On the reverse slope stood the remains of Picton's division and the Landwehr brigades of Best and Vincke, which consisted of inexperienced militia. They stretched from the crossroads to just above the collection of farmsteads of Papelotte, La Haye and Smohain, which were the bulwarks of Wellington's left (garrisoned by 4,000 experienced Nassau troops commanded by the Prince of Saxe-Weimar). To their right, as the ridge curved away, were the cavalry brigades of Vandeleur (three regiments of light dragoons) and Vivian (three regiments of hussars). In front, forming the first line, was Bylandt's brigade, which like Kempt's and Pack's brigades had also suffered severely at Quatre Bras.

A little after 11 o'clock, Napoleon's aide General de la Bedoyère brought Napoleon's instructions to General Comte d'Erlon. 1st Corps were to begin their attack at one o'clock in the afternoon, in the direction of the centre of Wellington's position at Mont St Jean. The attack was to start with Bourgeois' brigade on the left and the other divisons were to attack progressively from the left with Pegot's brigade from Durutte's division on the right attacking last. To prevent Wellington moving his troops from the right of his position there was to be a diversionary attack on the British outpost of Hougoumont. Such an attack, it was hoped, would persuade Wellington to move troops to his right, weakening his left even more. Although the attack on Hougoumont became a battle within a battle, sucking in more and more French troops, that was not Napoleon's intention. The hammer blow would be delivered by d'Erlon's corps.

Napoleon's master plan was for d'Erlon's corps to march up the ridge, break through Picton's division and then, turning left, roll up the British line, forcing Wellington's remaining divisions to disengage westwards and fall back on the Channel ports. Napoleon would then be able to enter Brussels and hopefully persuade the coalition to sue for peace. This is not as far-fetched as it sounds and, but for Sir William's and Somerset's brigades, came very close to success. This was for the following reasons.

Firstly, the French attacking forces were very strong. D'Erlon's corps consisted of four divisions that had not fought at Ligny and were therefore close to full strength, numbering 14,000 men. Each division had four regiments grouped into two brigades of two regiments each. Charlet, with 2,000 men, half of the first division, was tasked with attacking and capturing the forward allied position at La Haie Sainte, while the other half, under Bourgeois and Quiot, were to push for the crossroads. The second division, under Donzelot, of 5,300 men was to attack and defeat Kempt's brigade. The third division, under Marcognet, of 4,200 men would attack and aim to defeat Pack's brigade. The fourth division, under Durutte, would divide in two. One brigade of 2,000 men would attack Best and Vincke's troops to prevent them coming to Picton's assistance. The other brigade would attack and isolate the other Allied forward position in the farmsteads at Papelotte, La Haie and Smohain. Each division would be preceded by the usual French skirmishers, the *tirailleurs*, who would be able to shoot any Allied officers attempting to rally their men. Thus, excluding the troops necessary to attack La Haie Sainte and those of Durutte, d'Erlon had 11,500 infantry at his disposal to smash through the Allied position to the east of the crossroads.

Secondly, d'Erlon's troops had good morale. They had not yet sustained any casualties, as they had not been engaged at either Ligny or Quatre Bras. Sleeping conditions during the night had been awful, but in the morning the troops had made their soup, had some meat and drunk a great deal of brandy. As Captain Martin of the 45th Ligne in d'Erlon's corps wrote: 'We were all getting ready, cleaning our weapons, urging one another to do well so we could finish this campaign with one stroke.'[7]

Thirdly, at least two of d'Erlon's divisions were in a new formation that was being used for the first time at Waterloo. Normally the Allied troops would enjoy the superiority in firepower that a long line of infantry gave against a narrow French column frontage. D'Erlon and his generals had decided, however, that for Donzelot's and Marcognet's divisions, which were going to break the Allied line, they would need to have a much longer frontage. So on 18 June these divisions were arranged in a formation called *colonne de division par bataillon* with a frontage of 140 men. This was different from a normal French formation of *colonne de bataillon par division* with a frontage of seventy men. This meant that Donzelot and Marcognet could bring twice the firepower to bear, and perhaps more than the Allied regiments weakened as a result of the fighting at Quatre Bras.[8]

Fourthly, Ney and d'Erlon had ensured that their infantry were protected from attack. Accompanying the troops were horse artillery that could be used against any compact infantry formations and would move with the infantry. Also accompanying the corps on its left and right were cavalry units. On the left were two regiments of cuirassiers numbering 780 men. On the right were chasseurs, the equivalent of light dragoons, and lancers commanded by General Jacquinot totalling 1,100 men. The cavalry units would deter other Allied infantry from coming to the help of the attacked Allied troops, as well as protecting d'Erlon's corps from a flanking attack by Allied cavalry.[9] No protection was made against a frontal cavalry attack.

The final advantage that d'Erlon had was artillery. Napoleon had constructed a great battery composed of his reserve artillery as well as d'Erlon's own artillery. In total this numbered eighty guns, made up of six and twelve pounders arranged in a single line. This battery was to wear down the enemy across the whole area that d'Erlon's corps would attack.[10] The impact would be psychological as well as physical. Napoleon instructed General de Sales, the commander of the Grand Battery, to open fire with all his guns at the same moment 'to surprise and shake the morale of the enemy.'[11] At about one o'clock the Grand Battery started shelling the British line.

All of this would have proved daunting enough against well formed regiments at full strength, but ironically Napoleon's strongest corps of 14,000 men was being flung against Wellington's weakest divisions. Firstly Wellington had positioned his army so there were twice as many men on the western side of the crossroads as there were on the eastern side. This was because he was expecting the number of men in this eastern sector to be increased once the Prussians arrived, which he hoped would be at one o'clock. Secondly, the infantry on his left were made up mostly of troops that had suffered heavily at Quatre Bras.

The first line consisted of Graf van Bylandt's Belgian and Dutch brigade of 2,500 men and 400 men of the first battalion of the 95th Rifles, commanded by Sir Andrew Barnard. The Dutch brigade consisted of inexperienced troops, mostly militia, and had suffered heavily at Quatre Bras where it had lost 25 per cent of its strength. The 95th Rifles were high-calibre marksmen, but the Baker rifle was slower than the French Charleville musket and therefore they could be overwhelmed by force of numbers.

The second line, commanded by the veteran Sir Thomas Picton, consisted of four brigades. Firstly, closest to the crossroads, was Sir James Kempt's brigade of the 95th, 32nd, 79th and 28th Foot, numbering 1,900 men. Next, on its left, was Sir Denis Pack's brigade of 1,700 men, made up of the 1st, 42nd, 92nd and 44th Foot. The troops in these two brigades were of high quality, but they had suffered severely during the battle of Quatre Bras.

Further to the left, close to where Frischermont convent now stands, were two brigades of inexperienced Hanoverian militia commanded by Colonel Best (approx 2,700 men) and Colonel von Vincke (approx 2,600 men). To their left were the light cavalry regiments of Vandeleur and Vivian, totalling approximately 2,800 men. But it was not against Best and Vincke's troops that the hammer blow would fall. 2,100 men from Durutte's division would deter the Hanoverians from intervening, while 11,500 French infantry commanded by Bourgeois, Donzelot and Marcognet would attack Bylandt's, Kempt's and Pack's brigades of 6,500 men.

However, there were some advantages for the Allied troops destined to receive d'Erlon's hammer blow. First there was their position. The ridge had a steep slope at the front which the French had to climb up, while the reverse was more gentle. Also, apart from part of Bylandt's brigade, all the troops were on the reverse slope and therefore out of sight of d'Erlon's corps and the Grand Battery. Picton's brigade could not be seen and, of equal importance, neither could the Union Brigade. The French did not know that there were cavalry perfectly positioned to attack them in the one area they had not considered, namely the front. Also in front of the Allied position was a sunken lane, the Chemin de

Ohain. It was paved, but on both sides of the road was a raised bank with a hedge on at least one of the two banks. To attack the Allied line the French troops had to get to the top of the ridge, get through a hedge, scramble down onto the sunken lane, clamber up the bank and get through a thorn hedge on the Allied side. Such an obstacle could cause disorder among the best trained troops.[12]

Then there was the fact that although the Allied artillery was small in number, it was positioned on the hedge line. Because of this the gunners could see the attacking French infantry and could shell them when they came into range. This they did first with solid shot, then grape and then, at a range of 50 yards or less, with canister. Because the canister shell burst overhead, this proved particularly effective against densely packed columns of infantry and made up for the Allied forces having fewer guns at their disposal.[13] However, by being placed on the hedge line they were in view of the gunners of the Grand Battery and some of the Allied guns would be quickly be put out of action.

But the greatest advantage was the condition of the ground. To this day the soil on the battleground can turn into glutinous mud very quickly after heavy rain. This not only slowed down the approach of d'Erlon's corps, but also meant that the impact of the Grand Battery was minimised. Cannonballs in those days did not explode, but ploughed through lines of troops and had their maximum impact when they bounced after hitting solid ground, just like skimming a stone on the water. Given the rain from the day before and during the night, many cannonballs did not ricochet but simply sank into the mud. Apart from the howitzer shells from the main battery that fired over the top of the ridge, the actual number of casualties after 30 minutes of intensive bombardment was a lot fewer than Napoleon would have hoped.

Nevertheless, the Grand Battery did have an impact, particularly on the Allied artillery which was visible to Napoleon's gunners. Artillery caissons blew up and some Allied batteries that had been retaliating started to run out of ammunition and were pulled out of the area.[14] Bylandt's brigade had been repositioned behind the hedge above the Chemin de Ohain, but that part situated close to Wellington's artillery started to be hit by the French bombardment. Then the howitzer shells started to hit the troops on the reverse slope.

It was now 1.30pm. D'Erlon began his attack by attacking La Haie Sainte with one of the two brigades that made up Quiot's division. The attack went well from the French point of view. The farmhouse was surrounded, supporting troops were driven back and the supporting artillery destroyed. An attempt to reinforce the garrison met with disaster when the relieving troops were caught out in the open by Crabbe's cuirassiers and slaughtered. The cuirassiers also forced back the 95th Rifles. With the farmhouse surrounded and isolated d'Erlon could start feeding in his other divisions.

The 2,000 French troops of Quiot's remaining brigade, commanded by Bourgeois, advanced forward, followed at 5-minute intervals by Donzelot's division of 5,300 and then that of Marcognet (4,200). They descended the slope, made their way through the Grand Battery, re-formed, crossed the boggy part at the bottom of the valley and started to climb up the Allied slope. It was now 1.55pm.

The men were in great spirits. The drummers beat the *pas de charge*. The troops shouted *Vive L'empereur!* Their officers rode in front of each battalion, shouting that the emperor would reward the first of the troops that reached the top of the slope. The troops started off at the regulation seventy-six steps per minute. They had to cover 600 metres to reach the ridge. They flattened the fields of rye, turning the slope into a muddy morass for those in the rear battalions, who sometimes had their shoes pulled off by the mud. Some of the troops fell victim to the Allied artillery, but because there were not enough Allied guns the damage was limited. The gaps created were closed and on they marched.[15]

Advancing in front of Bourgeois', Donzelot's and Marcognet's formations were thousands of *tirailleurs*, or skirmishers. Their job was to shoot the Allied officers, the artillery men and the Allied skirmishers.

Because Picton's men were lying down, at least 100 yards behind the sunken lane, the French reached the hedge unopposed. Some of the artillery men panicked and left their guns. It was now 2.15pm.

The French crossed the hedge. The first troops they came up against were Graf van Bylandt's Belgian-Dutch brigade. Bylandt was wounded and, with most of his officers wounded or dead, the Belgian-Dutch broke completely on their right and fled, leaving only a single Belgian battalion in the gap to face the largest French division of Donzelot.

The British troops were ordered to advance. On reaching the hedge they were deployed not in the normal two-line formation, but in four-deep ranks. This was perhaps because their commanders feared an attack by cavalry, and it was easier to move into square when in four lines. The downside was that they lost the overlapping fire that a two-line formation would give them. A firefight started to develop and the new French formation of Donzelot started to have an impact. General Picton attempted to regain the initiative by ordering Kempt's brigade to charge with the bayonet, but he was shot and killed. The gap started to widen as the last companies of Kempt's brigade, seeing the French advancing on their flank, turned towards their left.[16] It was about 2.20pm.

The two brigades commanded by Grenier and Nogues of Marcognet's division started to arrive. Marcognet's men were opposed by Sir Denis Pack's brigade, three-quarters of whom were Scottish veterans, but who had taken many casualties at Quatre Bras and were also in four-deep lines. The Black Watch, who only numbered 330 men due to the casualties they had sustained two days before, were stopped and pushed back by the enemy's fire.[17] Pack shouted at his next battalion, the 92nd or Gordon Highlanders, 'Ninety Second you must advance, everything has given way on your right and left and you must charge this column!'[18] Pack wanted his men to attack with the bayonet, but the 92nd opted for a firefight with the French instead and came off worse. They too started to fall back from the hedge and the 45th Ligne went through the hedge.

As Sir Horace Seymour, who had been next to Picton, wrote: 'the Highlanders were for the instant overpowered by the masses of French infantry'.[19] The Allied troops were starting to lose the fight. Casualties were mounting. More soldiers were helping their wounded friends to the rear as a means of saving themselves. Ammunition was running low. Wellington had not placed any reserves on this side of the battlefield and all it would take was for a few more men to break and then a battalion and there would then be a gap big enough for the French to surge through, turn the British flank and the French would have won the battle of Waterloo.

Lieutenant Martin, of the 45th de ligne, the lead regiment in Marcognet's division, wrote: 'They [some English battalions] were chased off with the bayonet, we continued the climb, crossed the hedge line that sheltered their guns; we were on the plateau, victory was ours![20]

It was about 2.25pm, and at that moment the Union Brigade, led by Sir William Ponsonby, charged.

Key to Waterloo maps:
French troops are represented in outlined squares and rectangles, which change to ovals if attacked and dispersed. Allied troops are represented in outlined boxes.

French troops on the French right wing
A – Artillery of the Grand Battery
B – Bourgeois
Ch – 3rd Chasseurs
D – Donzelot
Du – Durutte
M – Marcognet
85 – Square of the 85th de la ligne

Allied troops on Wellington's left wing
Be – Best
ID – Inniskilling Dragoons
Ke – Kempt
Pa – Pack
RD – 1st Royal Dragoons
SG – Scots Greys
Va – Vandeleur
Vi – Vinke

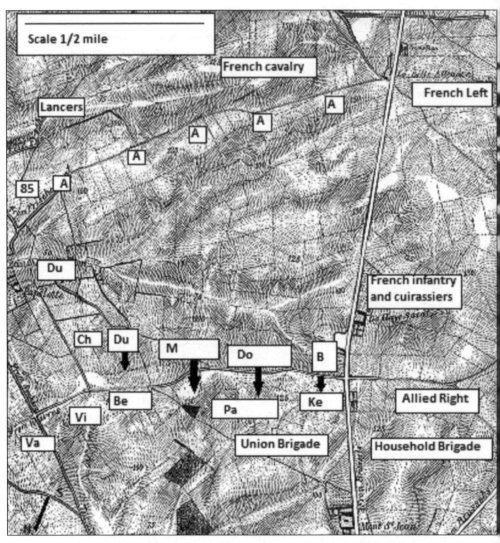

Simplified map showing the first charge of the Union Brigade repelling d'Erlon's corps

This is superimposed on Captain Siborne's own map of the battlefield.

Map 1 shows the success of the original French attack. Following the collapse of Bylandt's brigade Kempt's and Pack's brigades are unable to repel the French attack.

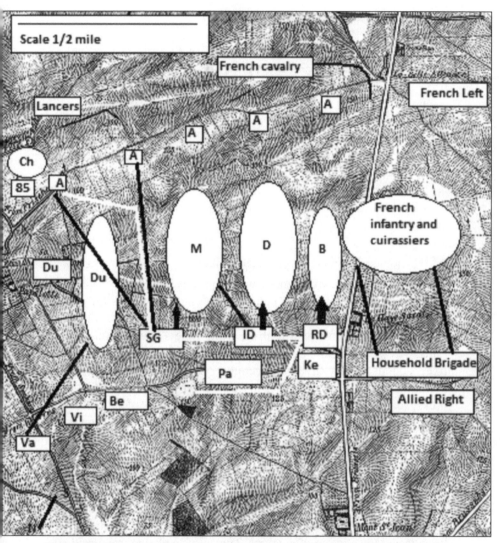

Scale 1/2 mile

French cavalry

French Left

Lancers

A

A

A

Ch

A

85

A

French infantry and cuirassiers

Du

Du

M

D

B

SG

ID

RD

Pa

Ke

Household Brigade

Be

Allied Right

Vi

Va

Map 2 The Union Brigade's charge is decisive in repelling the attack, but note the movement of part of Vandeleur's brigade to attack the French cavalry supporting Durutte. The repulse of Durutte and his retreating troops taking position close to the square of the 85th de la Ligne draws the attention of the bulk of the Scots Greys, while only part of the regiment, under Colonel Hamilton, attacks the Grand Battery. Sir William's route in the charge is represented by a white line.

Chapter 15

Waterloo, 2.20pm 18 June – the Battle Regained: the Charge of the Union Brigade

We can piece together what happened next from a variety of sources. For those who could write, many were so relieved to have survived the dreadful battle that over the course of the next few days they wrote letters home to friends and relations. Some letters were simply to announce that they were still alive, while others were more detailed. Later, others wrote more detailed accounts, trying to portray what it was like. The danger with these accounts is that sometimes they are inaccurate for a whole range of reasons. Over time the memory plays tricks; sometimes the account has been edited because of something the participant has read or heard; and sometimes, of course, the writer wants to portray themselves in the best possible light.

Sir William did not survive to write his own account and I have relied on those close to him on the day. Not all survived. A commander of a cavalry brigade had with him a small staff. First there was the brigade major, who was basically the general's chief of staff, responsible for the movement and deployment of the units of the brigade and the posting of picquets. They also tended to stay beside the commanding officer to ensure orders were carried out. In the Union Brigade this was Thomas Reignolds, a captain in the 2nd Dragoons, who was killed along with Sir William. Then the general had a personal aide de camp, who was very much the equivalent of the executive assistant in today's business world. Sir William's was Braithwaite Christie, who had been his ADC in the Peninsula after recovering from serious wounds he sustained at Salamanca. He was the third son of Admiral Alexander Christie of Baberton in Scotland. He is always referred to in accounts as the 'General's ADC'. But some generals had additional ADCs, including Sir William. His extra aide de camp was Major De Lacy Evans of the 5th West India Regiment. De Lacy Evans was born in Ireland and had served in the Peninsula and in the war of 1812 against the United States. He was known to Sir William, having been a lieutenant in the 3rd Dragoons, and therefore part of Sir William's brigade in the Peninsula. He had been wounded during the retreat from Burgos and was known for his bravery, and was wounded again in America. But he also had a reputation as an organiser, having fulfilled the role of quartermaster during the war in America. He had spent the evening of 15 June helping Wellington's quartermaster general de Lancey send out the orders to assemble the troops and on the 17th he had helped organise the fighting retreat of the cavalry through Genappe. He was 28 years old and would be commended for his actions at Waterloo by General Pack. In addition to these two ADCs William had an orderly, Archibald Hamilton, who had served in his brigade in the Peninsula as a lieutenant in the 4th Dragoons. He had recently transferred into the Scots Greys and was the son and heir of General John Hamilton of Dalziel. He stated that because he was the only subaltern in the brigade that Sir William knew 'he asked me to be with him on the 17th and on this day (the 18th) also.'[1] It seems clear that Sir William had assembled a small team that he could trust.

Hamilton left a detailed account of the battle, as well as writing a letter dated 24 June. De Lacy Evans wrote an account, years later, as part of his response to Siborne. Braithwaite Christie survived the battle, but no correspondence from him has yet come to light.

Hamilton says he joined Sir William, Reignolds and de Lacy Evans on the morning of 18 June. Braithwaite Christie had been sent by Sir William to Brussels that morning because, Hamilton says, Sir William had not expected the battle to begin 'so early, if at all that day.'[2] This was because there was the expectation that, as the Prussians had not arrived, the army would again retreat. Braithwaite Christie would rejoin this group before the charge began.

Hamilton records how Sir William looked over the brigade and left it 'drawn up close' at the bottom of the hill. He, Reignolds, de Lacy Evans and Hamilton then rode to the top, where they met the Duke of Richmond and his son with a number of officers peering through their telescopes to see if they could see the Prussians. All they saw was Napoleon's ride in front of the French army.[3]

Once the Grand Battery opened fire, some of the shots went over the ridge and started to fall among the brigade at the bottom. One of the two majors in the Scots Greys, Major Hankin, had his horse fall on top of him and he had to be carried to the rear. Two or three Scots Greys and a number of horses were severely wounded by cannon shot. Sir William sent Hamilton down to minimise the damage.

> The cannonade began on the right and increased every minute, till it was opposite to us, a gentle breeze wafting the smoke of the French guns towards us which wholly prevented our seeing anything in front of us. Our brigade continued drawn up at the bottom of the hill, and I was sent to desire the commanding officers of the different regiments to draw them up as close to the hill as possible, as they began to suffer both from shells and shot, the effects of the cannonade.[4]
>
> Upon my return to the General, a shell struck the ground in the middle of us and in an instant he threw himself to the ground, the brigade major an extra aide de camp and I did the same, while an orderly officer of the 6th Dragoons fell off his horse which took fright at our rapid movements. The shell did not burst! We were all therefore frightened but none of us hurt.[5]

D'Erlon's corps advanced with the success already mentioned. In a letter from his home at Beaudesert to Colonel Allan on 18 December 1815 Uxbridge, or Anglesey as he then was, wrote the following:

> The most destructive attack was made perhaps about 2 o'clock upon two very large movements of infantry and cavalry who tried to force our centre. I ordered Sir William Ponsonby (a most gallant officer and excellent fellow) to fall upon them with his brigade. Almost at the same moment I took down Lord Edward Somerset with the Household Brigade for the same process.[6]

In 1839, as part of Siborne's enquiries, Uxbridge elaborated:

> I had been visiting the extreme right of the cavalry, and those placed in support of Hougoumont when on returning to the centre of the position, I observed very large masses of the enemy both cavalry and infantry (supported too by a tremendous discharge of artillery from all parts of their line) moving upon our left but principally on La Haie Sainte, the road from Genappe to Brussels appearing to be nearly the centre of their advance.

I immediately galloped to the heavy cavalry and ordered the Household Brigade to prepare to form line, passed on to Sir William Ponsonby's and having told him to wheel into line when the other brigade did, I instantly returned to the Household brigade and put the whole in motion.[7]

Neither Hamilton or de Lacy Evans mention the role of Lord Uxbridge, but it is very unlikely that Sir William would have put the Union Brigade in motion without Uxbridge's permission. But the exact timing of the charge would be decided by Sir William, particularly as Uxbridge had galloped back to join Somerset and the 1st Heavy Cavalry Brigade. Hamilton again:

Our General observing what was about to take place, immediately sent me down to bring up the brigade with all speed. I did so, the General met us just before we reached the summit of the hill.[8]

Corporal John Dickson, moving as part of Captain Vernor's troop of the Scots Greys, remembered seeing Sir William, who must have moved over to the left of the brigade.

Immediately after this, the General of the Union Brigade, Sir William Ponsonby, came riding up to us on a small bay hack. I remember that his groom with his chestnut charger could not be found. Beside him was his aide de camp De Lacy Evans. He ordered us forward to within fifty yards of the beech hedge by the roadside. I can see him now in his long cloak and great cocked hat as he rode up to watch the fighting below.[9]

With Pack's brigade heavily engaged, Sir William rode back to the right of his brigade where the Royals were situated. Dickson again: 'At this moment our General and his Aide de Camp rode off to the right by the side of the hedge; then suddenly I saw de Lacy Evans wave his hat.'[10]

The reason for de Lacy Evans waving his hat is covered in a letter he wrote to Siborne.[11] It was the signal for the brigade to be put in motion, for as Hamilton said:

had we been five minutes later, it would have been too late to have effected what we did, as the French had charged our infantry with the bayonet, who fled through the intervals of our squadrons, but immediately rallying advanced again with us to the hedge, a little way down the hill, where they fired a volley at the French, when they were close to each other. Our three regiments of dragoons were not quite in line: the 1st Dragoons were on the right and some yards in advance, so that the General placing himself in front of them, they charged a little before the other regiments did, the French gave us only a partial volley, being in some disorder in consequence of their previous exertions against our infantry, and from having no idea of our brigade being so near at hand. We accordingly went right through them, not a horse as is usually the case went round from the fire, and the enemy through down their arms.

The other two regiments came up in succession, but were a little delayed by the hedge, we again charged – the General riding along the whole line to the left of the brigade – so that we saw the whole three regiments charge: the result in each instance the same – namely the enemy threw down their arms, and begging their lives.[12]

This was a technique known as an echeloned line attack formation. The first clash took place on the crest itself. Sir William and the Royals struck Bourgeois' division and its leading regiment, the 105th de la Ligne. Clark Kennedy stated that the French:

had forced their way through our line – the heads of the column were on the Brussels side of the double hedge.. in fact the crest of the height had been gained and the charge of the cavalry at the critical moment rescued it…The charge took place on the crest not on the slope of the ridge though it was followed up to the hollow ground between the two positions.[13]

As the Royals had to ride up the reverse slope and then attack the French on the crest they had to ride uphill, so the impact would not have been from a gallop but from the sheer surprise and the weight of the horses. Momentum would only be gained once the cavalry crossed the sunken way, broke through the other hedge and started down the front slope. Colonel Muter, in command of the Inniskillings, stated that they came into contact with Donzelot's division 'almost immediately after clearing the hedge and I should call it 'chemin creux'. We all agree in thinking that the French columns had nearly gained the crest.'[14]

The front regiments of Bourgeois' brigade managed to get off a volley, which brought down twenty of the Royals including Major Radclyffe. Two squadrons attacked Bourgeois' brigade and the French fell back down the slope, pushed by the cavalry whose charge was gaining momentum as they rode downwards. Captain Clark Kennedy had been engaged in fighting the enemy for 5 or 6 minutes when he spotted an eagle, and with his troops captured it and had it taken to the rear. With their blood up, the two squadrons of Royals pressed on:

> and went a little further than we ought to have done perhaps, getting under the fire of fresh troops stationed on the opposite heights and losing a good many men. About half way between the two positions we endeavoured to collect our squadrons but we were so much scattered that few could be got together and with these few we retired slowly towards our own position under a pretty severe fire, driving as many prisoners before us as we could.[15]

Thanks to Uxbridge's charge with the Household Cavalry, which had swept aside the French cuirassiers, there was no enemy cavalry to intervene. Indeed, the Royals had been followed down the ridge by some of the British infantry, who helped them secure the French prisoners. Because of these factors their casualties were not as great from this charge as those of the other units of the Union Brigade.

Sir William did not see the impact of the Royals' charge. He had passed on to the Inniskillings. They and the third squadron of the Royals had struck Donzelot's division. This was nearly three times the size of Bourgeois' brigade, but the French troops, using their new formation, had not practised deploying into square to resist cavalry and were therefore particularly vulnerable. As one of the squadron commanders of the Inniskillings, Major Miller, commented:

> So over the hedge I went and waited a moment or two for the men to collect, and then we were into the column in a second. Here it was I received my bayonet wounds and lost my horse. From our scattered state in getting over the hedge I do not conceive we should have made any impression on our opposing column had they not been inclined to retire.[16]

Some of the Inniskillings were brought down by enemy fire, but they also suffered less in losses than the third regiment, the Scots Greys.

Although a great deal of ink has been spent debating whether the Scots Greys had been ordered to provide a reserve to the other two regiments, this is in reality a pointless exercise. This is because also on the crest was the third main French column of Marcognet, which was successfully being deployed in the new formation against Pack's brigade. Someone had to charge this column or there would have been 4,200 Frenchmen successfully deployed on the crest. This is precisely what the Scots Greys did.

Sergeant Anton, who was with the Black Watch at Waterloo, published his account of the Scots Greys' charge in 1841:

> What pen can describe the scene? Horses hooves sinking in men's breasts, breaking bones and pressing out their bowels. Riders' swords streaming in blood, waving over their heads and descending in deadly vengeance. Stroke follows stroke, like the turning of a flail in the hand of a dexterous thresher, the living stream gushes red from the ghastly wound, spouts in the victor's face, and stains him with brains and blood... Such is the music of the field![17]

The best account, however, which gives a feel for the thrill of the charge, was noted down years later, in 1855, from the reminiscences of Corporal John Dickson, who was in the second rank of the Scots Greys.

> I saw De Lacy Evans wave his hat, and immediately our Colonel Inglis Hamilton shouted out, 'Now the Scots Greys charge!' and waving his sword in the air he rode straight at the hedges in front which he took in grand style. At once a great cheer arose from our ranks, and we too waved our swords and followed him. I dug my spur into my brave old Rattler and we were off like the wind. I felt a strange thrill run through me, and I'm sure my noble beast felt the same for, after rearing for a moment she sprang forward uttering loud neighings and snortings and leaped over the holly hedge at a terrific speed. It was a grand sight to see the long line of grey horses dashing along with flowing manes and heads down, tearing up the turf about them as they went. The men in their red coats and tall bearskins were cheering loudly and the trumpeters were sounding the 'charge'. Beyond the first hedge the road was sunk between high sloping banks and it was a very difficult feat

to descend without falling but there were very few accidents to our surprise.

All of us were greatly excited and began crying 'Hurrah Ninety Second! Scotland for Ever'.

As we crossed the road… Our colonel went on before us, past our guns and down the slope and we followed… As we tightened our grip to descend the hillside among the corn, we could make out the feather bonnets of the Highlanders and heard the officers crying out to them to wheel back by sections. Poor fellows some of them had not time to get clear of us and were knocked down.

The French were uttering loud discordant yells. Just then I saw the first Frenchman. A young officer of fusiliers made a slash at me with his sword, but I parried it and broke his arm; the next minute we were in the thick of them. We could not see five yards ahead in the smoke. I stuck close by Armour; Ewart was now in front.

The French were fighting like tigers. Some of the wounded were firing at us as we passed. Poor Kinchant who had spared one of these rascals was himself shot by the officer he had spared. As we were sweeping down a steep slope on the top of them they had to give way. Then those in front began to cry out for 'quarter' throwing down their muskets and taking off their belts. The Gordons at this rushed in and drove the French to the rear. I was now in the front rank for many of ours had fallen. …We now came to an open space covered with bushes and then I saw Ewart with five or six infantry men about him slashing right and left at them. Armour and I dashed up to these half-dozen Frenchmen, who were trying to escape with one of their standards. I cried to Armour to 'Come on!' and we rode at them. Ewart had finished two of them and was in the act of striking a third man who held the eagle; next moment I saw Ewart cut him down and he fell dead. I was just in time to thwart a bayonet thrust that was aimed at the gallant sergeant's neck. Armour finished another of them.

We cried out 'well done my boy!' and as others had come up we spurred on in search of like success. Here it was that we came upon two batteries of French guns which had been sent forward to support the infantry. They were now deserted by the gunners and had sunk deep in the mud.

We were saluted with a sharp fire of musketry and again found ourselves beset by thousands of Frenchmen [this was the 21st

Regiment in Nogues' brigade – the second brigade in Marcognet's division]. We had fallen upon a second column; they were also fusiliers. Trumpeter Reeves of our troop who rode by my side, sounded a Rally and our men came swarming up from all sides, some Eniskillens and Royals being amongst the number. We at once began a furious onslaught on this obstacle and soon made an impression; the battalions seemed to open up for us to pass through and so it happened that in five minutes we had cut our way through as many thousands of Frenchmen. We had now reached the bottom of the slope. There the ground was slippery with deep mud.[18]

It was 2.45pm. In a space of twenty minutes the Union brigade had destroyed five French infantry brigades, inflicting 5,000 casualties.[19] Thousands of prisoners had been taken and were being shepherded to the rear of the battlefield by the relieved British infantry, who fifteen minutes earlier must have thought themselves beaten. In addition thousands had been wounded and killed. Napoleon's masterstroke to secure victory had been defeated and, as Uxbridge wrote:

When I was returning to our position I met the Duke of Wellington, surrounded by all the Corps diplomatique militaire, who had from the high ground witnessed the whole affair. The plain appeared to be swept clean, and I never saw so joyous a group as was this Troupe dorée. They thought the battle was over.[20]

Sir William and the Union Brigade had pulled off a success more crucial than three years previously at Salamanca. Sir William had timed the charge perfectly and his close control, by riding from his most experienced regiment on the right (the Royals) via the Inniskillings to the Scots Greys on the left, had ensured all three regiments had played their part as expected. What was now crucial was for the Union Brigade to re-form and return to the British lines. But unlike at Salamanca, fate was not on Sir William's side.

Chapter 16

18 June – The Wheel of Fortune Turns Again

By this time the Union Brigade had accomplished its great objective. Many sources record that 2,000 prisoners were taken, but this ignores the much harder to establish figures for wounded and killed as well as those prisoners that were originally captured and subsequently escaped. It is probable that 5,000 of d'Erlon's corps (the equivalent of one third of his troops) were killed, wounded or captured as a result of the Union Brigade's charge. The remainder took time to regroup, but many were not effective for the rest of the day. What is certain is that the hammer blow which Napoleon had intended to deliver to defeat the Allied army had been decisively defeated after coming very close to success. What happened next was due to three key individuals, one British and two French.

Good practice dictated that, after a successful cavalry attack, the engaged troops would withdraw, protected by the cavalry reserve. Inevitably, once the fighting started after a while all formation was lost. Troops and squadrons lost their cohesion and broke into small groups, which could be picked off by an enemy counterattack. The heavy cavalry at Salamanca had become fragmented despite having squadrons in support, but this had not mattered as there was no French cavalry close by to attack them. After Waterloo there were a lot of allegations as the surviving commanders tried to blame each other for the fact that the Union Brigade did not have a reserve. Uxbridge stated he had ordered the Scots Greys to be the reserve, and some officers of the Royals said they heard him. Surviving officers of the Scots Greys said they had never received such an order. Such an order, if it had ever been given, was impractical. D'Erlon's attack was so well planned, and the number of troops engaged so great, that in order to defeat it the whole Union Brigade had to be committed.

There were other cavalry regiments that could have acted as a reserve, for example those under the command of Vivian and Vandeleur. However, as we will see, Vandeleur might already have had some of his troops committed against Durutte's infantry, and Vivian was further away from the action at the end of Wellington's left wing and had been instructed by Wellington not to leave his position. He would not want to risk Wellington's displeasure if he acted independently of his, or Uxbridge's, orders.

In the absence of such a reserve the essential action was to halt the advance, rally the troops and withdraw. The Royals, who were the most experienced of Sir William's three regiments, were already doing this. As Clark Kennedy wrote to Siborne:

About half way between the two positions we endeavoured to collect our squadrons as well as we could; but we were so much scattered that few could be got together and with these few we retired slowly towards our own position, under a pretty heavy fire driving as many prisoners before us as we could. No cavalry was opposed to that part of the brigade with which I was; but I was told that the left suffered greatly when retiring from an attack of lancers.[1]

This point he reemphasised in a subsequent letter:

No cavalry checked the right flank of the brigade. It retired from exhaustion and from getting under the fire of fresh troops on the opposite ridge. It was not attacked in retiring only fired upon. The left of the brigade I understand was followed and suffered severely from a body of lancers.[2]

Another factor that protected the retreat of the Royals was that Picton's infantry had advanced to secure prisoners and the formations they adopted would have deterred any cavalry from attacking.

Our infantry, which we passed at the hedge, now proved of essential service to us. They had formed small bodies or squares following in the rear of the charge, and not only checked pursuit but without their support and assistance I am satisfied we should not have got back as well as we did and certainly we could not have secured one half of the prisoners taken in the charge.[3]

For the Greys, fate in the shape of a senior officer dealt a severe blow. As Lieutenant Hamilton, Sir William's extra ADC, recalled:

After passing through and killing, wounding and making prisoners the whole of the advanced column of the French, we ought to have stopped and reformed the brigade: but our men were not contented with what they had done, they still went on. The General, his Aide de Camp and I got however about thirty of them collected together, in the hope of reassembling all who remained of those who had come on, for a great many, particularly of the officers had remained with the prisoners, when Colonel XX of the xx dragoons came past us at full gallop with about twenty men of his regiment following him. In a second all the men which we had collected set off in the same direction. In the hopes of stopping them we followed.[4]

Thanks to Corporal Dickson, we know who this individual was:

At this moment Colonel Hamilton rode up to us crying 'Charge! Charge the guns', and went off like the wind up the hill towards the terrible battery that had made such deadly work among the Highlanders. It was the last we saw of our colonel, poor fellow! His body was found with both arms cut off. I once heard Major Clarke tell how he saw him wounded among the guns of the great battery going at full speed with the bridle reins between his teeth, after he had lost his hands.[5]

Colonel Hamilton paid the price for his insubordinate behaviour with his life. But his intervention was disastrous. By attacking the Grand Battery he led approximately fifty Scots Greys further away from safety. The Grand Battery was approximately 1,900 yards (over a mile) from the Allied ridge line and half a mile from where Sir William had attempted to re-form the Scots Greys.

It is almost an accepted fact among historians that Hamilton took all the Scots Greys with him on his disastrous charge, but this is not the case. Lieutenant Ingilby of the Royal Horse Artillery, stationed with Sir Hussey Vivian's cavalry, was in a perfect position to see what happened. He wrote:

An inconsiderable party of Sir William Ponsonby's brigade after this success, or in continuation of the charge, wheeled to their right and rode amongst the Guns of the right flank of the great French Battery, and kept undisturbed possession of them for a quarter of an hour or twenty minutes.[6]

The second blow was, however, not long in coming and that came from Napoleon himself.

Watching the charge, Napoleon ordered some of his cuirassier brigades to attack both Somerset's Household Brigade and Sir William's Union Brigade. The 7th and 12th regiments of cuirassiers, numbering 440 men, were dispatched against those members of Somerset's Household Brigade that were in the valley. The 5th and 10th regiments of cuirassiers, made up of six squadrons totalling 875 men, attacked the Union Brigade. Other cuirassier regiments had come off worse when they had been charged by Uxbridge and the Household Brigade, but this had been when the Household Brigade was fresh and had the momentum of charging downhill. Now the cuirassiers were fresh and the Union Brigade troopers were tired, on tired horses. The cuirassiers outnumbered the soldiers of the Union Brigade that were still at the bottom of the slope and their swords were longer. They could have easily finished the job. However, the final blow was just about to fall, and that came from the cavalry on the French right.

When General Durutte had advanced as the right wing of d'Erlon's attack he had been supported by the light cavalry of General de Division Baron Charles Claude Jacquinot, a fact very much ignored by historians. Jacquinot was a very experienced cavalry commander, having served in Austria, Poland, Prussia and Russia as well as in the 1814 campaign on the French frontier. He had at his disposal two cavalry brigades. The first cavalry brigade was the equivalent of the British Light Dragoons and comprised three squadrons of the 3rd Chasseurs à cheval and three squadrons of the 7th Hussars – although by the time of the Union Brigade's charge the 7th, commanded by Marbot, had been sent to counter the Prussian advance. The 3rd were commanded by Colonel Lawoestine, with General Bruno as brigade commander. They had supported Pegot of Durutte's division when he had threatened the large square numbering 5,000 men formed by Best and Vincke's battalions. As Adjutant von Berckefeldt of the Munden Landwehr Batallion, commanded by Colonel Best, wrote:

This middle column was preceded in the tall corn of Smohain by a skirmish line and it was followed by the French 3rd and 7th Chasseur regiments, they rode up to the large square and seemed determined to launch their first attack against it.[7]

The second brigade under General Gobrecht comprised two dragoon regiments that had been converted into lancer regiments in 1811, the 3e and 4e Regiments de Chevaux-Légers, who numbered 700 men. The 4th Lancers were commanded by Colonel Bro. Bro was known as a vigilant and experienced officer.[8]

Jacquinot's two brigades numbered 1,100 men and he was in a perfect position to deploy them. Durutte always claimed that Jacquinot did not support his attack as well as he should have done. This does seem unfair, particularly as we know that the 3rd Chasseurs and some lancers supported Pegot. It must be remembered that the countryside around Papelotte and the other farms on the extreme left of the Allied left was unsuitable for Jacquinot's cavalry. The area round Papelotte and Smohain has been described as bocage country of uneven ground, deeply sunken lanes with high banks and dense tree coverage. Both Durutte and Jacquinot knew this from a reconnaissance that Jacquinot's lancers had made earlier that day. As a result of this, or because he had quarrelled with Durutte two days previously,[9] Jacquinot simply did not commit all his cavalry to support Durutte's attack on the Allied line. The rest, particularly the 4th Lancers, he had positioned on high ground before the land fell away into the bocage country.[10] As such he was able to see the Union Brigade attack and take steps to counter it. For this his lancers would be ideal, although he needed to deal with another British cavalry attack first.

What many historians have not realised is that the Household and the Union Brigade's charges were not the first cavalry attacks on d'Erlon's corps. Adjutant von Berckefeldt of the Munden Landwehr Battalion again:

> The outward faces of the square made ready to receive the approaching cavalry when the 4th English Cavalry brigade appeared and charged the French cavalry with great vehemence a short distance in front of us, scattered it and took a large number of prisoners, including several staff officers.[11]

Captain William Hay in *A Few Reminiscences and Anecdotes* recalls how a couple of squadrons of the 12th Light Dragoons under Frederick

Ponsonby had already charged the cavalry supporting Durutte's regiments that were advancing to attack the Hanoverian troops of Best and Vincke.

> I observed on our left, three or four squares of French infantry were drawn up at the bottom of the ridge and ending with their rear up the sloping ground in their front which was covered thickly with skirmishers employed in firing across the lane at our infantry who were returning the compliment from behind the small enclosures…so near was I that I never thought for a moment we could have been brought there for any other purpose than to charge the square. So much was I impressed with this idea that, when the colonel placed himself in the centre of the square to lead into action, and the word of command *Forward* given, I gave the word *Right shoulders forward* and in a second more would have dashed at the square next me, when I heard called out to me *Not that, not that Hay!* I then for the first time discovered just in our front were moving on to the flat ground several squadrons of the French cavalry composed of lancers and light dragoons, we had no time for reflection. On we went at a gallop, sweeping past, and close to the muskets of the French and over the skirmishers, who were running in all directions to seek shelter.[12]

Hay talks about charging lancers as well as chasseurs. Other squadrons charged Durutte's infantry. This account is supported by Mauduit, who says that the leading two regiments of Durutte's brigade had been so badly disorganised by English cavalry that their actions had no impact for the rest of the day.[13] Frederick Ponsonby then ordered Hay to withdraw, and it was having done this that he witnessed the Union Brigade charge:

> On glancing round I saw two lancers coming full tilt at me, one instant more and both their lances would have been in the small of my back; one spring into the hollow deprived them of their prey and, I have little doubt that the well directed aim of some of our noble infantry who saw the whole transaction, accounted for them and made them pay for their temerity, by leaving their carcasses where they intended mine should be laid.
>
> No sooner had I got down into the road than several of their brave hands were held out to pull me up, amongst them a little

stout sergeant, who congratulated me on my narrow escape and placed me in safety amongst his men. For the two or three moments I stood with them till I recovered my horse, I had the opportunity of seeing a noble sight – which was – the Charge of the Union Brigade… at that moment they came down the slope a little to the right of the infantry, where I was standing, like a torrent, shaking the very earth, and sweeping everything before them.

Our equally brave fellows, who had done their utmost to stand against the superior weight of the French cavalry, intermixed with them and fought man to man; but the heavy brigade from their weight went over them and through them, bringing back many prisoners.[14]

Jacquinot seems therefore to have supported Durutte, but he held some of his force back and this was likely to be the 4th Lancers under Colonel Bro. Interestingly this is supported by a sketch of the action by Colonel Bro, showing only one regiment of lancers and one of chasseurs being used in Jacquinot's counterattack on the Scots Greys.[15] Nevertheless the impact of the two regiments would be devastating.

The chasseurs were the equivalent of light dragoons and carried sabres, pistols and cavalry carbines. They were experienced troops but, due to being mounted on inferior horses to those of heavy dragoons, they were not likely to come off best unless they considerably outnumbered the heavy cavalry they were attacking, and they had already suffered casualties at the hands of the 12th Light Dragoons. It was, however, the impact of the 4th Lancers that everyone remembered. The lancers carried lances in addition to sabres, pistols and cavalry carbines. As Hervé de Montmorency observed, they were physically very fit and very well trained.[16] They wore green uniforms with coloured facings – crimson for the 4th – which explains why some of the Union Brigade referred to them as 'red lancers', which was a different lancer regiment entirely clothed in red. The 4th Lancers' headgear was a brass helmet with the lower part covered in panther skin for the officers. The lance was of hardened wood, usually black in colour and nearly nine feet long from point to butt. At the point of balance a wrist strap of white leather was attached. The strap was also wound round the lance to provide a hand grip. A pennon was attached, which was not only decorative, but could also be used to terrify enemy horses. The British army had not made the decision to create lancer regiments in 1815, but the impact that French lancer regiments could have had already persuaded other European powers to emulate the French example.

Jacquinot could deploy his lancers in a number of ways. Ideally he would have liked to have deployed in lines, with lancers in the first line using their lances and the lancers in the second line either using their lances or slinging them and using their sabres. He was aware that he had difficult country to negotiate. It was a tangle of sunken roads, tracks and thick hedges, only flattening out when it reached the valley. So Jacquinot would use squadrons where he could and, where he could not, he would attack '*en fourrageur*', 'the swarm attack'. This deployed his lancers in small groups, still sufficiently numerous to outnumber the small groups of the Union Brigade. Colonel Muter of the Inniskillings referred to his regiment as suffering severely 'both in pursuit and return from Pelotons (platoons), Clouds or small bodies of French lancers.[17]

Although attacked by chasseurs as well as lancers, for the survivors of the Scots Greys it was the memory of the lancers that stayed uppermost in their minds. Dickson, who was with the breakaway group of Scots Greys that attacked the Grand Battery, recalls:

> But you can imagine my astonishment when down below, on the very ground we had crossed appeared at full gallop a couple of regiments of cuirassiers on the right and away to the left a regiment of lancers. I shall never forget the sight. The cuirassiers in their sparkling steel breastplates and helmets mounted on strong black horses with great blue rugs across the croups, were galloping towards me, tearing up the earth as they went, the trumpets blowing wild notes in the midst of the discharges of grape and canister shot from the heights. Around me there was one continuous noise of clashing arms, shouting of men, neighing and moaning of horses. What were we to do?... There being no officers about, we saw nothing for it but to go straight at them and trust to Providence to get through. There were half a dozen of us Greys and a dozen of the Royals and Eniskillens on the ridge. We all shouted 'Come on lads; that's the road home!' And dashing our spurs into our horses' sides set off straight for the lancers. But we had no chance. I saw the lances rise and fall for a moment, and Sam Tar, the leading man of ours go down amid the clash of steel... The crash as we met was terrible; the horses began to rear and bite and neigh loudly, and then some of our men got down among their feet, and I saw them trying to ward off the lances

with their hands. 'Stick together lads', we cried and we went at it with a will slashing about us right and left over our horses necks. The ground around us was very soft and our horses could hardly drag their feet out of the clay. Here again I came to the ground for a lancer finished my new mount and I thought I was done for… It was just then I caught sight of a squadron of British Dragoons making straight for us. The Frenchmen at that instant seemed to give way and in a minute more we were safe. The Dragoons gave us a cheer and rode on after the lancers. They were the men of our 16th Light Dragoons of Vandeleur's brigade who not only saved us but threw back the lancers into the hollow.[18]

Dickson managed to scramble up the slope and rejoin the regiment, which was being mustered by Major Cheney. He lived to fight during the rest of the day, but just before the 16th Light Dragoons intervened, after he had to get off his second horse, he had come to a ploughed field and there he saw:

A spectacle I will never forget. There lay brave old Ponsonby, the General of our Union Brigade beside his little bay, both dead. His long fur lined cloak had blown aside and at his hand I noticed a miniature of a lady and his watch; beyond him our brigade major Reignolds of the Greys.[19]

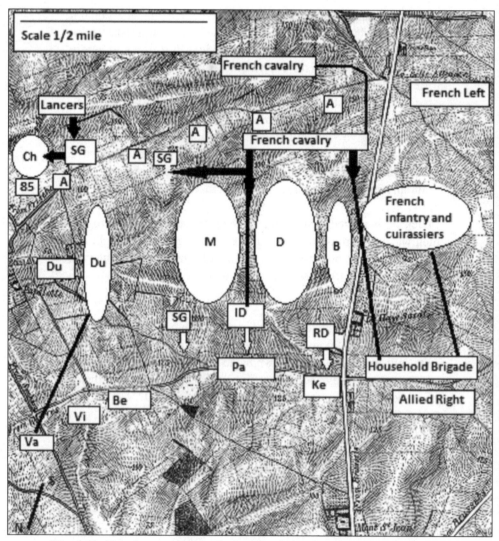

Map 3 The French counterattack. The Royals are already withdrawing, shepherding their prisoners back to Allied lines, as are some of the Inniskillings. The bulk of the Scots Greys are fired on by the 85th and in moving away attack the reforming 3rd Chasseurs. At that moment Bro attacks with his 4th Lancers and, following Sir William's death, the 4th Lancers from the left and the cuirassiers from the right sweep the valley of any British cavalry from the Union and Household brigades.

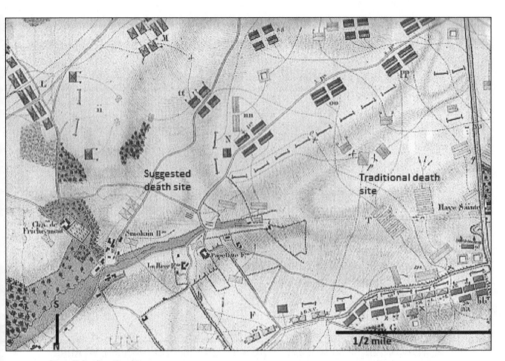

Possible death site

Most books assume Sir William's death to have occurred in front of the Grand Battery in a fairly central position. This assumes that he was cut down on his return from being in the Grand Battery, which we now know was not the case. Participants in the charge reported that most casualties were incurred among those who turned eastwards to return to the Allied position. General Pack simply wrote to Richard Ponsonby that Sir William's body had been found 'half a mile in front of our position', but that could have been anywhere in front of the Allied line. Colonel Best, who found the body the next day, does not say where. We know that Sir William was with the bulk of the Scots Greys, who had attacked the square of the 85th de la Ligne and, on being repulsed, had attacked the 3rd Chasseurs who were re-forming in the vicinity of the 85th. From the account of Colonel Bro and the sketch he drew in 1819 it is clear the lancers attacked from the south. Bro mentions the Scots Greys being to the right of a 'small wood' as he approached, and the only wood in proximity to the French appears on the 1774 Ferraris map and the map drawn in 1816 by the Dutch surveyor Willem Craan. Bro never mentions the Grand Battery and we should assume Sir William and the Scots Greys were closer to the wood than the Grand Battery, otherwise Bro would have mentioned the Grand Battery to place the action. Interestingly, Siborne missed the wood off his later map. Local legend has it that some form of formal planting took place as a memorial to Sir William, and a geophysics survey in 2015 revealed formal planting in the wood.

Chapter 17

How Did Sir William Die?

To Dickson, staggering back to the Allied lines, it was all too clear what had happened. Sir William and Reignolds had been killed by the lancers.

> They both had been pierced by the lancers a few minutes before we came up. Near them was lying a lieutenant of ours Carruthers of Annandale. My heart was filled with sorrow at this, but I dared not remain for a moment.[1]

Anyone who has seen the wonderful film *Waterloo* is all too aware of what is supposed to have happened. In the film Michael Wilding, playing Sir William, accompanied by a trooper, is chased by a number of lancers across a ploughed field. Wilding gives the trooper some of his possessions, asking him to give them to his son, and says 'Save yourself'. He then draws his sabre and, as his horse struggles through a muddy bog, he is stabbed to death by the lancers, as is the unfortunate trooper.

Apart from ignoring the inaccuracies of the film, such as handing over mementos to be given to a son that did not exist, and telling Uxbridge before the start of the charge that his father had been killed in battle by lancers due to riding an inferior horse, when his father was actually a civilian who never had any combat experience, do we actually know what happened? In the last few years letters have emerged claiming that Sir William was shot rather than lanced to death, but was he killed trying to get back to the British lines, or attempting to do something else?

The popularly accepted account of Sir William's death has its origin in the *Gentleman's Magazine*, an eighteenth/nineteenth-century equivalent of the *Spectator*. It was produced a month in arrears, so June 1815's *Magazine* was sold towards the end of July 1815. The June 1815 edition carried Wellington's Dispatch and an obituary of Sir William, recording his funeral on 10 July. This gave no details of his actual death besides saying:

> It is said (but we hope untruly) that he lost his life in consequence of the indiscreet valour of two of his regiments, who contrary to his orders, continued the pursuit nearly two miles beyond the infantry; and that, whilst restraining their rashness, he fell covered with wounds and with glory in his 43rd year. Most of those who thus led to the death of their Commander shared his fate.[2]

When August's magazine was released in September the *Gentleman's Magazine* stated that the cause of Sir William's death had been 'erroneously reported'. The reality was that it:

> was occasioned by his being badly mounted. He led his brigade against the Polish lancers, and checked at once their destructive charges against the British infantry; but having pushed on at some distance from his troops, accompanied only by one aide de camp, he entered a ploughed field where the ground was excessively soft. Here his horse stuck, and was utterly incapable of extricating himself. At this instance a body of lancers approached him at full speed. Sir William saw that his fate was decided. He took out a picture and his watch and was in the act of delivering them to his aide de camp to deliver to his wife and family, when the lancers came up; they were both killed on the spot. His body was found lying beside his horse, pierced with seven lance wounds. Before the day was over the Polish lancers were almost entirely cut to pieces by the brigade which this brave officer had led against them.[3]

Thus the popular version was changed, from Sir William losing his life due to some of his troops' indiscretions, to it being his own fault that he was badly mounted and had become separated from his men. He had, the *Gentleman's Magazine* decided, died a tragic hero's death, which his troops had avenged later in the day. We do not know who came up with the second report, but it achieved great currency, being repeated verbatim in many of the accounts written in the five years after the battle, such as Mumford's.

Thanks to the *Gentleman's Magazine* regimental honour had been protected, but myths had been created. Not the least of these was the claim that Sir William met his death at the hands of Polish lancers. This was untrue. There were 125 Polish lancers at Waterloo, but they formed part of Napoleon's bodyguard and were on another part of the battlefield. The French had converted many of their light dragoon regiments into lancers, and it was these that were involved in the attack on the Union Brigade. The Polish lancers had a legendary reputation. They had, after all, decimated English troops at Albuera in the Peninsular War, so perhaps it was felt that the British public wanted the Union Brigade to have suffered at the hands of the best. But this is not what happened.

Also, if both Sir William and his ADC were killed, how did the story of the handing over of his picture and watch arise? Further, none of Sir William's ADCs were killed at Waterloo.

There is also doubt about the number of lance wounds Sir William received. Major General Pack reported one, but Frenchman Lieutenant Martin had heard there were seven.[4] There are no accounts of a medical examination, although one would have been undertaken, just as with the body of Lieutenant Colonel Hamilton of the Scots Greys, so again we don't actually know for certain.

To find out what actually happened we have to dig deeper and try and find alternative accounts not based on the *Gentleman's Magazine* or from before September 1815. Sadly some of the key individuals who could have told us were killed in the battle, or were too busy fighting for their own lives to notice what happened.

From the English accounts we know that Sir William had his staff with him. When we left Sir William he and his staff (Hamilton, de Lacy Evans, Braithwaite Christie and Reignolds) had collected a group of thirty troopers before Colonel Hamilton recklessly intervened. Archibald Hamilton said that Sir William and his staff followed them: 'in the hopes of stopping them we followed and passed between the columns of the French infantry, when their Red lancers closed behind us.'[5] Archibald Hamilton then had to fight off a lancer, which meant he could not see what was happening to the general. 'Upon getting quite clear of the French, the first person I saw was Captain de Lacy Evans, our General's extra aide de camp, who had lost sight of the General some minutes before I had.' Hamilton then says that he rode to other senior officers, to persuade them to intervene to 'recover the General and such other of our officers who were in the hands of the French.'[6]

So both Hamilton and de Lacy Evans believed Sir William was a prisoner, not that he had been killed. They cannot therefore have seen his body alongside those of Reignolds and Carruthers on the ploughed field.

Where Sir William was killed is important. Dickson described the ploughed field where he saw the body as not being in the hollow, but it was also not where the Grand Battery was, as he passed through it on his way back from the Grand Battery. There were guns there, and we now know that some of the Grand Battery pieces were moved forward to further support d'Erlon's corps and that some guns had been left further forward by Durutte.[7]

De Lacy Evans, riding with Sir William, never refers to their position as being among the Grand Battery. He says:

> We ascended the first ridge occupied by the enemy and passed several French cannon, on our right hand towards the road abandoned on our approach by their gunners, and there were some French squares of infantry in rear.[8]

He also says 'the spot where Sir William fell, and his body was found by us the next morning, was… on the ridge to which I have before alluded and on which the enemy had I think occasionally their advanced batteries in the early part of the battle.[9]

We know that this first ridge was 500–600 metres from the ridge occupied by the Allies. The Grand Battery was originally further back, and most of the guns would stay in their original position. De Sales, the French commander of artillery, stated he planned to move the whole Grand Battery forward to better support d'Erlon's attack, but he was attacked by the Union Brigade when only some had been moved forward. The soldiers and artillery men fled. The only people who seemed to keep their cool were the 85th de Ligne, arranged in square protecting twelve of Durutte's guns that did not belong to the Grand Battery.[10]

The role of the 85th is of critical importance. The regiment was weak in numbers, about 600 men, and therefore deemed by Durutte not to be strong enough to take part in the attack up the slope. However, as Chapuis, captain of the 85th grenadiers, wrote, many of the men had been prisoners of war in England and they were thirsting for revenge. The 85th was commanded by an enterprising colonel called Masson, who had recently been appointed to the command from his previous regiment, the 3rd Tirailleurs de la Garde. The 85th's designated task was to protect twelve of Durutte's own guns that he had left behind to serve as support for his advancing division. They were on an advanced slope some distance in front of the Grand Battery and were placed to the left of Durutte's division. It was Masson who had decided the 85th should be in a square of two ranks.[11]

De Lacy Evans' account of Sir William's body being found on this advanced ridge is corroborated by Sir Denis Pack, William's friend, who wrote the very day after the battle to Sir William's brother Richard, the Bishop of Londonderry: 'His body was found this morning about half a mile in front of our position pierced through the breast with a lance and he died seemingly without pain.'[12] What was Sir William doing on this advanced slope or ridge?

Sir William had certainly been with the Scots Greys. Sergeant Ewart, who captured the eagle of the French 45th de Ligne, says in a letter written on 16 August 1815 that after he had had captured the eagle he was attacked first by a lancer, then by an infantry soldier, and that after he had disposed of these two attackers he showed the captured eagle to Sir William. As the lancers only put in an appearance as part of the counterattack, it seems that Ewart took the eagle a little later than previously believed.

> I presumed to follow my comrades Eagle and all but was stopped by the General saying to me 'You brave fellow, take that to the rear, you have done enough until you get quit of it' which I was obliged to do but with great reluctance.[13]

Certainly Sir William was not a spectator general. He was fighting alongside his men. Sergeant William Clarke of the Scots Greys, who had ridden in the charge, wrote in a letter to his parents in July 1815: 'And brave General the Honourable Sir William Ponsonby being at our head the whole time, fought like a lion.'[14]

It seems clear from Lieutenant Ingilby's account, quoted in the previous chapter, that Lieutenant Colonel Hamilton took only a small number of Scots Greys with him in his crazy charge to the Grand Battery.[15] Up to this moment casualties had been light among the Scots Greys in their attack on Marcognet's division, so even allowing for those troops shepherding prisoners back there were probably still 150–200 Scots Greys on this part of the battlefield. They did not participate in the attack on the Grand Battery, but do seem to have joined in the attack on other French troops in that area of the battlefield. Lieutenant Wyndham of the Scots Greys states in a response to Siborne:

In descending the hill, about three or four hundred yards from the hedge, the Greys came into contact with a second French column or square, regularly formed, the fire from which they received [and which] did great execution. The loss at this moment in men and horses was most severe. The column was nearly destroyed and the remainder of it were taken prisoners.[16]

Wyndham states that these French troops were not the same as the ones from whom the eagle was captured, and therefore did not belong to Marcognet.[17]

French accounts of the battle fortunately give us a clear picture of what Sir William was doing on this ridge. Hyacinthe-Hippolyte de Mauduit (1794–1862) covers this in his indispensable work *Les Derniers Jours de la Grande Armée*: Hippolyte had joined the French Army in 1813 and had fought in Germany and in the campaign for France in which he had been wounded. He gave up his rank of sous lieutenant to become a sergeant in the grenadier regiments of the Old Guard and fought at Ligny and Plancenoit during the Hundred Days. After the Bourbons had been forced to abdicate in 1830 and the new Constitutional Monarchy was trading off the legendary heroics of the period Mauduit became the editor of a French military journal. In *Les Derniers Jours* he reproduced key documents from the lead up to the battle and the battle itself. He also corresponded with and interviewed a lot of the French survivors. Mauduit writes of the attack of cavalry on Durutte's brigade: 'the squadrons of this brigade which made for the column of General Durutte paid dearly for the part they would play in that bloody action.'[18]

He adds:

Colonel Masson feeling that his isolated position would be dangerous made his regiment form a single square of two ranks its numerical weakness preventing it from being three ranks deep. But full of confidence in himself this brave colonel passed on this feeling to his soldiers and it was in this fortunate situation that the English dragoons found this small phalanx, at the moment of the disorganisation of the six other battalions of the division.[19]

Mauduit says that Durutte's division was:

suddenly surprised on the march by a column of dragoons who appear on the summit of the ridge, swoop down on it, and take it from the front and on its left flank and throw it into great confusion. In this brawl Durutte's division loses at least 300 men, of whom about 200 are taken prisoners and taken behind the wood forming the fulcrum of the allied line.[20]

Audaciously pursuing their success these dragoons arrive on the first side of the square of the 85th but a lively and organised fire stops them short. The ground is strewn with men and horses. The energetic cries of '*Vive l'empereur!*' ring from everyone in this small but formidable human fortress, proving to the bold cavalrymen the uselessness of their attempts. There, their charge broken, they are forced to swirl about until the time when in their turn they are charged wholeheartedly by the 3rd regiment of chasseurs à cheval of Jacquinot's division.[21]

Durutte says that his artillery was attacked by 150 dragoons who: 'sabre some of the gunners, the others take flight, the drivers cut the traces from the horses and ride off so that the artillery remains without horses.'[22]

Those historians who have paid any attention to this action have assumed this was Frederick Ponsonby's regiment of the 12th Light Dragoons from Vandeleur's brigade, and this would certainly tie in with the account of Durutte's column being surprised, but it is quite clear from the 85th's officers that there were a lot of Scots Greys involved as well. Captain Chapuis was the captain of the grenadier company of the 85th de ligne, present in the square of the 85th, and he states:

> The English cavalry arrive at the first side of the square and are held off by lively fire. The ground is strewn with red jackets and grey horses and our cries of '*Vive l'Empereur*' proved to them that it would not be easy to beat us. They whirled around us.[23]

The Light Dragoons were in blue uniforms, so Scots Greys were clearly involved and in substantial numbers. It seems that the 12th Light Dragoons attacked Durutte's attacking division and pushed them down the slope, then attacked the front of the 85th while the Scots Greys attacked the 85th from the flank, which would tie in with Mauduit's account.

The resistance of the 85th was the first check that the Union Brigade had sustained. What they experienced was what was going to happen to the French cavalry later on in the day when they tried in vain to break the English squares. Horses, as the French cavalry would find out, would not charge a square that preserved its formidable formation of men in rows with bayonets attached to their muskets and a supply of ammunition. Against such a formation cavalry were relatively helpless. They could ride around the square looking for a gap, or attempt to pressurise the infantry to break ranks so they could enter. They could fire their pistols and carbines, but given the lack of precision of these weapons the cavalry were at the mercy of the infantry, who although their weapons were imprecise, given the fact that they were wedged together in a square, could fire more shots than the cavalry and would inevitably hit something.

Over the last few years my friend Gareth Glover has brought inestimable benefits to Waterloo research by searching archives for unpublished accounts of the battle. During this research he has come across a number of letters written by Scots Greys who claim that Sir William was shot rather than lanced to death. If this is true, it is likely to have occurred during the attack on the square of the French 85th.

Sergeant William Clarke of the Scots Greys wrote a letter to his parents on 8 July 1815:

> And brave General the Honourable Sir William Ponsonby being at our head the whole time, fought like a lion and when he was in the act of crying out 'Well done Greys this will be a glorious day' he received a musket ball through his heroic breast which laid him lifeless on the ground. Colonel Hamilton our first colonel was likewise killed on the same spot and 7 more of our officers.[24]

Another sergeant in the Scots Greys, Archibald Johnston, wrote a similar account. As his account contains brigade orders up to December 1815, it cannot be his immediate reminiscences, but it is nevertheless important. He states:

> I have to observe that on our advance to charge, the brave Sir W Ponsonby who was charging at the head of his brigade, after he had the satisfaction of seeing his brigade annihilate the first line of Bonaparte's chosen troops, and advancing upon the second, while crying out 'Well done my brigade' was shot through the breast by a musket ball and instantly expired.[25]

Lieutenant George Gunning of the 1st Royal Dragoons, also writing some time after the battle, wrote:

At the moment Corporal Styles left me going to the rear with the eagle General Ponsonby rode up to me by himself and said 'For God's sake Sir collect your men and retire on the brigade.' At this moment the French infantry on our left advanced rapidly and fired a volley of musketry among the scattered cavalry. By this volley General Ponsonby was killed, within 20 yards of me. I saw him fall from his horse at the bottom of the hollow way to the left of General Picton's Division. The ridiculous story about the General's horse being unmanageable was all a farce to please the lovers of the marvellous. I was severely wounded by the same volley of musketry and in a few seconds afterwards my horse had his near fore leg struck by a cannon ball. I then made my way into the square of the 28th Regiment of Foot (General Picton's division) with several other dismounted men, and remained there till the evening before I could get a horse to go to the rear.[26]

Then there is the account of Captain Charles Methuen, also of the Royals. This was written from Brussels on 27 June 1815:

Soon after the first charge General Ponsonby, in endeavouring to reform the men, received a shot through the head which deprived the brigade of a most gentlemanlike and excellent officer.[27]

There are a number of problems with Gunning's and Methuen's accounts. Firstly there is the position of the Royals at the right of the brigade, compared to the Scots Greys on the left, and the Scots Greys are adamant that Sir William was with them when he was shot. Although some Royals did get mixed up with the Scots Greys, they did tend to stay closest to the crossroads. According to Gunning Sir William's death seems to occur early on in the charge, before he had moved over to the Inniskillings and then the Scots Greys. Gunning could have joined the Scots Greys, but the fact that he states he took refuge in the square of the 28th, which was in the centre of Kempt's brigade, suggests he didn't. As for Captain Methuen, he was not at Waterloo, and obtained his account from speaking to wounded officers who did take part in the battle. One of these might have been Gunning. Secondly, there is the nature of the wound itself. Given that the body was examined the next day, such an obvious wound as a shot in the head would have been noticed and commented on – but it wasn't.

Coming up against the gunfire from an infantry square was not the only thing the Scots Greys were going to experience in this small area of the battlefield. As Captain Chapuis noted 'and everything that our fire spared was soon destroyed by a regiment of lancers and a regiment of chasseurs a cheval that were a short distance behind the 85th'.[28]

We know that the two regiments involved were the 3rd Chasseurs and the 4th Lancers. The 3rd chasseurs, having lost men due to Allied artillery and to the earlier charge of the light dragoons, numbered fewer than 350 men. Mauduit credits General Bruno with the decision to split his force and attack some of the Scots Greys frontally, and some in the flank: 'The charge executed with great energy had full success. The English column was shattered and to avoid destruction it changes its direction to the left and retires in great disorder.'[29]

Unfortunately, the Scots Greys ran into the lancers. This was the blow that everyone remembered and it came from the 300 men of the 4th Lancers, commanded by Colonel Bro. Bro himself wrote an account that explains what happened:

The Marcognet division speeds up but can't save a battery taken by the troops of Ponsonby who charges at the head of the grey dragoons of Scotland. Our infantry, cut into pieces, breaks up. Drouet d'Erlon orders the cavalry to charge. A waterlogged terrain doesn't allow us to manoeuvre with ease. I reposition my 4th lancers. To the right of a small wood we notice the English cavalry which promptly re-formed are threatening to outflank the 3rd chasseurs. I put myself at the head of the squadrons shouting 'Let us go my children, we must overthrow this rabble.' The soldiers reply 'Forward. Long live the Emperor!' Two minutes later impact occurs. Three ranks of the enemy are overturned. We hit the others badly. The mêlée is becoming terrible. Our horses crush dead bodies and the cries of the wounded come from everywhere. For a moment I'm like someone lost in the powder smoke. When it clears I notice some English officers who surround Second Lieutenant Verranne the eagle bearer. Rallying some men I go to his rescue. Sergeant Major Orban kills General Ponsonby with a blow of his lance. My sabre cuts down three of his captains. Two others are able to flee. I return to the front to save my adjutant major. I had emptied my second pistol when all of a sudden I felt my right arm paralysed. With my left hand I cut down the aggressor who defied me. A dizzy spell forces me to grab hold of my horse's mane. I had the strength to say to Major Perrot 'Take command of the regiment'. General Jacquinot having arrived sees the blood soaking my clothes, takes hold of me and says 'Withdraw' and leaves for the charge. Major Motet cut my dolman and applied a shredded linen bandage saying 'This isn't fatal but you mustn't stay here'. I am so furious at leaving my squadrons I weep.[30]

So the French commander on the spot gives us a new account. Sir William is not alone. He has reformed enough English cavalry in three ranks to threaten to overthrow Jacquinot's first attacking regiment, the chasseurs, and to inflict damage on two squadrons of lancers. In this area the lancers are not in small groups, but in two squadrons numbering 300 men. The clash happens close to a wood and visibility is obscured by smoke, probably from the infantry square of the 85th. We are also given the name of the man who kills Sir William, Sergeant Major Orban.

It seems to me that there is a great deal of truth in Bro's account. Besides the obvious point that he had no reason to falsify it, he gives us two key pieces of corroborative information. Firstly he pinpoints the action, not near the Great Battery but close to a small wood. The Ferraris map of the area, supplied to me by Robert Pocock and produced in the 1770s, shows a small wood in this area. It also appears in the Craan map of 1816 but not in Siborne's. Close to it today is another wood, which a local guide, Alasdair White, says has a formal element to it, which locals say was planted after the battle to commemorate the place where Sir William was slain. Secondly, there is the name of Sir William's killer. There was a marechal de logis in the 4th Lancers called Orban (sometimes referred to as Urban) at Waterloo. Thanks to French Napoleonic websites we know something about him. He was born François Orban on Thursday 15 January 1778 at Bettant in eastern France, and had made his career in the military. He served in the 9th Dragoons and was made a Chevalier of the Legion d'Honneur on 28 September 1813. He had become a sergeant in the first company of the first squadron of the 4th regiment of chevaux-léger lancers in March 1815. After Waterloo he lived in retirement on his parents' small landholding in St Denis en Bugey and died in 1848 in Bettant.[31]

Mauduit gives further details of Orban's actions and it is quite clear that he spoke to or corresponded with Orban after the Battle of Waterloo. In *Les Derniers Jours*, having noted Napoleon's orders for the cuirassiers to charge, he states:

But already the divisions of Subervie and Jacquinot by a manoeuvre as usefully executed as it was bold hit the line of retreat of the English Dragoons and charged them with such impetuosity that they created disorder in their squadrons. About 40 of the lancers from the 4th regiment were killed or disabled in this fight. Colonel Bro received for his part a sabre blow of such violence on his right arm that he almost lost his shoulder and fell on the field of battle. Three officers were equally wounded and a fourth was captured. The other regiments also took losses in this hand to hand combat.

Le Marechal de logis Urban from the elite company of the 4th lancers, already a recipient of the legion d'honneur, gave on this occasion new evidence of his skilfulness and boldness which merits its place in this book.

Having noticed at the head of the English dragoons, a general officer, Urban goes straight at him and takes him prisoner, not on foot, as several historians have said but on horseback and sabre in hand. Some seconds later, some dragoons rush to the aide of their chief. Urban, fearing that they are going to snatch his prisoner who is already looking to see if he can escape from him, decides to his great regret to strike him down [à le renverser sur les pieds]. It was General Ponsonby.

Among the dragoons who advance one of them still holds in his hand the flag of the 45th which he is looking to take away. Urban swoops down on him like the speed of lightning, with a blow of his lance directed at the defective shoulder of his horse he unhorses him and in a second, powerfully strikes, and kills the soldier who is trapped under his horse.

Urban now turns on a second adversary who wanted to avenge his general and his comrade, Urban kills him as well and crowns his prodigious exploits by retaking the eagle of the 45th and takes it to his colonel at the gallop.[32]

Again, there are some discrepancies in Mauduit's account. Colonel Bro survived Waterloo and therefore did not fall on the field as Mauduit claims, although we know from Bro's own account that he was seriously wounded. Secondly, the French recapturing the eagle of the 45th did not occur, but other French accounts claimed that other French standards were recaptured.[33] So what about the rest of Mauduit's account?

I believe there are a number of points that support the claim that

Orban killed Sir William. First is the fact that he admits to killing Sir William in cold blood (a dishonourable act given the concept of honour of those times). Orban is unlikely to have admitted this if it was not true.

Second, Orban obtained Sir William's sword. Having been defeated in combat, Sir William would have offered his sword to Orban. In 1928 Sir John Ponsonby, who subsequently wrote the family history, was then a major general who had served in the First World War. He was approached by a former French cuirassier officer called T. Barbet de Vaux. Barbet de Vaux, who was also a military collector, claimed he had Sir William's sword, which he subsequently gave to Sir John as a sign of France and England being allies in the First World War. Previously he had shown the sword to Sir Douglas Haigh and a French general. He claimed that when Orban retired the sword was mounted above the fireplace in Orban's home. When Orban died, he had no direct descendants so the sword was sold and went through a number of hands until Barbet de Vaux acquired it.[34] (See Appendix C)

The sword is still in the family's possession. It is a Spanish blade and is dated to the time Sir William was in Madrid after Salamanca. It was made for either a French senior officer or a Spanish sympathiser, as it has inscribed in Spanish on the blade 'Long Live the Emperor'. The scabbard bears the Ponsonby arms and is dated to the time Sir William was in Madrid. It is possible that Sir William, when he was in Madrid, rode past a sword shop and decided after the events at Salamanca and Majalahonda that he would buy a blade of Toledo steel. No doubt the sword manufacturer was willing to sell it as he did not believe the French would return and all his handiwork would be wasted. It is a superb piece.

Thus I believe there is enough evidence to suggest that Sir William did die a hero's death, but not as the writer of the second account in the *Gentleman's Magazine* envisaged. After the success of the charge, in which Sir William had ridden from the right to the left of his brigade, he was with the Scots Greys. He had seen Lieutenant Colonel Hamilton take some of the Scots Greys on a wild goose chase towards the Grand Battery, despite his and his staff's best efforts to stop them. He then moved on, with the main part of the Scots Greys, to attack the French guns of Durutte and the square of the 85th de ligne. He had seen Jacquinot's cavalry move to prevent the Scots Greys from retreating to the Allied position on the ridge. He had managed to pull together sufficient men to attack the French chasseurs, and also the lancers, in an attempt to get the rest of his troops back to safety. It was bad luck for him that some of his men thought so highly of him that they wanted to rescue him, and his captor would not let them do that.

It is also possible to reconcile the two differing accounts of him being shot or lanced to death. You could be shot without being killed. We have already dismissed Methuen's claim that Sir William was shot through the head, as that would have been known on the 19th when the body was found and General Pack would have reported it to Richard Ponsonby as the cause of death. The sergeants in the Scots Greys, however, have a stronger argument. Although there were widely differing accounts of people's deaths at Waterloo,[35] the sergeants are unlikely to have mistaken someone else for Sir William when they stated he was shot.

Sir William was well known to the Scots Greys. They had been reviewed by him on a number of occasions and the sergeants talk about him in their accounts. The language they record him using fits in perfectly with what we know of him from other accounts. We also now know that the shot could have come from the square of the 85th, which was very close to the action against the 4th Lancers of Colonel Bro.

It is possible that Sir William was first wounded by a musket shot and then killed by a lance. The close proximity of the 85th de Ligne infantry regiment, in square to the counterattack of the 4th Lancers, makes this a distinct possibility. It is also supported by what happened to James Carruthers of Annandale, a lieutenant in the Scots Greys. Dickson says he saw Carruthers' body near those of Sir William and Reignolds. Sergeant Johnston of the Scots Greys recorded that the day after the battle he had found Carruthers before he died. Carruthers had told him his horse had been brought down by a musket shot and that, lying trapped, he had later been stabbed by a man with a spear, in other words, a lance.[36]

So perhaps Sir William received a musket ball wound from the 85th, but it was not fatal. A musket ball wound in the main part of the body is much less noticeable than a head wound, particularly if there is another, more noticeable wound, such as that from a lance. If Sir William had been wounded by a musket ball it would have made it easier for Orban to take him prisoner. There is some circumstantial evidence to support this. In Mauduit's account Orban says that after taking Sir William prisoner Sir William looked to see if he could escape. Again this is contrary to the concept of honour of the time, as Sir William would have given his parole and could only be released from it with Orban's agreement. Could Sir William's movements be explained by his body's reactions to the effects of the musket wound?

That Sir William could have been wounded twice is also supported by Lady Conyngham's account, in which she wrote: 'I saw a man who was by Sir W Ponsonby when he fell he says he suffered nothing that his death was instantaneous that he never spoke after the first wound.'[37]

This individual was Braithwaite Christie, Sir William's aide de camp. Unlike Hamilton and de Lacy Evans, who believed Sir William might have been taken prisoner, Braithwaite Christie was under no such illusion. Sergeant Ewart recorded in a letter:

About two or three o'clock in the afternoon of the 18th I was ordered by an officer of the 42nd to take the eagle to Brussels. General Ponsonby's aide de camp overtook me and passed me on the road and informed me first that the general was killed.[38]

Unfortunately no letter from Braithwaite Christie has survived which could confirm all this. We will never really know whether Sir William was shot before being lanced to death, but it is a possibility. One wound from a musket ball could have easily been followed by the fatal blow from a lance. Certainly the lance wound alone caused a great deal of damage. Colonel Best, who found the body the next day, referred to Sir William's shirt as being 'entirely soaked in blood', having been 'struck through the chest and body' (see pp214–215).

Regardless of whether he had both gun and lance wounds, or just a lance wound, what we do know is that Sir William died bravely after leading a brilliant charge which destroyed Napoleon's main attack, caused many casualties and saved Wellington's army from defeat.

Chapter 18

'Dulce et Decorum est pro Patria Mori'

At Waterloo soldiers were no respecters of the dead bodies of comrades or enemies. Sir Thomas Picton's aide recounted that he had to stop an English soldier rifling the general's pockets as he slumped dead off his horse at Waterloo, and they hastily buried his body to prevent it suffering any indignities.[1] Soldiers recounted tales of robbing dead friends and enemies indiscriminately.[2] We have to remember that life was cheap, existence hard and if you did find anything of value – well the deceased didn't need it anymore, and it would be more useful to you. When night fell the situation worsened as the camp followers and local peasants scoured the battlefield to take anything they could use: uniforms, trousers, shoes. Men of the Scots Greys were found the next day having been stripped so they only wore their shirts.[3] Lieutenant Carruthers, whom Dickson had seen lying near Sir William, had his watch and other possessions stolen and was stripped of all but his shirt before he was found the next day.[4]

A general's body was more conspicuous than most for pillaging. Orban had retained Sir William's sabre,[5] and I do wonder if the account of Sir William attempting to hand over his watch derives from Dickson seeing it lying on the ground after someone had been disturbed rifling the body. Sir William's body lay on the battlefield for up to eighteen hours before it was found. It was an area crossed by the French, the Prussians, the British and the scavengers and we have to accept that it was subjected to all sort of indignities. Indeed Lady Conyngham's account stated that Sir William was recognised by his features, implying not from his uniform.

Wellington received a report that Sir William was dead early on the morning of 19 June while he was writing his report to Lord Bathurst, and immediately added a postscript:

Since writing the above, I have received a report that Major General the Hon Sir William Ponsonby is killed; and in announcing this intelligence to your Lordship, I have to add the expression of my grief for the fate of an officer who had already rendered very brilliant and important services and who was an ornament to his profession.[6]

Lord Stanhope, in his conversation with the Duke of Wellington on 4 October 1839, obtained more information on the effect the news had on the Duke:

He had begun writing the Waterloo Dispatch very soon on the morning of the 19th, a little later Doctor Hume informed him of the death of Gordon and other losses; but when he learnt later that Ponsonby was fallen, he stopped, feeling that it was no longer possible to write. He did not start writing it again until after arriving in Brussels later in the morning.[7]

However, the body was probably not found until first light, by Braithwaite Christie and Sir William's servant, who were deliberately looking for it. Lady Conyngham stated that Braithwaite Christie had ridden to Brussels after Sir William's death to inform Lord Conyngham and then returned to the battlefield. In this extract from a letter from Marchioness Conyngham, dated 6 August 1815 from Brussels, she writes:

His Aide de Camp came to Brussels more dead than alive. My son saw him immediately and thought he would have fainted as he walked upstairs he wanted to see Lord C who was out and wished him to write to the family, he went the next morning and found the body, it was known by the sweet smile which was still visible on his fine countenance where goodness and kindness were marked with such strong lines that it was impossible to mistake them.[8]

Very recently a letter from Colonel Charles Best was sold at Bonham's. In it is the following statement:

I also found Major General William Ponsonby who was struck through the chest and body – he was stripped except his shirt which was entirely soaked in blood. I ordered my men to remove it to a farmhouse, his poor servant having recognised his master came to me to request this favour.[9]

Once found, due respect could be paid and the body was placed in a coffin and escorted by Braithwaite Christie to Ostend and then via gun brig to Deal. The 'Shipping News' in the *Times* for 7 July 1815, recorded that on 5 July at Deal:

Arrived the Urgent gun brig with the body of the gallant Sir William Ponsonby from Ostend. It has been landed at the Navy yard attended by all the officers here, and remains for further arrangements at the barracks.[10]

Obviously, William's family had to be informed. General Pack wrote a letter to Sir William's brother Richard, the Bishop of Derry, from a 'Bivouac near Jenappe (sic)' on 19 June:

My Dear Sir

You may well conceive the feelings with which I take up my pen to tell you of the fall of my dear friend William in the glorious but murderous battle of yesterday.

He was immediately in rear of my Brigade with his Cavalry, and on our advancing to support the first line (Dutch troops) which had given way to a furious attack on that part of the position in our front, he followed up our advance by an instantaneous and most gallant charge by which nearly 1,000 Prisoners and 3 eagles were taken. The numbers of the enemy were immense both cavalry and infantry, and the impetuosity of his men carried them beyond support and their loss in consequence was dreadfully severe.

His body was found this morning about half a mile in front of our position pierced through the breast with a lance and he died seemingly without pain.[11]

We don't know for certain who had the horrendous task of breaking the news to Georgiana, pregnant with Sir William's child, and to his daughters. But a series of letters to Mary Lady Grey gives us an idea of the catastrophic blow that fell on the family and how they reacted to it. On 30 June the Earl of Somerset wrote to Charles Grey:

My Dear Lord

I can no longer delay taking up my pen to ask you how Lady Grey is? I heard of the sad loss she has sustained with the most heartfelt sorrow but I could not resolve to intrude upon your time till now. Pray give me one line this is not an enquiry of design be assured. I feel the liveliest interest in everything that affects you and yours and no calamity can reach Lady Grey without my seemly participation in the same. I must beg you also to tell me how Lady Ponsonby is? From what I have heard of her I fear this stroke will go very deep indeed. These are sad times – I feel so exceedingly when is this effusion of blood to stop? And for what are we marching to Paris? After all our professions are we now to force a government upon France? But enough – forgive my troubling you to write. Believe me to remain with the greatest regard

Sincerely yours

Friday 30th

Lord Somerset

Bulstrode

Gerrards Cross[12]

Monday

My Dearest Cousin Mary

You shall not answer me mind – for I only take this scrap of paper to ease my own mind – by telling you that I think of you continually and of poor Lady W Ponsonby though I have never seen her since she was at Margate in love with him she has now lost – of your good mother too! In short it is painful to refrain any longer from saying something to you and a folly to say anything – Lord Ponsonby too! So uncomfortably separated from you all, to reflect alone on all this misery! I am afraid I shall not see you before you leave London. We shall only pass through town on Saturday on our way to the Court and I must look at our next meeting at Howick. I had proposed to myself the greatest delight in this but now I feel you will not have recovered your spirits and indeed in these dreadful times we may expect fresh horrors every day and one domestic calamity only effaced by another, till that accursed little man who was sent into the world to destroy the human race shall himself share the fate of humanity. I cannot bear fine words and sighings on this occasion particularly as all was over. Perhaps someone would have the goodness to tell me how you all are for I will not not have you write. Kindest love to all and forgive me being a bore. Your most affectionate BW[13]

Certainly it was believed that the news of William's death would adversely affect the chances of his cousin Frederick Ponsonby, Lieutenant Colonel of the 12th Light Dragoons, from recovering from his wounds sustained at Waterloo. Lady Caroline Lamb wrote to her brother Lord Duncannon from Ghent on 2 July 1815:

With what joy after hours of agony I now write to tell you that Tournier whom we sent express from hence last night is just returned with news that Fred is at Bruxelles doing well, quite well. Only think what William suffer'd they told him he was dead last night.[14]

Publicly there were mixed emotions: joy at the defeat of Napoleon, but horror at the price that had been paid. The Duke of York led the way:

The triumph of success cannot lessen the regret which must be felt by all, for the loss of the very many valuable lives which has unavoidably attended the accomplishment of this great achievement, and I particularly deplore the fall of Lt General Sir Thomas Picton and Major General Sir W Ponsonby.
I am my lord Duke
Yours sincerely
Frederick Commander in Chief[15]

Lord Edward Somerset, commander of the Household Brigade at Waterloo, wrote to his mother after the battle:

I am truly concerned to say that poor General Ponsonby was killed. I lament him exceedingly he was a most excellent good sort of man and having served three or four campaigns together we were good friends.[16]

The House of Commons voted for memorials to be placed in St Paul's for both Sir William and Sir Thomas Picton. Sir William has the more elaborate memorial, produced by Theed and Bayly. He is portrayed as a typical classical hero from antiquity, having died sword in hand beside his dead horse. Sir William's old regiment, the 5th Dragoon Guards, recorded in their records that they lamented they had not been present at Waterloo to avenge him.

Sir William was not buried in Ireland, but instead at the Molesworth family vault at St Mary's, Kensington. *The Morning Chronicle* on Saturday 15 July recorded the following for 10 July:

On Monday last, the 10th of July the remains of the gallant Major General Sir William Ponsonby were deposited in the family vault at Kensington, belonging to his noble ancestors in the female line. The funeral was conducted with a taste perfectly conformable to the life of the deceased; and was therefore plain, simple and correct; indeed it was so private that the inhabitants within sight of the church knew not for whom it was designed, until the ceremony was over. It was attended by Earl Grey, two of the brothers of the deceased, the Hon General Fitzroy and a few officers and select friends. To bestow high sounding epithets upon the departed and not unfrequently upon those who, whilst living, were thought to be amongst the worthless, is no very infrequent practice; but upon the present occasion it is no bombast to say that England had not within its service a more accomplished officer, nor society within its circle a more amiable man, than Sir William Ponsonby. He was naturally diffident, well bred and unassuming, with a singleness of mind and a simplicity of character, and both of which were so strongly expressed in his countenance, that his appearance induced a prepossession which his genuine worth secured.

He has left four sweet infant daughters but who fortunately for themselves are too young to appreciate their loss and a beautiful widow who is no less sensible of their misfortune than her own; indeed affliction and firmness, grief and resignation, anguish and fortitude, were never more strongly shown than by her Ladyship. She is the daughter of a former Lord Southampton and it is understood her Ladyship is now pregnant and if a son he will be heir presumptive to the title and estates of the present Lord Ponsonby, who has no children.[17]

One person who did not attend the funeral was William's despicable elder brother John. Despite everything William had done for him, John would not appear in England to honour his brother if it meant incurring the risk of imprisonment from his creditors. As he had the gall to write to Mary:

June 30th
My Dearest Mary
Your accounts of my Mother's insistence to preserve some show

of tranquillity have given me the greatest pleasure. I confess I trembled for the effect the shock might have upon her. I hope and trust you also have exerted your fortitude and are composed – have no alarms about me it is true I have now experienced almost the greatest misfortune I could suffer but I submit you must keep your promise of writing to me. I have not courage to remain in uncertainty about your welfare I was on the point of going to London but prudence which is in my situation a necessity made me alter my intention. Adieu my dear Mary. You know how I loved William and preferred him to all and can guess his loss to me but say nothing, poor Georgiana

P[18]

As after all deaths, the living got on with the job of living and the world moved on. On 11 July writs were ordered for a new election for Sir William's parliamentary seat at Londonderry, made vacant by his death. On 6 February 1816 Georgiana gave birth to William's son, whom she called after his father. Young William was a disappointment. He is referred to as keeping bad company and seems to have led an irresponsible existence. He joined the 3rd Light Dragoons as a cornet but did not make a success of his military career. He incurred gambling debts and ultimately had to flee England to avoid his creditors. In 1851 he married Maria Theresa Duerbeck of Munich and settled in Bavaria. They had no children. Georgiana never remarried. She moved from Hampstead into a house at Earls Court with her children. She sometimes attended receptions at Court and died in 1835. All William's daughters married.[19]

Remembrance became an annual event. On Tuesday 18 June 1816 the gentlemen of the County of Roxburgh held a meeting at Jedburgh to commemorate the battle of Waterloo. One toast was to 'Major General Sir William Ponsonby's brigade'.[20] Those who attended agreed that the anniversary should be made permanent. Similarly, in Edinburgh a dinner was held in the Assembly Rooms, one of the toasts being: 'The Memory of Sir William Ponsonby – drunk in silence – Tune Patrick's day in the morning.'[21]

Printmakers had a field day portraying Sir William's death at the hands of the lancers. After the Duke of Wellington's death Wellington College was founded as a memorial to him. A bust of Sir William was placed in the quadrangle alongside those of the senior British commanders. In death Sir William had earned a place among the Waterloo heroes.

Chapter 19

Postscript

*'The ills men do live after them, the good is oft interred
with their bones'*

With the passing of time, the recriminations started. Why did the Scots Greys not form the reserve to counter the cavalry attacks? Why was the charge allowed to get out of hand? Accounts of the battle stoked up the desire among those that were left to safeguard personal reputations. Uxbridge claimed he had ordered the Scots Greys to form a reserve. Scots Greys officers claimed he had not. The surviving senior officers: Clifton of the Royals, Muter of the Inniskillings and de Lacy Evans, now a general, kept silent. Lieutenant Colonel Hamilton of the Scots Greys, Reignolds the brigade major, the ADC Braithwaite Christie (d.1825) and Sir William himself were all dead and could make no reply.

A flurry of armchair historians pronounced their own verdicts. To this day a misinformed critic can refer on a website to Sir William's 'incompetent charge'. Jac Weller stated:

Uxbridge himself, as gallant and dashing a man as ever lived, led the Household Brigade, but lost all control of it. Ponsonby led his own with equal bravery and even less knowledge of his job.[1]

Alessandro Barbero, who has written the best book on the subject in recent years, was encouraged to claim that Sir William was deliberately poorly mounted at Waterloo so he wouldn't suffer financial loss if his best horse was killed.[2] In doing so he ignored all the reasons contemporaries gave for why Sir William was poorly mounted, as well as the common sense observation that no one, and certainly not a cavalry general or a member of the Irish landowning class, would put his own life at risk by being poorly mounted if he could avoid it.

Other historians quoted the losses the Union Brigade suffered at Waterloo, not realising that in comparing the numbers at the start of 18 June with those at the start of 19 June they were ignoring the fact that the charge against d'Erlon's infantry was just one of many charges the

Union Brigade made that day. The Union Brigade in fact made up to six more charges, and also suffered severe casualties from artillery fire when the brigade had to stay in line in the late afternoon, exposed to cannon shot in order to steady Wellington's line. Indeed Uxbridge commented: 'Sir William Ponsonby's brigade was very much exposed and constantly engaged during the day, charged very often and always with success.'[3]

The Regimental Records of the Inniskilling Dragoons recorded:

> At about four o'clock the Brigade moved across the Charleroi Road in support of the infantry on the right of the position, where it was again formed in the hottest part of the Battle and where it remained till late in the evening, exposed to the incessant fire of cannon, bombs and musketry, which killed and wounded great numbers.[4]

In fact, the Inniskilling's colonel and its lieutenant colonel were both wounded and forced to quit the field after 6.30pm – not during the Union Brigade's first charge.

Only a few commanders who had been present continued to give Sir William and the Union Brigade credit. Sir Hussey Vivian, the commander of the 6th Cavalry Brigade at Waterloo, who could see all from his position on the Allied left flank, wrote to William Siborne in 1830:

> the desperate attack of the Brigade of Heavy Cavalry under the command of Major General Sir William Ponsonby on the columns of French infantry advancing against our position on the left of the road, and its complete success, had an influence on the battle infinitely greater than has ever been admitted; indeed, having myself witnessed from my position on the left the complete success of the charge, and the consequences to the French infantry I cannot but consider it as one of the most important features of the battle.[5]

At the beginning of the 20th century, as historians wrote new accounts of the Peninsular War, due recognition was given to Sir William's success as a brigade commander. Fortescue wrote:

> Of the brigadiers the names of hardly one has survived, or deserved to survive. The Germans Bock and Arentschildt were probably the best and next after them William Ponsonby, Le Marchant and Vivian.[6]

Hopefully this book has helped to redress the balance.

Appendix 1

Sir William's Brothers and Sister

John Ponsonby (1770?-1855)

John Ponsonby was William's elder brother by one year and his father's heir. He was very handsome and charming. He was very attractive to women, knew it and treated them badly. There is a story that during the French Revolution he was actually going to be hanged as an English aristocrat but was saved at the last moment by a group of French women who claimed he was too handsome to die.

His father had hopes that John would interest himself in politics, but John had an aversion to public speaking and although he sat in the Irish House of Commons twice he never spoke, saying to a friend 'it is all I can do to find nerve for *yes* or *no* when there is a question in the House and that is in a whisper'. He was indolent and it was only much later in life that he discovered he had skills for diplomacy, becoming Envoy Extraordinary to Brazil in 1826, Buenos Aires 1826–28, securing recognition by Great Britain of the independence of Uruguay, Brazil again in 1828–1829, Belgium 1830–1831 and Sicily in 1832–1833. In 1833 he became Ambassador at Constantinople, a position he held until 1841. He was later Ambassador to the Austro-Hungarian Empire (1846–1850). He died in Brighton on 21 February 1855.

In the early part of the nineteenth century John played the role of the 'young man about town', having a house at Curzon Street in Mayfair. Being also financially irresponsible he incurred great debts. But in earlier life he could at least be expected to play his part in widening the Ponsonby family's connections by making a good marriage. He easily seduced Elizabeth Denison, the daughter of a wealthy banker and, given the fact that the Ponsonby family outspent its income, this would have been a very good match. Unfortunately there were no political advantages and John's father ordered him to break off the match. John transferred his attentions to the most notorious courtesan in England, Harriette Wilson, and features prominently in her *Memoirs*, in which she claimed he was the great love of her life and that she was heartbroken when he broke off their affair as he could no longer afford her. On 13 January 1803 he married Lady Frances Villiers, seventh daughter of George Bussey, 4th Earl of Jersey, and his wife Frances, daughter and heiress of Philip, Bishop of Raphoe. Although Lady Frances was a beauty she was unfortunately deaf and the family not as wealthy as had been hoped. So John took solace with Elizabeth Denison again, even though his first rejection of her had almost made her go mad. He would reject her for a second time. In all of this his behaviour was no worse than many of his contemporaries. But it was in stark contrast to William's.

John spent much of his life outside England, firstly avoiding his creditors and secondly as a diplomat. He persuaded William to guarantee some of his debts on the promise that he would repay these. He never did and so when William returned from the Peninsula War in 1814 not only was he put under pressure by his mother to resolve the family's financial problems, but he also found he was still liable for John's debts. On William's death John left the sorting out of the family's financial problems to his youngest brother Frederick, and very rarely replied to any of Frederick's letters.

William's elder brother was a charming rogue with no moral scruples, financial or otherwise.

Richard Ponsonby born at Kildare 5 October 1772, died 27 October 1853

William's younger brother Richard Ponsonby was destined for the church. Again this was an unusual step for the Ponsonby family. None of them to that date had followed an ecclesiastical career. Richard was educated at Trinity College, Dublin. He was ordained in 1795 and appointed Prebendary of Tipper in St Patrick's Cathedral. In 1828 he became Bishop of Killaloo and in 1831 Bishop of Derry. He was also, from 1834, Bishop of Raphoe. In 1804 he married Frances, the fourteenth daughter of the Rt Hon John Staples, and had five children. His wife was reputed to be beautiful, but the worst housekeeper in Dublin. Richard was reputed to be handsome, and a man of talent with courtly manners, but lazy in business. He also gambled heavily, but although not having excessive wealth his income from the Church and his wife's family reduced financial pressures.

George Ponsonby (1773–1863)

George made his life in England and would become a Lord of the Treasury. He was educated at Trinity College, Dublin and Lincoln's Inn. He represented the family in the English House of Commons, sitting for County Kilkenny in 1806, County Cork 1806–12 and Youghal 1826–32. He had a reputation for doing as little work as he possibly could, although he was a member of Lord Grey's cabinet at the time of the Great Reform Bill of 1832. Like other members of the family he was addicted to gambling, but made an advantageous second marriage to Diana, daughter of the Hon Edward Bouverie, brother of the Earl of Radnor. George was a great friend of Edward Bouverie, who left him his estate at Woolbeding in Sussex. He died in 1863.

Frederick Ponsonby (1774–1849)

Frederick, the last son, took on the role of a local squire in later life, becoming saddled with the immense responsibility of running the Bishopscourt estate, which was massively encumbered by his father's and eldest brother John's debts. Frederick was well known and a popular figure in County Kildare and a great sportsman. He presented the Ponsonby Bowl, to be run for by the farmers of Kildare at the Kildare Hunt Races. If it was won three years in succession it became the property of the winner. He was the last Master of the Bishopcourt Hounds and spent his time at home, rarely going away even for a night, and devoted his time to the enjoyment of country pursuits. The local population called him 'The Old Master' and he was a popular figure; when he died, his funeral cortège was met by local people at Rathcoole, where the coffin was taken from the hearse and carried to the chapel at Oughterrard Hill, where he was buried. However, Frederick's life was not without sorrow and bitterness. His letters to his eldest brother, held in Durham University Library, show he felt lonely, put upon, constantly victimised and ignored. He was given to outpourings of bitterness and, unbelievably, was extravagantly delighted to receive any communications from his wayward eldest brother. He sat in Parliament between 1811 and 1813 for the Borough of Galway. Despite his best efforts he had to sell the Bishopscourt estate, amounting to 1,958 acres, in 1838. After that he lost interest in life and died in Dublin in 1849.

Mary Elizabeth Ponsonby (1776–1861)

Louisa's final child was a girl, Mary, who was known for her beautiful and gentle nature. In 1794 she married William's friend, Whig politician

Charles Grey, who would eventually be remembered for posterity as the Prime Minister who ensured the passing of the Great Reform Bill. Charles Grey was twelve years older than Mary, but it was very much a love match and the marriage produced fifteen children. Because of this they were not very wealthy and Mary spent her time between the Grey estate at Howick in Northumbria and their London residence at Portman Square. William's mother spent time with them at Howick. Mary was very supportive of her husband. She and Charles believed in educating their children at home and during the troubles of the Great Reform Bill Mary and her daughters wrote out much of the confidential correspondence. Charles Grey suffered from stomach attacks and it is said that Mary produced a tea blend to soothe this, which is now of course known as Earl Grey tea. It is fitting that recently Twinings have produced Lady Grey tea in her memory.

The 5th Dragoon Guards When William Joined

In 1793 the regiment's authorised establishment was six troops of fifty men each, with a total strength of 363 officers, NCOs and men. The men were very tall. In 1792 only six were shorter than 5ft 9in. The regiment had the reputation for being the best mounted regiment in Ireland, with no horse below 15.2 hands. Troops were armed with swords, pistols and a firelock with bayonet. The officers wore a plain scarlet coat with dark green lapels, white waistcoat and breeches, gold buttons and gold-laced hats. The lapels were changed to yellow between 1791 and 1800. However, green was restored in 1800, leading to the regiment being called 'the Green Horse'.

The pay for a private was one shilling and a halfpenny a day. Captains earned twelve shillings and fourpence per day. Majors had a daily wage of seventeen shillings and fourpence, and lieutenant colonels nineteen shillings and fourpence.

Inspections by Inspecting Generals were uniformly positive, but to prevent staleness the troops were rotated each year through a different area of Ireland. Although some towns had barracks, most troops were lodged in private houses. In the West of Ireland the barracks consisted of thatched cottages for the men and sheds for the horses. The only proper parade ground was in Dublin. Bizarrely, manuals for a standardised form of training cavalry did not exist at that time.

In 1796 the 5th Dragoon Guards, comprising nine troops and totalling approximately 330 men, marched to Bantry Bay to oppose a French landing. However, stormy weather conditions forced the invasion fleet to return to France and the regiment went into camp on the Curragh with other cavalry regiments. There it was inspected and General Wilford, one of the inspecting generals, said it was the best mounted regiment in the camp. In the autumn of 1797 the regiment was moved to Dublin and it was there that William Ponsonby joined it in March 1798.

Appendix 3

Sir William's Sword – The Barbet de Vaux Correspondence with Sir John Ponsonby

Translated from the letters in French appearing in the appendices to Sir John's book *The Ponsonby Family*, pages 221-223.

National Federation of the French Cuirassiers
Paris
22 March 1928

General!
I have neither the honour nor the great advantage of having been presented to you.

For more than 20 years I have been the owner of the battle sabre of your great uncle, Sir William Ponsonby. Surrounded in my collection of the sabres of the most famous generals and French marshals of the Revolution and the First Empire it holds for me the place of honour. It rests on a red velvet display cloth trimmed with gold braid between the sabres of honour of the valorous major generals Thomas Picton and Alexander Mackenzie Fraser: often when I am reading or writing at my desk – which belonged to a marshal of the empire – it pleases me to contemplate this sacred object which I cover with all respect and admiration and not without reason, since by thinking I see your heroic ancestor at the head of the Scots Greys, the Inniskillings and the Royals fighting as a lion for the greater glory of your great country. Frequently also in looking at it I remembered, not without emotion, that the so lamented General Earl Douglas Haigh, accompanied by our General Maugin during a long visit that they made to me at the end of the army in 1918, had taken up this sabre and was pleased to hold it in his hands for several minutes without saying a single word. He then put it back and gave me thanks for preserving it so religiously.

General, permit me now as I was pleased to say to Major Astor that as I see it you have no need to thank me. During the Great War we have been allies to save the world from barbarism; on many occasions I have had the great patriotic joy of seeing your fine troops in action as formerly I had the honour to fight at their side against the Boxers in the column commanded by Admiral Seymour for the taking of Peking. English and French we are now brothers in arms in the purest sense of the term. If therefore you would like me to provide your very illustrious family and you General with the means to have returned to their possession this ancestral weapon, my dearest wishes are satisfied and I will be happy as a collector that this great satisfaction has been given in my life time.

Please accept the expression of my very living gratitude, and the assurance of my great and profound respect to you and your noble family.

T Barbet de Vaux
47 Boulevard de la Chapelle, Paris 10At

Paris
12 April 1928

General!
I am writing concerning the battle sabre of your glorious ancestor General Sir William Ponsonby. The only information I have are the notes that have come down to me. After Waterloo in 1815 the marechal des loges Urban, who had killed him with a lance blow as you know, and took possession of his sabre, was at that time thirty years old. He was made redundant from the army at the beginning of the Restoration and returned to his parents, who were small farmers. On the death of his father in 1824 he succeeded to his property and himself died in 1842 without leaving any children. In accordance with the law at his death the sabre, with the other objects of the estate, was sold to people outside the family, then acquired in their turn by collectors, but at what time I can't tell you.

It is to be presumed, it is certainly to be expected, that when this sabre belonged to your great uncle, like all generals' sabres from this period, it would be covered with a rich gilding. But as Urban, during the twenty-seven years that he survived after the Battle of Waterloo, had kept this glorious trophy well on view at his home, probably above the big fireplace of the farm, little by little the gilding was altered by the air, humidity and smoke.

General, I thank you for the great honour that you have given me in asking for my photograph and my heart of an old soldier takes a great pride in being persuaded by the idea that the sword would stay in your noble family and perpetuate my gesture as I said.

T Barbet de Vaux

Notes

Chapter 1

1. Cooke to Nepean 27 January 1795 (Chatham Papers P.R.O. 8/30/327)
2. Quoted in Wilson F *The Courtesan's Revenge*, Faber & Faber, London 2004.
3. There is a family legend that when challenged by a Royalist friend about how he could support Parliament when his family motto was '*Pro rege, lege, grege*' which most people would have translated as 'For the King, the Law and the People', he immediately responded 'You translate it wrongly, the word *lege* means read and the motto runs thus: *For the king read the people*'. Ponsonby, Sir J. *The Ponsonby Family*, The Medici Society, London, 1929 p15.
4. Ponsonby, Sir J. *The Ponsonby Family*, The Medici Society, London, 1929. Appendix 1 p207.
5. There were very few Parliamentarian families in Cumberland – the Briscoes of Crofton and John Ponsonby being the only examples. As C.B. Phillips showed in his article 'The Royalist North: The Cumberland and Westmorland Gentry 1642–1660' (pages 239–260 R.C. Richardson (ed) *The English Civil Wars Local Aspects*, Sutton Publishing Ltd, 1997) the bulk of Cumberland families were apathetically Royalist. Representatives of some families fought on the Royalist side in the first Civil War, but not in the second, and vice versa. The families' position seemed to be Cumberland first and the king second. This meant that, with a few exceptions, the Royalist families did not do enough to have their lands sequestered and offered for sale by Parliament to its own supporters. Those lands that were sold John Ponsonby could not afford to buy. Also the English government could not afford to remove any of the local families from power, because it needed them to control dissatisfaction in an area that was far from London but at the same time very close to the new problem area of Scotland. Apart from levying some fines –few of which were punitive in nature – and seizing some estates, the Parliamentarian government left West Cumberland in the hands of the royalist Curwens, Huddlestons, Lamplughs, Lowthers, Musgraves and Senhouses, who had ruled the area since medieval times. John Ponsonby was an ambitious man. He looked elsewhere and in Ireland

he believed he would be able to seize an opportunity that was not available in West Cumberland.

It is also possible that as his second wife Elizabeth, daughter of Henry Lord Ffolliot, came from Ballyshannon in Ireland, he might have started to look at Ireland as a land of promise, allowing him to leave Cumberland and Haile and the memories of his deceased first wife Dorothy Briscoe. Whether he was escaping from Cumberland, or attracted to Ireland, we will never know; perhaps it was a mixture of both.

6. Morrill, J. 'Introduction' to Kenyon, J. and Ohlmeyer, J. (joint editors) *The Civil Wars A Military History of England, Scotland and Ireland 1638-1660*, Oxford University Press, 1998
7. Ponsonby, Sir J. *The Ponsonby Family*, The Medici Society, London, 1929, pp 37-38
8. Ibid. pp 39-40
9. Ibid. pp 41-42
10. Ibid. p56
11. Ibid. p62
12. Ibid. 1929 p63
13.This was further increased when Louisa's father died. Lord Bessborough to Lady Bessborough, Holyhead, July 13 1793 (Bessborough, *Lady Bessborough and her family circle*, John Murray, 1940, p96-97) 'I left Mr Ponsonby in London. I believe I told you so. He got a third of Lord Molesworth's estate.'
14. A writer described the Bishopscourt Hunt as follows:
Although the turn out of the Bishopcourt Hunt itself in the four days about which I am thus irregularly jotting down my recollections, was not from the sombre uniform of its members, as flashing and as striking to some eyes who like to dwell on some hundred to hundred and fifty cavaliers decked in scarlet and gold, yet to my eye which was caught more by the aristocratic Master himself, than the coat he had on, the splendid and numerous pack of well bred, well matched, English hounds, the blue coat and velvet cape lined with buff, the broad striped blue and buff waistcoat, yellow buckskins, in fact the dress of the Fox Club with a large yellow button, in which was embossed a fox's pate around which in large legible characters *Bishopcourt Hunt* appeared quite as aristocratic as anyone need wish. Although the right honourable owner of these hounds seemed to take as much satisfaction and delight in the way he was surrounded, yet nothing I could plainly

see was at all to be compared to the marked joy mingled with love and respect which you saw in every member of the Hunt's countenance when riding up to greet their admitted leader in both the house and the field.

Ponsonby, Sir J. *The Ponsonby Family*, The Medici Society, London, 1929, p65

15. Ibid. pp 66–68)

16. Lord Bessborough to Lady Bessborough, Bessborough, July 21 1793 (Bessborough, *Lady Bessborough and her family circle*, John Murray, 1940, p98) 'The house is very large and comfortable but as you may suppose very old-fashioned. There are about 10 or 11 good bed-chambers... The extent of the estate about it is very great, there are 27,000 English acres all lying near together here belonging to me, but a good deal of it in long leases and you must not from that suppose me very rich.'

Chapter 2

1. William's date of birth is given usually as 1772. But if this was the case it would have to be early 1772, as his younger brother Richard was born on 5 October 1772. William's elder brother John died aged 84 on 21 February 1855, which puts his birth date between March 1770 and February 1771.These facts, together with the age given when he matriculated at Cambridge, mean that William must have been born between March 1771 and January 1772.

2. Information courtesy of Adam Green, Assistant Archivist and Manuscripts Cataloguer, Trinity College, Cambridge.

3. The Royal Navy had its own process for educating its officers. Only one notable officer, Homes Riggs Popham, attended Cambridge at this time.

4. The best book on the 1798 rebellion is still Thomas Pakenham's *The Year of Liberty*, Hodder and Stoughton Ltd, London, 1969.

5. Froude, J.A. *The English in Ireland in the 18th Century*, New York, 1874, p185.

6. *The London Gazette* p247.

Chapter 3

1. Pomeroy, Hon. Ralph Legge *The Story of a Regiment of Horse being the regimental history of the 5th Princess Charlotte of Wales Dragoon Guards*, William Blackwood and Sons, Edinburgh and London, 1924. Reprinted Naval and Military Press, p116.

2. Maguire, W.A. *Up in Arms – The 1798 Rebellion in Ireland* The Ulster Museum, 1998, p155.

3. Pomeroy, op.cit., p116.
4. I am indebted to Captain Alan Henshaw, Curator of the 5th Dragooon Guards Museum in York, for his assistance and his putting the regiment's records at my disposal.
5. Pomeroy, op.cit, p117.
6. Pakenham, T. *The Year of Liberty The Great Irish rebellion of 1798*, Hodder and Stoughton Limited, 1969, p 343.

Chapter 4

1. Uglow, J. *In these Times – Living in Britain through Napoleon's Wars* Faber & Faber, London, 2014, Chapter 24. This is a wonderful book drawing on first-hand accounts to portray what it was like to live through this period.
2. Heathcote, R. *Letters of a Young Diplomatist and Soldier during the time of Napoleon*, John Jane, The Bodley Head, London, 1907, p120-138.
3. Ibid. p120-138.
4. Mrs G. Clark (ed) *Gleanings from an Old Portfolio* D. Douglas, Edinburgh, 1896, Vol 3, p134.
5. Evans, R. Major *The Story of the 5th Royal Inniskilling Dragoon Guards*, Gale and Polden Ltd, Aldershot, 1951.
6. Mitchell, L. *The Whig World* Hambledon and London, London, 2005.
7. Mrs G Clark , op.cit, pp 45-46. In 1785 Lady Portarlington wrote to Lady Louisa Stuart: 'and then on another day we went to see Besborough which is a charming place with fine old timber and a very good house with some charming pictures and it felt as warm and as comfortable as if the family had left it the day before and it has not been inhabited these forty years, which I think does great credit to the maid who looks after it.'
8. *The Morning Chronicle*, Tuesday 2 December 1806.
9. Papers of John Viscount Ponsonby, University of Durham GRE/E/ 487/2.
10. Ibid. GRE/E492
11. Ibid. GRE/E487/7

Chapter 5

1. Pomeroy, Hon Ralph Legge *The Story of a Regiment of Horse being the regimental history of the 5th Princess Charlotte of Wales Dragoon Guards*, William Blackwood and Sons, Edinburgh and London, 1924. Reprinted Naval and Military Press, Vol 2 Chapter 4 pages 89-188.

2. Ibid. p248.

3. Ibid. p89-188.

4. Ibid p89-188.

5. Ibid. 89-188.

6. NAM 6807-213 'Anonymous memoirs of a Dragoon'.

7. *Hampshire Telegraph and Sussex Chronicle*, 1811.

8. *Hampshire Telegraph and Sussex Chronicle*, 1811.

9. NAM 6807-213 'Anonymous memoirs of a Dragoon'.

10. Ibid.

11. Ibid.

12. Ibid.

13. Memoirs and Correspondence of Field Marshal Viscount Combermere, London, Hurst and Blackett, 1866, p217.

14. Anon *The British Cavalry on the Peninsula by an officer of Dragoons 1831*, Mark Thompson Publishing, 1996, p78.

15. Ibid. p78.

16. 4) Wellington's dispatches, 1 October 1811 quoted in Pomeroy Hon Ralph Legge, op.cit, p128.

17. General Orders 13 October 1811 and 16 November 1811.

18. NAM 6807-213 'Anonymous memoirs of a Dragoon'.

19. Ibid.

20. Ibid.

21. Cannon, R: *Historical Record of The Fifth or Princess Charlotte of Wales' Regiment of Dragoon Guards*, Longman Orme & Co., London, 1839, pp 54-55.

Chapter 6
1. NAM 6807-213 'Anonymous memoirs of a Dragoon'.

2. Ibid.

3. Muir, R. *Salamanca 1812*, Yale University Press, New Haven and London, 2001. This is by far the best book on the Salamanca campaign, using French sources as well as the traditional English ones.

4. Ibid., Chapter 3.

5. NAM 6807-213 'Anonymous memoirs of a Dragoon'.

6. Le Marchant, D. *Memoirs of the late Major General Le Marchant 1766-1812*, Spellmount Ltd, Staplehurst, 1997, p277.

7. Muir, R. op. cit, Appendix 3.

8. Le Marchant, D. op. cit, p289. Cotton was known as capable and brave, but not a genius and there seems to have been no love lost

between him and Wellington and also between him and Le Marchant. Cotton's wife wrote much later: 'It would appear from what we can gather that though always on friendly terms with Lord Combermere and fully appreciating his value Wellington entertained no personal regard for him – perhaps indeed slightly the contrary.' (*Memoirs and Correspondence of Field Marshal Viscount Combermere*, London, Hurst and Blackett, 1866.)

9. Mattingly, B. *Wellington's Field Trumpeter?*

10. Douglas, J. (ed. S. Monlick) *Tale of the Peninsula & Waterloo*, Leo Cooper, London, 1997.

11. Napier, W.E.P. *History of the war in the Peninsula and the south of France from the year 1807 to the year 1814*, Vol 5, Constable, London, 1993, p172.

12. NAM 6807-213 'Anonymous memoirs of a Dragoon'.

13. Norcliffe, Lieutenant N. *A Dragoon's experiences at Salamanca*, ed C. Dalton, *Cavalry Journal*, October 1912, pp458-460.

14. Ibid. pp458-460.

15. Muir, R., op.cit, Chapter 6.

16. The staff is long with a giant silver head bearing the words '66me Regiment d'Infanterie de Ligne'. It is enriched with silver criss-cross chains and silver eagles. On the silver band below the head is the following inscription: 'This trophy was taken in the charge of the 5th Dragoon Guards at the Battle of Salamanca July 22 1812 in which among others the 66 French Regiment was annihilated. Major General Ponsonby begs leave to present it to the 5th Dragoon Guards to be carried by the trumpet major on all occasions of review as a memory of that glorious day.' Evans, Major R. *The Story of the 5th Royal Inniskilling Dragoon Guards*, Gale and Polden Ltd, Aldershot, 1951, p55.

17. Cobbett's *Weekly Political Register*

18. Ibid.

19. Cannon, R. *Historical Record of The Fifth or Princess Charlotte of Wales' Regiment of Dragoon Guards*, Longman Orme & Co., London, 1839, p60.

20. NAM 6807-213 'Anonymous memoirs of a Dragoon'.

Chapter 7

1. Le Marchant, D. *Memoirs of the late Major General Le Marchant 1766-1812*, Spellmount Ltd, Staplehurst, 1997, p305.

2. Ponsonby, Major General Sir John, *The Ponsonby Family*, The Medici Society, 1929, p216.

3. Cannon, R. *Historical Record of The Fifth or Princess Charlotte of Wales' Regiment of Dragoon Guards*, Longman Orme & Co., London, 1839, pp61-62.

4. Muir, R. *Salamanca 1812*, Yale University Press, New Haven and London, 2001, pp230-231.

5. NAM 6807-213 'Anonymous memoirs of a Dragoon'

6. Maxwell, *Peninsular Sketches*, pp372-374, Reprinted Naval and Military Press Ltd, 2002.

7. Napier, W.E.P. *History of the war in the Peninsula and the south of France from the year 1807 to the year 1814*, Vol 5, Constable, London, 1993, p191-192. Oman, C. *A History of the Peninsular War*, Vol 5, Greenhill Books, London, 2005, pp 508-513. Uffindell, A. *The National Army Museum's Book of Wellington's Armies*, Sidgwick and Jackson, London, 2003, p135 for Wellington's quote.

8. Stephenson, W. *A Short account of the 3rd or Kings Own Dragoons through Portugal, Spain and commencing from that time it left Guildford in Surrey for embarkation at Portsmouth in July 1811 until its return in July 1814 giving the exact distances of each day's march* (NAM 1968-07-215)

9. I am indebted to Stephen Drake Jones, President of the Wellington Society in Madrid, for this information. Stephen also helped me discover the route used by Wellington's troops to enter Madrid and where the cavalry were based when they were in the city.

10. NAM 6807-213 'Anonymous memoirs of a Dragoon'.

11. NAM6807-213 'Anonymous memoirs of a Dragoon'.

12. Cassels, S.A.C. (ed) *Peninsular Portrait 1811-1814 The Letters of Captain William Bragge, Third (Kings Own) Dragoons*, Oxford University Press, London, 1963, p69.

13. Gurwood, J. *The Dispatches of Field Marshal the Duke of Wellington during his various campaigns from 1799 to 1815*, Vol 9, p351.

14. Bessborough *Lady Bessborough and her family circle*, John Murray, 1940, p225.

15. Napier, op. cit, p259.

16. D'Urban, B. *The Peninsular Journal 1808-1817*, Greenhill Books, London, 1998, p288.

17. Stephenson, op. cit.

18. Longford, E. *Wellington – The Years of the Sword*, The Literary Guild, London, 1969, p296.

19. Cassels, op. cit, p79.

20. Cassels, op cit, p76.

21. Napier, op. cit, p281.

22. Bessborough, op. cit, p228.

23. Cassels, op. cit, p75.

24. Glover, G. (ed) *Eyewitness to the Peninsular War and the Battle of Waterloo The Letters and Journals of Lt Col The Honourable James Stanhope*, Pen and Sword, Barnsley, 2010, pp94-95.

25. Stephenson, op. cit.

26. Cassels, op. cit, p83.

27. Burroughs, G.F. *A Narrative of the retreat of the British Army from Burgos*, 1814, reprinted by Ken Trotman Military Monographs, 2004.

28. Douglas, J. (ed. S. Monlick) *Tale of the Peninsula & Waterloo*, Leo Cooper, London, 1997.

29. Oman, C. *A History of the Peninsular War*, Vol 6, Greenhill Books, London, 2005, pp77-79.

30. Stephenson, op. cit.

31. Ibid.

32. Ibid.

33. Wellington correspondence.

34. Cassels, op. cit, pp81-82.

35. Thomas Creevey wrote to his wife on 19 October 1812:

> Let me not omit to mention to you that Colonel Gordon, who you know is with Wellington, is in constant correspondence with both Grey and Whitbread and that his accounts are of the most desponding caste. He considers our ultimate discomfiture as purely a question of time and that it may happen on any day, however early. That our pecuniary resources are utterly exhausted and that the [.....] of the French in recovering from their difficulties is inexhaustible; that Wellington himself considers this resurrection of Marmont's broken troops as an absolute miracle in war and in short Gordon considers Wellington is in very considerable danger. Of course you will not use this information but in the most discrete manner.

Creevey Papers *A Selection from the correspondence and diaries of the late Thomas Creevey MP edited by Rt Hon Sir Herbert Maxwell*, John Murray, London, 1903.

36. Stephenson, op. cit.

37. Uffindell, A. *The National Army Museum's Book of Wellington's Armies*, Sidgwick and Jackson, London, p151. There are no accurate figures for the losses sustained by the Spanish.

38. Cannon, op. cit, pp64-65.

Chapter 8
1. Cassels, S.A.C. (ed) *Peninsular Portrait 1811-1814 The Letters of Captain William Bragge, Third (Kings Own) Dragoons*, Oxford University Press, London, 1963, p90.
2. Ibid, p88.
3. Stephenson, W. *A Short account of the 3rd or Kings Own Dragoons through Portugal, Spain and commencing from that time it left Guildford in Surrey for embarkation at Portsmouth in July 1811 until its return in July 1814 giving the exact distances of each day's march* (NAM 1968-07-215)
4. Pomeroy, Hon Ralph Legge *The Story of a Regiment of Horse being the regimental history of the 5th Princess Charlotte of Wales Dragoon Guards*, William Blackwood and Sons, Edinburgh and London, 1924. Reprinted Naval and Military Press, Vol2, p36.
5. Cassels, op. cit, p91.
6. Graham, W. *Travels through Portugal and Spain, during the Peninsular War* Sir Richard Phillips & Co., London, 1820. Reprinted General Books LLC, Memphis, USA, 2012, p19.
7. Cassels, op. cit, p98.
8. Graham, op cit, p19.
9. Ibid. p20.
10. Green, J: *The Vicissitudes of a Soldier's life*, Simpkin and Marshall, London, 1827, p149.
11. Graham, op. cit, p20.
12. Oman, C. *A History of the Peninsular War*, Vol 6, Greenhill Books, London, 2005, p352.
13. Graham, op. cit, p21.
14. Stephenson, op. cit.
15. Graham, op. cit, p21.
16. Hunt, E. *Charging against Napoleon*, Leo Cooper, Barnsley, 2001, p93.
17. Graham, op. cit, p21.
18. NAM 6807-213 *Anonymous memoirs of a Dragoon*
19. Napier, W.E.P. *History of the war in the Peninsula and the south of France from the year 1807 to the year 1814*, Vol 5, Constable, London, 1993, p559.
20. Fletcher, I. *Vittoria 1813*, Osprey Campaign Series, Reed International Books Ltd, 1998, p61. The Great Road had been cut by Longa's Spanish, but he was unable to exploit this.
21. Cassels, op. cit, p102.
22. NAM 6807-213, op. cit.

Chapter 9

1. Glover, G. (ed) *Eyewitness to the Peninsular War and the Battle of Waterloo The Letters and Journals of Lt Col The Honourable James Stanhope*, Pen and Sword, Barnsley, 2010, p117.
2. Fortescue *A History of the British Army Vol 9*, The Naval and Military Press Ltd, Uckfield, 2004.
3. King Joseph's silver gilt service is no longer with the family. Some pieces were sold by Sir William's spendthrift son and the remainder was stolen in a break in at Haile Hall following the death of Lady Molly Ponsonby.
4. Graham, W. *Travels through Portugal and Spain, during the Peninsular War* Sir Richard Phillips & Co., London, 1820. Reprinted General Books LLC, Memphis, USA, 2012, p23.
5. Oman, C. *A History of the Peninsular War*, Vol 6, Greenhill Books, London, 2005, p455.
6. Graham, op. cit, p24.
7. Ibid. p24.
8. Ibid. p24.
9. Ibid. p26.
10. Haggard, Captain D.J. 'With the 10th Hussars in Spain: Letters of Edward Fox Fitzgerald', *Journal of the Society for Army Historical Research*, Vol xliv, no 178, June 1966.
11. Graham, op.cit, p26.
12. Ibid. p27.
13. Ibid. p32.
14. Ibid. p32.
15. *Caledonian Mercury*
16. *London Gazette*
17. Cassels, S.A.C. (ed) *Peninsular Portrait 1811-1814 The Letters of Captain William Bragge, Third (Kings Own) Dragoons*, Oxford University Press, London, 1963, p124.
18. Robertson, I. *Wellington invades France*, Greenhill Books, London, 2003, p250.
19. Birks, M. *The Young Hussar – The Peninsular War Journal of Colonel Thomas Wildman*, Book Guild Publishing, Sussex, 2007, p141.
20. Quoted in ibid. p142.
21. Ibid. p152.
22. Hunt, E. *Charging against Napoleon*, Leo Cooper, Barnsley, 2001, p222.
23. Cannon, R. *Historical Record of The Fifth or Princess Charlotte of*

Wales' Regiment of Dragoon Guards, Longman Orme & Co., London, 1839, pp69-70.

Chapter 10
1. Borthwick Institute for Archives, University of York, ref Halifax A1/4/29.
2. Danniell, W. *A Voyage around the coast of Great Britain*, published by the Folio Society, London, 2008.
3. Borthwick Institute for Archives, University of York, ref Halifax A1/2/4.
4. Horner, F. *Memoirs and Correspondence of Francis Horner MP Vol 2*, Little, Brown and Co., Boston, 1853.
5. Borthwick Institute for Archives, University of York, ref Halifax A1/2/4.
6. Borthwick Institute for Archives, University of York, ref Halifax A1/2/4.
7. Gurwood, Lt Col *The Dispatches of Field Marshal the Duke of Wellington during his various campaigns from 1799 to 1815*
8. *London Gazette*, 16 November 1814.
9. *London Gazette*, 6 April 1815.
10. 5th Dragoon Guards website.
11. Borthwick Institute for Archives, University of York, ref Halifax A1/2/4.
12. Borthwick Institute for Archives, University of York, ref Halifax A1/2/4. It was true that the Bessboroughs had large estates. Their Irish lands amounted to 27,000 acres. In England besides Roehampton and Cavendish Square there were also estates in Cambridge, Leicestershire and Northamptonshire. But as in so many of the leading families at that time a combination of long leases with no opportunity to increase the rents and massive gambling debts meant that the Bessboroughs were not as wealthy as everyone (including William) imagined. Indeed in 1798 they had had to take substantial loans from the Spencers, the Duke of Bedford and Lord Fitzwilliam to stave off their creditors.
13. Borthwick Institute for Archives, University of York, ref Halifax A1/2/4.
14. Borthwick Institute for Archives, University of York, ref Halifax A1/2/4.
15. Borthwick Institute for Archives, University of York, ref Halifax A1/2/4.
16. Borthwick Institute for Archives, University of York, ref Halifax A1/2/4.

17. Borthwick Institute for Archives, University of York, ref Halifax A1/2/4.
18. Borthwick Institute for Archives, University of York, ref Halifax A1/2/4.
19. Borthwick Institute for Archives, University of York, ref Halifax A1/2/4.
20. Borthwick Institute for Archives, University of York, ref Halifax A1/2/4.
21. Borthwick Institute for Archives, University of York, ref Halifax A1/2/4.
22. *Caledonian Mercury* Monday Jan 9th 1815, Supplement to the *London Gazette* of 3rd January, Wednesday Jan 4th 1815.
23. Borthwick Institute for Archives, University of York, ref Halifax A1/2/4.
24. Borthwick Institute for Archives, University of York, ref Halifax A1/2/4.
25. Borthwick Institute for Archives, University of York, ref Halifax A1/2/4.

Chapter 11
1. *Le Moniteur*, 1815.
2. Borthwick Institute for Archives, University of York, ref Halifax A1/2/4.
3. Gurwood, Lt Col. *The Dispatches of Field Marshal the Duke of Wellington during his various campaigns from 1799 to 1815*, Vol 12, p337.
4. Gurwood, Lt Col. *The General Orders of Field Marshall the Duke of Welllington*, W. Clowes & Sons, London, 1837.
5. Ibid.
6. Dawson, P. *Au Gallop! Horses and Riders of Napoleon's Army*, Black Tent Publications, Stockton on Tees.
7. Glover, G. *The Waterloo Archive Vol 3*, Frontline Books, Barnsley, 2011, p27.
8. Ibid. p67.
9. Siborne, Major General H.T., *Waterloo Letters*, Greenhill Books, London, 1993, p85.
10. Mercer, General C. *Journal of the Waterloo Campaign*, Greenhill Books, London, 1985.
11. Ibid. p54.
12. Ibid. p56.

13. Ibid. p76.
14. Ibid. p60.
15. Ibid. pp48-49.
16. Ibid. p83.
17. Glover, Vol 3 op. cit, p29.
18. Ibid. p43.
19. Glover, Vol 1 op. cit. p43.
20. Ibid. p43.
21. Letter of Sir William Ponsonby to Lt General Sir H. Fane. National Army Museum NAM 1963-10-36. Found by Gareth Glover.
22. Mercer, op. cit, p117.
23. Ibid. pp117-118.
24. Glover, Vol 1 op. cit, p44.
25. Sabine, Major General E. (ed) *Letters of Colonel Sir Augustus Simon Frazer KCB*, The Naval and Military Press Ltd, Uckfield, pp522-523.
26. Glover, Vol 1 op. cit, p44.
27. Borthwick Institute for Archives, University of York, ref Halifax A1/4/29.
28. Gurwood, *Dispatches* op. cit, p337
29. Ibid. p344.
30. Ibid. p373.
31. Ibid. p373.
32. Ibid. p438.
33. Ibid. p462.
34. Grey Papers, University of Durham GRE/E/400/1.
35. Borthwick Institute for Archives, University of York, ref Halifax A1/2/4.

Chapter 12

1. Quoted in Robinson, M. *The Battle of Quatre Bras 1815*, The History Press, Stroud, 2009. The full text in Jackson, B. *Notes and Reminiscences of a Staff Officer*, John Murray, London, 1903, states: 'For two or three hours I was engaged with others in writing our orders for the several divisions to march which were expedited by means of hussars, men selected for their steadiness. Each was told the rate at which he was to proceed and time for reaching his destination. It was his duty to bring back the cover of the despatch on which the officer receiving it had to state the exact time of its delivery. I thought my duty for the day was ended when the despatches had been sent off, but my friend Colonel Torrens whispered in my ear that he had put me in for a

ride and Sir William Delancey handed me a packet saying *I am told you know the road to Ninove, here is a letter for Colonel Cathcart (later Lord Greenock); be as speedy as possible. In a few minutes I was in the saddle wending my way in the darkness to Ninove by a crossroad.'* pp12-13.

2. Jackson, op. cit, pp12-13.

3. Duke of Argyll (ed)(Elibron Classics: *Intimate Society Letters of the 18th century vol 2.* pp671-674

4. Duke of Argyll (ed) Elibron Classics: *Intimate Society Letters of the 18th century vol 2,* pp671-674.

5. Borthwick Institute for Archives, University of York, ref Halifax A1/2/4.

6. Miller, D. *The Duchess of Richmond's Ball 15 June 1815,* Spellmount, Staplehurst, 2005.

7. Braithwaite Christie was the 3rd son of Admiral Alexander Christie of Baberton in Scotland. He had joined the 5th Dragoon Guards and had been severely wounded at the Battle of Salamanca. On returning to the regiment after recovering he became Sir William's ADC for the rest of the war. He was present when Sir William was killed at Waterloo and found his body the next day and brought it back to England. The Dragoon Guards' Museum at York displays a Legion d'Honneur medal from a French officer that Braithwaite Christie captured. After Waterloo he became ADC to General Pack and was known as a capable officer. He became a captain in the 5th Dragoon Guards in 1817 and was the senior captain in 1824. Sadly he died from a wasting illness at his father's home at Belmont in Bath in 1825. Thomas Reignolds was killed with Sir William at Waterloo, leaving behind orphaned children. He had joined the 2nd Dragoons in December 1804.

8. Glover, G. *The Waterloo Archive Vols 1-6,* Frontline Books, Barnsley, 2011. In particular vol 1 pp32 and 44, and Clark-Kennedy, A.E. *Attack the Colour! The Royal Dragoons in the Peninsula and at Waterloo,* The Research Publishing Company, London, 1975, p92.

9. Jackson, op. cit, pp12-13.

10. Ibid. p14.

11. Glover, op. cit, p24.

12. Ibid. p.24.

13. Field, A.W. *Prelude to Waterloo Quatre Bras – The French Perspective,* Pen and Sword, Barnsley, 2014, p80.

14. Mercer, General C. *Journal of the Waterloo Campaign,* Greenhill Books, London, 1985, p130.

15. Siborne, Major General H.T., *Waterloo Letters,* Greenhill Books, London, 1993, p66.
16. Radclyffe Journal quoted in Atkinson *History of the Royal Dragoons,* Robert Maclehose and Co., University Press, Glasgow, 1938.
17. Field, op. cit, p172.
18. Adkin, M. *The Waterloo Companion,* Aurum Press, 2001, p74.
19. Colburn, H. *United Services Journal 1838, Part 2,* London, p432. John Williamson, the regimental quartermaster of the 30th, as a non-combatant would remain in the rear of the army during the battle.
20. Barbero, A. *The Battle A History of the Battle of Waterloo,* Atlantic Books, London, 2006, p189.
21. Gerald Ponsonby in 1915 wrote an article in the *Journal of the Kildare Archaeological Society* entitled 'Bishopscourt and its Owners'. In it he recorded the family tradition that Sir William's charger was returned to Ireland after Waterloo and lived out its days at Bishopscourt.

Chapter 13
1. Clark Kennedy, quoted in Siborne, Major General H.T., *Waterloo Letters*, Greenhill Books, London, 1993, p66. Captain Clark added Kennedy to his surname afterwords but I have kept the traditional spelling.
2. Clark Kennedy quoted in Ibid. p66.
3. Evans, Major R. *The Story of the 5th Royal Inniskilling Dragoon Guards*, Gale and Polden Ltd, Aldershot, 1951, p60.
4. Tondeur, J., Courcelle, P., Meganck, P., Pattyn, J. *Genappe Le 17 Juin et la nuit du 18 au 19*, Tondeur editions, Bruxelles, 2007, p83.
5. Vivian quoted in Siborne, op. cit, p148.
6. Hay, Captain W. *Reminiscences 1808-1815 Under Wellington*, Ken Trotman Ltd, Cambridge, 1992, pp168-169.
7. Mercer, General C. *Journal of the Waterloo Campaign*, Greenhill Books, London, 1985, p150.
8. Tondeur, J. et al, op. cit, p88.
9. Glover, G. *The Waterloo Archive Vol 1*, Frontline Books, Barnsley, 2011, p32.
10. Ibid. p46.
11. Mercer, op. cit, p150.
12. Simmons, G. *A British Rifleman*, Greenhill Books, London, 1986, p364.
13. Lt J. Banner, 23rd Light Dragoons, quoted in Siborne, op. cit, p94.
14. Lt J. Banner, 23rd Light Dragoons, quoted in Siborne, op. cit, p94.
15. Mercer, op. cit, p153.

16. Uxbridge quoted in Siborne, op. cit, p7.

17. Owen, E. *The Waterloo Papers*, AQ & DT Publications, 1997.

18. Uxbridge quoted in Siborne, op. cit, p7.

19. Glover, op. cit, p32.

20. *Radclyffe Journal* quoted in Atkinson *History of the Royal Dragoons*, Robert Maclehose and Co., University Press, Glasgow, 1938, and Glover, op. cit, p25.

21. Clark Kennedy quoted in Siborne, op. cit, p66.

22. Uxbridge quoted in Siborne, op. cit, p7.

23. Quoted in Tondeur, J. et al, op. cit, p102: 27 officers and men killed, 52 wounded and 36 missing. 45 horses killed, 20 wounded and 33 missing.

Chapter 14

1. Eaton, C.A.W. *Waterloo Days: The Narrative of an Englishwoman resident at Brussels in June 1815*, George Bell, London, 1888, reprinted General Books, Memphis, 2010, p65.

2. Howarth, D. *A Near Run Thing*, London, 1968.

3. *Radclyffe Journal*, quoted in Atkinson, *History of the Royal Dragoons*, Robert Maclehose, and Co., University Press, Glasgow, 1938.

4. Napoleonic Archive *Archibald Hamilton at Waterloo with the Scots Greys*, p4.

5. Glover, G. *The Waterloo Archive Vol 6*, Frontline Books, Barnsley, 2011, p55.

6. Glover, G. *The Waterloo Archive Vol 1*, Frontline Books, Barnsley, 2011, p48.

7. Field, A.W. *Waterloo: The French Perspective*, Pen and Sword, 2012, p30.

8. Ibid. p244-249.

9. Ibid. p84-85.

10. However, it is true that conditions were not as favourable as they could have been due to the position, Wellington's deployment and the weather conditions. The Grand Battery was firing up hill against a target they could not see due to Wellington deploying his troops as normal behind the ridgeline on the reverse slope. The ground was soft after the amount of rain during the previous 24 hours and this meant that cannonballs would not bounce and ricochet when they hit the ground. The damage they could inflict was limited to whatever they hit in their downward trajectory and therefore had a reduced effect. Nevertheless, the psychological power of the noise of so many guns firing on the troops behind the ridge was real enough and for the troops on the reverse

slope subject to shells from the French howitzers, and the Allied artillery situated in gaps in the hedge and therefore visible to the French artillery, the actual damage was very real.

11. Field, op. cit, p75.
12. Ibid. p104.
13. Lipscombe, N. (Col.) *Wellington's Guns*, Osprey Publishing, Oxford, 2013. Ross had three guns disabled within minutes and eight gun horses were killed, p372.
14. Field, op. cit, p78.
15. Field, op. cit, pp99-100.
16. Field, op. cit,
17. Field, op. cit, pp 105-106.
18. Siborne, Major General H.T., *Waterloo Letters*, Greenhill Books, London, 1993, p383.
19. Ibid. p19.
20. Field, op. cit, p102.

Chapter 15

1. Napoleonic Archive *Archibald Hamilton at Waterloo with the Scots Greys*, p8.
2. Ibid. p8-9.
3. Ibid. p9.
4. Ibid. p10.
5. Ibid. p10.
6. Anglesey, 'letter to Colonel Allan', 18 December 1815.
7. Siborne, Major General H.T., *Waterloo Letters*, Greenhill Books, London, 1993, pp7-8.
8. Napoleonic Archive op. cit, p10.
9. Low, E.B. *With Napoleon at Waterloo: The Greys at Waterloo Reminiscences of the last survivor of the famous charge*, Francis Griffiths, London, 1911, p141.
10. Ibid. p142.
11. Siborne, op. cit, p63-64. 'As to the person who took off his hat as a signal from the crest of the hill for the brigade to advance, I venture to think I was myself the individual who did so. It occurred thus: I accompanied Sir William Ponsonby to the crest to ascertain the proper time for the Brigade to come up. At the moment when he appeared of the opinion that this should be done, he himself met with a trifling interference. The Enemy just then redoubled their cannon fire against the crest. The General was mounted on a secondary untrained horse, and

some round shot frightened the horse and his cloak being loose flew off. He dismounted for a moment to get his cloak restored to its place. It was in that interval that he instructed me to make the signal alluded to.'

12. Napoleonic Archive op. cit, pp10-11.

13. Siborne, op. cit, p72.

14. Ibid. p85.

15. Ibid. p71.

16. Ibid. p89.

17. Anton, J. *Retrospect of a Military Life*, W.H. Lizars, Edinburgh, 1841, reprinted Ken Trotman Ltd, 1991, p210.

18. Low, op. cit, pp142-144. Dickson gave his account many years after the event and the details may well have got a bit muddled. The batteries referred to were probably protected by Durutte's troops (see later).

19. Martin, J, *Souvenirs d'un ex officier*, Librairie Cherbuliez, Paris, 1867, p292. He quotes 5,000 losses, of which 2,000 were prisoners.

20. Siborne, op. cit, p9.

Chapter 16

1. Siborne , Major General H.T., *Waterloo Letters*, Greenhill Books, London, 1993 p71.

2. Ibid. p73.

3. Ibid. p71.

4. Napoleonic Archive *Archibald Hamilton at Waterloo with the Scots Greys*, p11.

5. Low, E.B. *With Napoleon at Waterloo: The Greys at Waterloo Reminiscences of the last survivor of the famous charge*, Francis Griffiths, London, 1911, p144-5.

6. Siborne, op. cit, p199.

7. Glover, G. *The Waterloo Archive Vol 5*, Frontline Books, Barnsley, 2011, p88.

8. Mauduit, Hippolyte de *Les Derniers Jours de la Grande Armée, ou, souvenirs, documents et correspondence inédite de Napoleon en 1814 et 1815*, Paris, 1848, Vol 2, p286 and p304-5. Mauduit states that the night before Waterloo Bro had sent out a reconnaisance force, which had discovered the Allied artillery park, but his plan to attack it was vetoed by a French general. Mauduit also states that as early as 11am on the 18th Colonel Bro, on his own initiative, had detached some of his lancers further to the right of the French army and they had reported seeing Prussian Uhlans, which news he had passed on but seems not to have been acted on by the French high command. Bro was aged 34 at

Waterloo. He had served with the 1st Hussars in the San Domingo campaign and in Germany. He had been present at the battles of Eylau and Friedland and had distinguished himself at Wagram. In 1811 he had transferred to the 5th squadron of *chasseurs à cheval* of the Guard and saw action in Russia, Germany and the 1814 French campaign. He was promoted to colonel and Napoleon met him on his return in 1815 at the head of the 4th regiment de chevaux legers lanciers. He died in 1844.

9. Ibid. p286 and p304-5.
10. Field, A.W. *Waterloo: The French Perspective*, Pen and Sword, 2012, p114.
11. Glover, op.cit, p88.
12. Hay, Captain W. *Reminiscences 1808-1815 Under Wellington*, Ken Trotman Ltd, Cambridge, 1992, p177.
13. Mauduit, op. cit, p286 and p304-5.
14. Hay, op. cit, p181.
15. I am very grateful to Pierre de Wit for bringing to my attention Colonel Bro's map.
16. Montmorency, Lt Col R.H. de *Exercises and Manouevres of the Lance*, Longman, Hurst Rees Orme and Browne, London, 1820, reprinted by The Naval and Military Press Ltd in association with the Royal Armouries.
17. Siborne, op. cit, p87.
18. Low, op. cit, p145-6.
19. Ibid. p146.

Chapter 17
1. Low, E.B. *With Napoleon at Waterloo: The Greys at Waterloo Reminiscences of the last survivor of the famous charge*, Francis Griffiths, London, 1911, p146.
2. Sylvanus Urban *The Gentleman's Magazine*, vol 1, 1815, p644.
3. Sylvanus Urban *The Gentleman's Magazine* vol 2 1815, p179.
4. Martin, J. *Souvenirs d'un ex officier*, Librairie Cherbuliez, Paris, 1867, p292. He may have confused Sir William with his second cousin Frederick, commander of the 12th Light Dragoons, who was wounded a number of times by lancers but survived.
5. Napoleonic Archive *Archibald Hamilton at Waterloo with the Scots Greys*, p11.
6. Ibid. pp11-12.
7. Low, op. cit, p144-147.
8. Siborne , Major General H.T. *Waterloo Letters*, Greenhill Books, London, 1993, p62.

9. Ibid. p62.

10. Field, A.W. *Waterloo: The French Perspective*, Pen and Sword, 2012, p112-113.

11. Coppens, B. and Courcelle, P. *La Papelotte Waterloo 1815 Les Carnets de la Campagne No 4*, Bruxelles, 2000, pp47-48.

12. Ponsonby, Major General Sir John *The Ponsonby Family*, The Medici Society, 1929, p220.

13. C. Ewart, quoted in Brett-James, A. *The Hundred Days – Napoleon's Last Campaign from Eye Witness Accounts*, Macmillan and Co. Ltd, London, 1964, p120.

14. Glover, G. *The Waterloo Archive Vol 1*, Frontline Books, Barnsley, 2011, p30.

15. Siborne, op. cit, p199.

16. Ibid. pp 81-82.

17. Glover, Vol 6, op. cit, pp63-64.

18. Mauduit, Hippolyte de *Les Derniers Jours de la Grande Armée, ou, souvenirs, documents et correspondence inédite de Napoleon en 1814 et 1848*, Paris, 1848, pp304.

19. Ibid. pp307.

20. Ibid. p308.

21. Ibid. pp308.

22. Coppens, op. cit, p44.

23. Ibid. pp47-48

24. Glover, Vol 1 op. cit, p30.

25. Ibid. p51.

26. Glover, Vol 6, op. cit, pp55-57.

27. Glover, Vol 1, op. cit, p26.

28. Coppens, op. cit, p48.

29. Mauduit, op. cit, pp340.

30. Napoleonic Archive *Colonel Bro at Waterloo with the 4th lancers*, p11.

31. French Napoleonic website.

32. Mauduit, op. cit, pp299-303.

33. Some might think that Mauduit's report of Urban's claim that he recaptured the eagle of the 45th, which was safely in Ewart's hands, is preposterous and invalidates the rest of his account. Given the chaos occasioned by the charge, the eagle taken and then retrieved could have belonged to another regiment. Indeed Commandant Lachoque credits Bro's lancers with recapturing the eagle of the 55th de ligne (Lachoque, Commandant Henri *Waterloo*, Arms and Armour Press, 1972, p157) and

Brack with Orban recapturing that of the 44th (Teissedre, F. *Waterloo Recits de combatants*, Librairie Historique F. Teissedre, Paris, 1999, p153). Delort said the Union Brigade captured Durutte's eagles, so it may simply have been a question of mixing up numbers. Or it may not have been an eagle at all, but a flag as Mauduit first called it. Each French regiment carried two flags, one per battalion. One had an eagle, one did not. Given the number of French infantry regiments in disarray it is possible that others were seized and retaken.

34. Ponsonby, Major General Sir John *The Ponsonby Family*, The Medici Society, 1929. Appendices. I have translated the letters in Appendix C.in this book

35. Major Clarke, acting commander of the Scots Greys, wrote a letter on 19 June to Lieutenant James Carruthers' father, assuring him that from reports from colleagues who knew his son that his son's wound was not serious and he had been wounded by a musket shot in his right breast. This was despite the fact that it was known to other Scots Greys that he had died from a lance thrust and they had buried him! Another account had him killed by a cannon ball. Another example is that of the commander of the King's Dragoon Guards, who was reported as dying on three different parts of the battlefield. Glover Vol 1, op. cit, p55 and Vol 4, op. cit, p55.

36. Glover, Vol 1 op. cit, p55.

37. Borthwick Institute for Archives, University of York, ref Halifax A1/2/4.

38. Glover, Vol 3 op. cit, p34.

Chapter 18

1. Siborne, Major General H.T., *Waterloo Letters*, Greenhill Books, London, 1993, p21.

2. Field, A.W. *Waterloo: The French Perspective*, Pen and Sword, 2012.

3. Glover, G. *The Waterloo Archive Vol 1*, Frontline Books, Barnsley, 2011, p55.

4. Ibid. Vols 1 and 4, p55 and pp55-56.

5. See previous chapter.

6. Wellington, *Waterloo Dispatch to the Secretary of State for War*.

7. Stanhope, *Notes of Conversations with the Duke of Wellington 1831-1851*, Oxford, quoted in Philippe de Callatay *La Musée Wellington, trois siecles d'histoire au coeur de Waterloo*, Waterloo, 2015.

8. Borthwick Institute for Archives, University of York, ref Halifax A1/2/4.

9. I am very grateful to Pierre de Wit for drawing my attention to this,

and to Mathew Haley of Bonham's for allowing me to publish the extract. It is part of a letter written by Colonel Best to his cousin Charlotte between 5 and 28 July 1815. Best relates how at daybreak on the 19th he had ordered his men to move the wounded and then went for a walk on the battlefield. It will be remembered that he was positioned close to where I believe Sir William died.

10. *The Times* Ship News, 7 July 1815.

11. Ponsonby, Major General Sir John, *The Ponsonby Family*, The Medici Society, 1929, p220.

12. Borthwick Institute for Archives, University of York, ref Halifax A1/4/29.

13. Ibid.

14. Bessborough, *Lady Bessborough and her family circle*, John Murray, 1940, p243.

15. Glover, Vol 1, op. cit, p63.

16. Glover, Vol 6 op. cit, p19.

17. *Morning Chronicle*, July 1815.

18. Borthwick Institute for Archives, University of York, ref Halifax A1/4/29.

19. Anne Louisa married William Tighe Hamilton, a barrister, in 1832 and died at Nice in 1863. Charlotte Georgiana married twice: firstly Lieutenant Colonel John Stapleton and then Rear Admiral Sir Charles Talbot. She died in 1883 at Biggleswade, Bedfordshire. Mary Elizabeth married the Reverend Henry Talbot in 1835 and also died in 1883. Frances Isabella married the Reverend Windham Beadon and died in 1845 at Newton Abbott.

20. *Caledonian Mercury*, Edinburgh, Saturday 24 June 1816.

21. *Caledonian Mercury*, Edinburgh, Thursday 20 June 1816.

Postscript

1. Weller, J. *Wellington at Waterloo*, Longmans, London, 1967, p104.

2. Barbero, A. *The Battle A History of the Battle of Waterloo*, Atlantic Books, London, 2006, p189.

3. Anglesey, *Letter from Beaudesert to Colonel Allan*, 18 December 1815.

4. Jackson, Major E.S. *The Inniskilling Dragoons*, Arthur L. Humphreys, London, 1909.

5. Siborne, Major General H.T., *Waterloo Letters*, Greenhill Books, London, 1993, p158.

6. Fortescue, Hon. J.W. *A History of the British Army*, reprinted by The Naval and Military Press Ltd, Uckfield, 2004, Vol 10 p211.

Bibliography

A

Adkin, M. *The Waterloo Companion*, Aurum Press, 2001.

Almack, E. *The History of the Second Dragoons Royal Scots Greys*, Alexander Moring Ltd, London.

Anon, *The British Cavalry on the Peninsula by an officer of dragoons 1831*, Mark Thompson Publishing, 1996.

Anon, *Memoirs and Services of the Eighty Third Regiment, County of Dublin From 1793 to 1907*, Hugh Rees Limited, London, 1908.

Anton, J. *Retrospect of a Military Life*, W.H. Lizars, Edinburgh, 1841.

Anonymous Memoirs of a Dragoon, National Army Museum, NAM 6807–213.

Atkinson, *History of the Royal Dragoons*, Robert Maclehose and Co., University Press, Glasgow, 1938.

Argyll, Duke of (ed) Elibron Classics: *Intimate Society Letters of the 18th century vol 2*.

B

Bamford, A. *Gallantry and Discipline – the 12th Light Dragoons at war with Wellington*, Frontline Books, London, 2014.

Barbero, A. *The Battle A History of the Battle of Waterloo*, Atlantic Books, London, 2006.

Barthorp, M. *Men at Arms – Welllington's Generals*, Osprey Publishing Ltd, 1978.

Bessborough, *Lady Bessborough and her family circle*, John Murray, 1940.

Birks, M. *The Young Hussar – The Peninsular War Journal of Colonel Thomas Wildman*, Book Guild Publishing, Sussex, 2007.

Blacklock, M. *The Royal Scots Greys*, Leo Cooper Ltd, London, 1971.

Borthwick Institute for Archives, University of York, ref Halifax A1/2/4.

Borthwick Institute for Archives, University of York, ref Halifax A1/4/29.

Bourachot, C. *Napoleon La dernière bataille 1814-1815 Temoignages*, Omnibus, Paris, 2014.

Burnham, *Charging against Wellington, the French cavalry in the Peninsular War 1807-1814*, Frontline Books, 2011.

Brett-James, A. *The Hundred Days – Napoleon's Last Campaign from Eye Witness Accounts*, Macmillan and Co. Ltd, London, 1964.

Burroughs, G.F. *A Narrative of the retreat of the British Army from Burgos*, 1814, reprinted by Ken Trotman Military Monographs, 2004.

C

Cannon, R. *Historical Record of The Fifth or Princess Charlotte of Wales' Regiment of Dragoon Guards*, Longman Orme & Co., London, 1839.

Cassels, S.A.C. (ed) *Peninsular Portrait 1811-1814 The Letters of Captain William Bragge, Third (Kings Own) Dragoons*, Oxford University Press, London, 1963.

Clark, Mrs G. (ed) *Gleanings from an Old Portfolio*, D. Douglas, Edinburgh, 1896, vols 1-3.

Clark-Kennedy, A.E. *Attack the Colour! The Royal Dragoons in the Peninsula and at Waterloo*, The Research Publishing Company, London, 1975.

Cockayne, *The Complete Peerage of England, Scotland and Ireland*, Volume 4.

Cooper, L. *British Regular Cavalry 1644-1914*, Chapman & Hall, London, 1965.

Coppens, B. & Courcelle, P. *Le Chemin d'Ohain Waterloo 1815*, Tondeur Diffusion, Bruxelles, 1999.

—— *La Papelotte Waterloo 1815*, Tondeur Diffusion, Bruxelles, 2000.

Costello, C. *A Class Apart The Gentry Families of County Kildare*, Nonsuch Publishing, Dublin, 2005.

Craan, W.B. & A. Gore *A Historical Account of the Battle of Waterloo: Fought on the 18th of June 1815, intended to elucidate the topographical plan*, Samuel Leigh, London, 1817.

Creevey Papers *A Selection from the correspondence and diaries of the late Thomas Creevey MP edited by Rt Hon Sir Herbert Maxwell*, John Murray, London, 1903.

D

Dalton, C. *The Waterloo Roll Call*, Arms and Armour Press, London, 1971.

Dawson, P. *Au Galop! Horses and Riders of Napoleon's Army*, Black Tent Publications, Stockton on Tees.

—— *Charge the Guns! Wellington's cavalry at Waterloo*, Black Tent Publications, Stockton on Tees, 2015.

De Ainslie General *Historical Record of the 1st or the Royal Regiment of Dragoons*, Chapman and Hall, London, 1887.

Dempsey, Guy C. Jr *Napoleon's Army 1807-1814 as depicted in the prints of Aaron Martinet*, Arms and Armour, London, 1997.

Digby Smith *Napoleon's Regiments: Battle Histories of the Regiments of the French Army 1792-1815*, Greenhill Books, 2000.

Dewlly, E. *Dwelly's Waterloo Cavalry Roll*, Savannah Publications, 2002.

Douglas, J. (ed S. Monlick) *Tale of the Peninsula & Waterloo*, Leo Cooper, London, 1997.

D'Urban, B. *The Peninsular Journal 1808-1817*, Greenhill Books, London, 1998.

E

Eaton, C.A.W. *Waterloo Days; The Narrative of an Englishwoman resident at Brussels in June 1815*, George Bell, London, 1888, reprinted General Books, Memphis, 2010.

Evans, Major R. *The Story of the 5th Royal Inniskilling Dragoon Guards*, Gale and Polden Ltd, Aldershot, 1951.

F

Field, A.W. *Waterloo: The French Perspective*, Pen and Sword, Barnsley, 2012.

—— *Prelude to Waterloo Quatre Bras – The French Perspective*, Pen and Sword, Barnsley, 2014.

Fletcher, I. *Wellington's Regiments the men and their battles*, Spellmount Ltd, Staplehurst, 1994.

—— *Salamanca 1812*, Osprey Campaign Series, Reed International Books Ltd, 1997.

—— *Vittoria 1813*, Osprey Campaign Series, Reed International Books Ltd, 1998.

—— *Galloping at everything – The British Cavalry in the Peninsular War and at Waterloo*, Spellmount Ltd, Staplehurst, 1999.

—— *A Desperate Business Wellington, the British Army and the Waterloo Campaign*, Spellmount Ltd, Staplehurst, 2001.

Foreman, A. *Georgiana Duchess of Devonshire*, Harper Collins, London, 1999.

Fortescue, Hon. J.W. *A History of the British Army*, reprinted by The Naval and Military Press Ltd, Uckfield, 2004.

Fosten, B. *Soldiers of the Napoleonic Wars: 8) The Union Brigade*, Almark Publications, New Malden.

Froude, J.A. *The English in Ireland in the 18th century*, New York, 1874.
G
Givanangeli, B. *Waterloo, la campagne de 1815 racontée par les soldats francais*, Nouvelle Imprimerie Labellerie Clamercey, 2004.
Gleeson, J. *An Aristocratic Affair*, Bantam Press, London, 2006.
Glover, G. *The Waterloo Archive Vols 1-6*, Frontline Books, Barnsley, 2011.
—— *Letters from the Battle of Waterloo: Unpublished correspondence by allied officers from the Siborne papers*, Greenhill Books, London, 2004.
—— *Campaigning in Spain and Belgium: The Letters of Captain Thomas Fenton, 4th Dragoons & The Scots Greys 1809-1815*, Ken Trotman Publishing, 2010.
—— (ed) *Eyewitness to the Peninsular War and the Battle of Waterloo The Letters and Journals of Lt Col The Honourable James Stanhope*, Pen and Sword, Barnsley, 2010.
Graham, W. *Travels through Portugal and Spain, during the Peninsular War*, Sir Richard Phillips & Co., London, 1820, reprinted General Books LLC, Memphis, USA, 2012.
Grant, Charles S, *Wellington 1813 The Vittoria Campaign*, Partizan Press, Newthorpe, 2013.
Green, J. *The Vicissitudes of a Soldier's life*, Simpkin and Marshall, London, 1827.
Gurwood, Lt Col. *The General Orders of Field Marshall the Duke of Welllington*, W. Clowes & Sons, London, 1837.
—— *The Dispatches of Field Marshal the Duke of Wellington during his various campaigns from 1799 to 1815*

H
Haggard, Captain D.J. *With the 10th Hussars in Spain: Letters of Edward Fox Fitzgerald*, Journal of the Society for Army Historical Research, Vol XLIV No.178, June 1966.
Head, Michael G. *French Napoleonic Lancer Regiments*, Almark Publications, London, 1971.
Hills, R.J.T. *The Royal Dragoons*, Leo Cooper Ltd, London, 1972.
Harrington, P. *English Heritage: English Civil War Archaeology*, BT Batsford, 2004.
Hay, Captain W. *Reminiscences 1808-1815 Under Wellington*, Ken Trotman Ltd, Cambridge, 1992.
Heathcote, R. *Letters of a Young Diplomatist and Soldier during the time of Napoleon*, John Lane, The Bodley Head, London, 1907.

Horner, F. *Memoirs and Correspondence of Francis Horner MP Vol 2*, Little, Brown and Co., Boston, 1853.

Houssaye, H. *Napoleon and the Campaign of 1815 Waterloo*, The Naval and Military Press Ltd, Uckfield, 2004.

Howarth, D. *A Near Run Thing*, London, 1968.

Hunt, E. *Charging against Napoleon*, Leo Cooper, Barnsley, 2001.

J

Jackson B *Notes and Reminiscences of a Staff Officer*, John Murray, London, 1903.

Jackson, Major E.S. *The Inniskilling Dragoons: The records of an old heavy cavalry regiment*, Arthur L. Humphreys, London, 1909.

K

Kelly, Dr J. *Multitext Project in Irish history: The Ponsonby family* University College Cork.

Kelly, L. *A flame now quenched, Rebels and Frenchmen in Leitrim 1793-1798*, The Lilliput Press Ltd, 1998.

Kenyon, J. and Ohlmeyer, J. (joint eds) *The Civil Wars A Military History of England, Scotland and Ireland 1638-1660*, Oxford University Press, 1998.

L

Lachoque, Commandant Henri *Waterloo*, Arms and Armour Press,1972.

Le Marchant, D. *Memoirs of the late Major General Le Marchant 1766-1812* Spellmount Ltd, Staplehurst, 1997.

Lipscombe, Col. N. *Wellington's Guns*, Osprey Publishing, Oxford, 2013.

Longford, E. *Wellington – The Years of the Sword*, The Literary Guild, London, 1969.

Low, E.B. *With Napoleon at Waterloo*, Francis Griffiths, London, 1911.

M

Maguire, W.A. *Up in Arms- The 1798 Rebellion in Ireland*, The Ulster Museum, 1998.

Mann, M. *And they Rode on – The King's Dragoon Guards at Waterloo*, Michael Russell Publishing Ltd, Salisbury, 1984.

Maricourt, Baron A. *Memoires du General Nogues*, librairie Alphonse Lemerre, Paris 1922.

Martin, J. *Souvenirs d'un ex officier*, Librairie Cherbuliez, Paris, 1867.

Mattingly, B. *Wellington's Field Trumpeter?*

Mauduit, Hippolyte de *Les Derniers Jours de la Grande Armée, ou, souvenirs, documents et correspondence inédite de Napoleon en 1814 et 1815*

Maxwell, W.H. (ed) *Peninsula Sketches by actors on the scene Vol 2*, The Naval and Military Press Ltd, 2002.

Mayne, E.C. *A Regency Chapter Lady Bessborough and her friendships*, Macmillan & Co. Ltd, London, 1939.

McNally, M. *Ireland 1649-1652*, Osprey Publishing Ltd, 2009.

Mellor, S. *Greys Ghosts, Men of the Scots Greys at Waterloo 1815*, Savannah Publications, London, 2012.

Mercer, General C. *Journal of the Waterloo Campaign*, Greenhill Books, London, 1985.

Miller, D. *The Duchess of Richmond's Ball 15 June 1815* Spellmount, Staplehurst, 2005.

Mitchell, L. *The Whig World*, Hambledon & London, London, 2005.

Montmorency, Lt Col. R.H. de *Exercises and Manouevres of the lance*, Longman, Hurst Rees Orme and Browne, London, 1820, reprinted The Naval and Military Press Ltd, in association with the Royal Armouries.

Moody, T.W. and Vaughan, W.E. *A New History of Ireland Vol IV Eighteenth Century Ireland 1691-1800*, Oxford University Press, 1996.

Moore, Sir J. *The Diary of Sir John Moore vol 1*, reprinted by General Books, Memphis, USA, 2012.

Muir, R. *Salamanca 1812*, Yale University Press, New Haven and London, 2001.

Murray, V. *High Society, A Social History of the Regency Period 1788-1830*, Viking, 1998.

N

Napier, W.E.P. *History of the war in the Peninsula and the south of France from the year 1807 to the year 1814 Vol 5*, Constable, London, 1993.

Napoleonic Archive *Archibald Hamilton at Waterloo with the Scots Greys*

Napoleonic Archive *Colonel Bro at Waterloo with the French lancers*

Norcliffe, Lieutenant N. *A Dragoon's experiences at Salamanca* ed. C. Dalton, *Cavalry Journal*, October 1912 pp458-460.

O

Oman, C. *Wellington's Army*, Edward Arnold, London, 1912.

—— *A History of the Peninsular War*, Vol 5, Greenhill Books, London, 2005.

—— *A History of the Peninsular War*, Vol 6, Greenhill Books, London, 2005.

Owen, E. *The Waterloo Papers*, AQ & DT Publications, 1997.

P

Pakenham, T. *The Year of Liberty The Great Irish rebellion of 1798*, Hodder and Stoughton Limited, 1969.

Phillips, C.B. *The Royalist North: The Cumberland and Westmorland Gentry 1642-1660*, in R.C. Richardson (ed) *The English Civil Wars Local Aspects*, Sutton Publishing Ltd, 1997.

Pomeroy, Hon Ralph Legge *The Story of a Regiment of Horse being the regimental history of the 5th Princess Charlotte of Wales Dragoon Guards*, William Blackwood and Sons, Edinburgh and London, 1924, reprinted Naval and Military Press.

Ponsonby, Major General Sir John *The Ponsonby Family*, The Medici Society, 1929.

Ponsonby, John 1st Viscount *Collected Papers*, University of Durham Library.

Porter, S. *Destruction in the English Civil Wars*, Alan Sutton Publishing Ltd, 1994.

R

Reid, S. *Men at Arms- Armies of the Irish Rebellion 1798*, Osprey Publishing Ltd, 2011.

—— *Battle Orders Wellington's Army in the Peninsula 1809-1814*, Osprey Publishing Ltd, 2004.

Robertson, I. *Wellington invades France*, Greenhill Books, London, 2003.

Robinson, M. *The Battle of Quatre Bras 1815*, The History Press, Stroud, 2009.

Ross, C. (ed) *Correspondence of Charles First Marquis Cornwallis Vols 2 &3*, Cambridge University Press, Cambridge, 2011.

Royal Military Calendar or Army Service and Commission Book, A.J. Valpy, London, 1820, Vols 1-5, reprinted by The Naval and Military Press.

S

Sabine, Major General E. (ed) *Letters of Colonel Sir Augustus Simon Frazer KCB*, The Naval and Military Press Ltd, Uckfield.

Sadoun, B. (ed) *Waterloo le premier corps*, Gloire & Empire, Paris, 2010.

Siborne, Major General H.T. *Waterloo Letters*, Greenhill Books, London, 1993.

Simmons, G. *A British Rifleman*, Greenhill Books, London, 1986.

Stanhope, *Notes of Conversations with the Duke of Wellington 1831-1851*, Oxford quoted in Philippe de Callatay *La Musée Wellington trois siecles d'histoire au coeur de Waterloo*, Waterloo, 2015.

Stephenson, W. *A Short account of the 3rd or Kings Own Dragoons through Portugal, Spain and commencing from that time it left Guildford in Surrey for embarkation at Portsmouth in July 1811 until its return in July 1814 giving the exact distances of each day's march*, (AM 1968-07-215).

Summerville, C. *Who was who at Waterloo*, Pearson Education Ltd, Harlow, 2007.

T

Teissedre, F. *Waterloo Recits de combatants*, Librairie Historique F.Teissedre, Paris, 1999.

Tondeur, J., Courcelle, P., Meganck, P., Pattyn, J. *Genappe Le 17 Juin et la nuit du 18 au 19*, Tondeur editions, Bruxelles, 2007.

U

Uffindell, A. *The National Army Museum's Book of Wellington's Armies*, Sidgwick and Jackson, London, 2003.

Uffindell, A. and Corum, M. *On the fields of Glory* , Greenhill Books, London, 1996.

Uglow, J. *In these Times- Living in Britain through Napoleon's Wars*, Faber & Faber, London, 2014.

Urban, S. *The Gentleman's Magazine*, Vols 1 & 2, 1815.

W

Weller, J. *Wellington at Waterloo*, Longmans, London, 1967.

Wilson, F. *The Courtesan's Revenge*, Faber and Faber Ltd, London, 2003.

Index